Motivation in
Work Organizations

Motivation in Work Organizations

Edward E. Lawler III

Jossey-Bass Publishers
San Francisco

Substantial discounts on bulk quantities of Jossey-Bass books are available to corporations, professional associations, and other organizations. For details and discount information, contact the special sales department at Jossey-Bass Inc., Publishers. (415) 433-1740; Fax (415) 433-0499.

For sales outside the United States, contact Maxwell Macmillan International Publishing Group, 866 Third Avenue, New York, New York 10022.

Manufactured in the United States of America. Nearly all Jossey-Bass books and jackets are printed on recycled paper that contains at least 50 percent recycled waste, including 10 percent postconsumer waste. Many of our materials are also printed with vegetable-based ink; during the printing process these inks emit fewer volatile organic compounds (VOCs) than petroleum-based inks. VOCs contribute to the formation of smog.

Library of Congress Cataloging-in-Publication Data

Lawler, Edward E.
    Motivation in work organizations / Edward E. Lawler, III. — 1st [Classic] ed.
       p.   cm. — (The Jossey-Bass management series)
    Includes bibliographical references and index.
    ISBN 1-55542-661-1
    1. Psychology, Industrial. 2. Employee motivation. I. Title.
II. Series.
HF5548.8.L2973 1994
658.3'14 — dc20   93-50160
                                                          CIP

FIRST EDITION
HB Printing   10 9 8 7 6 5 4 3 2 1   *Code 9458*

The Jossey-Bass
Management Series

To three beautiful human beings—
Leslie, Cindy, and Eve.
I love them and miss them more than
my words can express.

Contents

Introduction
to the Classic Edition

The publication of *Motivation in Work Organizations* in 1973 marked an important point of change in my research work. Prior to 1973, a majority of my work focused on the theoretical issues that are the subject of the first four chapters of the book. In several respects, writing this book helped me to summarize the work I had done on motivation theory and to translate it into practical and usable material. In the preface to the book, I note that it represents the summation and integration of many years of research. Looking back at *Motivation in Work Organizations,* I am struck by how true this is. However, it also began a new phase of my research — one that has been more focused on organizational change and management practice.

Much of my work since the publication of *Motivation in Work Organizations* has involved the issues discussed in Chapters 6, 7, 8, and 9. Indeed, I have much more to say about these issues than I did when *Motivation in Work Organizations* was originally published. The world of management has changed dramatically in the last two decades, and I believe that we know a great deal more now about how to effectively manage large, complex organizations and how to motivate the employees who work for them.

In this introduction, I will briefly discuss recent developments in motivation theory; mainly, I will consider the new developments in management and organization design that are relevant to motivation and organizational effectiveness. The reason for this emphasis is very straightforward: much more has been learned and much more has changed in the area of management and organization than in our basic understanding of motivation. In many respects this is not surprising, since motivation has been studied for decades — even centuries — and human behavior has, to some degree, remained constant. New technologies, new performance demands, new research, and a host of other factors, however, have influenced organizational design, and have changed substantially the predominant logic about how complex organizations should be managed.

Although my research during the last two decades has not focused on motivation theory, I have not stopped focusing on the motivation issues that are discussed in this book. Quite to the contrary, I still use these theories regularly; in fact, they form the basis for most of my work in the areas of pay and reward systems, employee involvement, organization design, and organization change. Since motivation is a core issue in any organization design, I use the motivation ideas covered in this book to decide which organization designs and management practices make sense and to predict what their impact will be on individual and organizational behavior. As I wrote in the original preface to *Motivation in Work Organizations,* understanding motivation theory is critical to thinking analytically about all behavior in organizations and to making organization-design decisions.

Motivation Theory and Research Today

Any motivation theory must answer three questions: (1) What activates behavior? (2) What directs behavior? and (3) What reactions do individuals have to the outcomes that result from their behavior? I believe that the expectancy-theory framework presented in *Motivation in Work Organizations* continues to represent the best overall theoretical approach to answering these three questions.

The idea that people have needs continues to be the best explanation for what activates behavior. Since the publication of *Motivation in Work Organizations,* considerable attention has been given to the work of Bandura and its focus on efficacy (Bandura, 1986). In many respects, this work is a continuation of a long chain of research suggesting that individuals have a need to experience a sense of competence, effectiveness, and achievement in their lives. It represents a valuable addition to our way of thinking about what motivates individuals and why they seek to accomplish particular goals, but it does not cause me to reconceptualize or change fundamentally the ideas in Chapter 2 about the role of needs in motivating human behavior. It does serve to further establish that individuals are motivated by both extrinsic rewards, such as pay, and intrinsic rewards, such as feelings of achievement and competence. It further highlights the point that effective organizations need to use both intrinsic and extrinsic rewards to motivate their members.

The increased diversity of the work force has brought into even sharper focus the issue of individual differences in people's needs. There seems little question that there are national differences in the types of rewards that individuals seek from work. This has led to the development of highly publicized work systems, such as those in Japan, which are quite different from those in the United States. If anything, these systems serve to emphasize the tremendous importance of understanding what individuals want from the workplace, and the central role that individual differences need to play in determining organization-design and reward-system practices.

The expectancy-theory model, which is offered in this book as the explanation of what directs behavior, has stood up well in the two decades since the book was published. Considerable research has been done on what determines people's perceptions of how likely their effort is to lead to successful performance, and on the connection between performance and reward. This research has clearly pointed out that an individual's effort/performance expectancies and performance/outcome beliefs are not always accurate and are influenced by a number of factors, including an organization's culture and the individual's past experiences. These are important additions to the theory but do not change the fundamental proposition that expectancies are critical in directing behavior. They also do not change the point that organizations need to be designed so that individuals can perceive a connection between performing well and obtaining the rewards that they value. In the area of reward systems, "line-of-sight" is an increasingly popular term used to capture the expectancy-theory view that, in order to be a motivator, a reward must be seen as important and obtainable by an organizational member.

The work of Locke and Latham (1990) has helped clarify the importance of goals in determining motivation. It has been particularly effective in contributing to our understanding of how and why people become committed to goals, and it has helped clarify the way participation and extrinsic rewards affect the performance goals that individuals establish. Fundamentally, however, it has not persuaded me that the basic concepts of expectancy theory need to be changed. Quite to the contrary, it has emphasized that individuals' cognitive beliefs about the consequences of their actions and the likelihood that those actions will be successful are the major determinants of motivation in both work and nonwork settings.

Motivation in Work Organizations places substantial emphasis on the role of job satisfaction. At the time the book was published, it was unusual to view satisfaction primarily as a consequence of performance, since many still argued that it was often a *cause* of performance. Since then, there has been increased acceptance of the view that satisfaction is best thought of as a consequence of performance that is influenced by the types of rewards that individuals receive and their connection to performance.

The idea that job satisfaction influences people's decisions about where to work and whether to stay in their present job still appears to be valid. Job satisfaction has, if anything, grown in importance in both managerial and organizational practice. Organizations increasingly conduct attitude surveys to determine their employees' feelings of satisfaction, to understand how the organization operates, and to determine the effects of particular management practices and organization designs. A rather large consulting industry has developed to support the use of attitude surveys. In many respects, this industry has become quite sophisticated in interpreting the results of job satisfaction surveys and in determining how the results are fed back to the organization. National norms have been developed, making it possible for organizations to compare their employees' satisfaction with a number of aspects of the work organization to a national average. In addition, most surveys are analyzed to compare different parts of an organization. Results from the survey are often given to employees, who are asked to participate in discussions about how things can be changed. In other cases, management may simply use satisfaction survey data as one indicator of how things are going in the organization.

It is particularly important that job satisfaction data be interpreted with a comparative standard in mind. There are essentially two kinds of comparisons that are relevant for any job satisfaction data. The first is how an organization compares with other organizations. This comparison is particularly critical in evaluating how the organization is likely to fare relative to others in terms of turnover, absenteeism, and work culture. Perhaps even more valuable is the second kind of data, which show how satisfaction levels have changed as a consequence of particular organizational actions. By systematically gathering survey data, organizations can assess the effectiveness of their experiments with new policies and organization designs — not just in terms of immediate productivity outcomes, but in terms of human outcomes as well. This can help organizations develop a learning approach to their management practices and designs.

All too often, the wrong kinds of comparisons are made in interpreting data on job satisfaction and data concerned with the importance that individuals attach to particular aspects of their work environment. Comparisons are made on the relative satisfaction levels reported by individuals on factors such as their pay, their supervisor, and the nature of their work. The assumption seems to be that individuals who report that pay is more important or more satisfying than job security (or some other work factor) are more satisfied or place more importance on this factor. It is further assumed that this factor must, therefore, deserve special attention or is potentially a more powerful motivator of behavior than other factors. Unfortunately, this conclusion is too simplistic.

Years of research have shown that the relative importance ratings and relative satisfaction ratings that individuals assign to different factors in the work environment are very much a function of how the questions are worded. Further, individuals consistently tend to report that some items are more satisfying or more important than others, regardless of existing organizational conditions. For example, it is dangerous to assume that because individuals report more dissatisfaction with their pay, this is necessarily a higher-priority item for action than one for which individuals report less dissatisfaction. In situation after situation, almost regardless of how well individuals are compensated, pay is mentioned as a source of dissatisfaction. In most cases, the key issue is how pay satisfaction in one organization compares with pay satisfaction in another, or how it varies within the same organization at different points in time or among different parts of the same organization. This kind of comparison can often yield valid data about whether a particular job factor stands out or deserves special attention. This is in contrast to the more simplistic approach of comparing individuals' responses on one item with their responses on another item.

Because of increasing global competitiveness, the last decade has seen a decreased focus on job satisfaction and quality of work life and an increased focus on issues of organizational effectiveness. The decreased focus on satisfaction is unfortunate, because the quality of work life has a very powerful influence on people's quality of life in general, and is a societal outcome worth seeking in its own right. Thus, research on job satisfaction remains important, both because of the insights it provides into quality-of-work-life issues, and because of its impact on organizational effectiveness.

Extrinsic Rewards

Since writing *Motivation in Work Organizations,* a substantial amount of my work has focused on the role of extrinsic rewards, particularly financial rewards. Much of this work is summarized in my book, *Strategic Pay* (Lawler, 1990). Building upon the basic concepts presented in *Motivation in Work Organizations,* the work analyzes the way extrinsic rewards systems can and should be designed to fit different management systems. My work, and that of many others, continues to show that money can be an important motivator when a line of sight exists for individuals. The challenge in complex organizations is to find ways to reward individuals that allow for enough money to be involved so that the reward is important, and to deliver the reward in a way that ties it clearly to performance. This challenge has led me to do considerable research on individual-performance appraisal systems, since one way to distribute rewards is to focus on individual performance and to have supervisors judge performance and distribute rewards. Much of my research in this area was summarized in *Designing Performance Appraisal Systems,* a book that I coauthored with Allan Mohrman and Susan Resnick-West (Mohrman, Resnick-West, & Lawler, 1989). It emphasized that effectively appraising individual performance is a complex task that is often done poorly by managers. It also suggested that combining a discussion about pay with a performance appraisal is particularly difficult. Nevertheless, it stressed that if pay is to be a motivator, it must be discussed in conjunction with performance. Finally, it recommended separating skill- and career-development issues from discussions of past performance and related financial rewards.

The many difficult issues surrounding the effectiveness and practicality of individual pay-for-performance approaches have increasingly led me to focus my research on group and organizationwide pay-for-performance systems. There is still little question that, where appropriate, individual pay-for-performance is the most powerful motivator, because it has the strongest line of sight. However, there are many situations where because of work-design and organizational issues, individual pay-for-performance is simply not the best approach. This is particularly true when teams and highly participative management systems are used. In these situations, the best solution is often a pay-for-performance plan based on teams or business units.

My research, and that of others over the last decades, has shown that gainsharing plans, which reward whole plants or business units on the basis of their controllable operating results, can be quite effective if they are combined with participative-management and open-communication systems (Lawler, 1990). Although it is difficult to establish a line of sight for large numbers of individuals, the evidence suggests that this can be done if the organization openly provides business information and gives individuals a chance to influence organizational performance through suggestion systems and joint decision-making processes. This discovery has led an increasing number of companies to use gainsharing plans; the popularity of stock-ownership and profit-sharing plans has also increased (Lawler, Mohrman, & Ledford, 1992). A note of caution is in order, however: the evidence continues to show that employee-ownership and profit-sharing plans are effective only when there is strong employee involvement in a wide range of business decisions, and when employees have good access to business information. In the absence of these, there is no line of sight and therefore little or no impact on motivation.

My work has also increasingly focused on the role of pay in motivating individuals to acquire new skills and abilities. This approach to pay is usually called skill- or competency-based pay. In its simplest form, it rewards individuals for gaining increased competencies in a technical area or for learning new skills that broaden their abilities to perform organizational tasks. Paying individuals for their skills has proved to be particularly popular in team-oriented organizations that generally favor an employee-involvement approach to management.

Overall, my research on reward systems has increasingly suggested that extrinsic rewards, such as pay and promotion, can play a very important role in influencing motivation and in setting the overall culture of an organization. Extrinsic rewards help to define which behaviors are valued, motivate particular kinds of performance and management styles, and ultimately play a key role in determining how satisfied individuals are with their work experiences. It has also become more apparent that what is appropriate in the area of reward systems is significantly influenced by an organization's approach to work design and organization design.

Work Design

Motivation in Work Organizations argues convincingly that job design has an important impact on motivation, job satisfaction, and job performance. The subsequent research of Hackman and Oldham (1980) and others has confirmed this view. Indeed, I think it is fair to say that when *Motivation in Work Organizations* was written, our understanding of how the particular characteristics of a job influence motivation was just developing; still, the material on job design covered in Chapter 7 has stood the test of time. Today there is little doubt that job characteristics are critical in influencing motivation, and that the types of characteristics identified in Chapter 7 are the critical ones. For work to be motivating, individuals need to feel personally responsible for the outcomes of the work, need to do something that they feel is meaningful, and need to receive feedback about what is accomplished. This conclusion has been substantiated by hundreds of studies since the publication of *Motivation in Work Organizations,* some of which have pointed out that an individual's perception of a job is only partly determined by its objective characteristics (Griffin, 1987). The social setting of the job, as well as the past experiences of the individual, also play a role; thus, a one-to-one relationship between a job's characteristics and its impact on the motivation of individuals may not exist.

Chapter 7 correctly emphasizes that technology can limit the available job-design options. For example, in many mass-production situations it is difficult for individuals to have an "enriched" job — one in which they take a whole project from beginning to end. Recognition of this limitation may be partly responsible for the popularity of problem-solving groups and other approaches that give individuals a chance to perform nonroutine activities and to influence decisions. It also has led to the realization that some jobs should be automated rather than enriched. Substituting machines for people is increasingly popular and viable due to the rapid development of computer technology: many simple jobs can now be done by computers, thereby freeing people to do more challenging work.

Motivation in Work Organizations does not give much attention to the approach of making self-managing work teams responsible for whole products, services, or parts of the work process. Although there was research literature on "semiautonomous teams" at the time that *Motivation in Work Organizations* was written, few organizations had made use of teams. Today the situation is dramatically different. Most large corporations are at least experimenting with self-managing work teams, and some have decided to consistently organize themselves around work teams. A number of converging forces have led to the increased popularity of work teams.

Clearly, one contributing force is the complexity of the work done in most organizations today. A second is the high level of interdependence that exists among various tasks. Given high levels of complexity and interdependence, it is often hard to design individually enriched jobs, and thus organizations are faced with the challenge of either having relatively simple repetitive work, which is not motivating, or assigning meaningful pieces of work to teams and asking them to produce whole products or whole services.

The research evidence on teams suggests that teams are more complex to manage than individuals doing enriched jobs, but that many of the same principles that apply to individual work design also apply to team-based design. Teams can be intrinsically motivated to perform work if they receive a whole and meaningful piece of work to do, have considerable autonomy or discretion in how they carry out the work, and receive feedback about the effectiveness of their work (Hackman, 1987). Because teams provide a superior motivational structure, a team-based approach often leads to significant gains in performance output, quality, and employee satisfaction (Galbraith, Lawler & Associates, 1993).

Today, information technology is being used to provide teams and individuals with the information they need to be more self-managing and to receive valid feedback (Zubhoff, 1988). With such technology, it is possible to provide individuals and teams with the information they need to make decisions that previously were made only by top or middle management. It also can be used to combine tasks that were previously done by separate departments or individuals. The net effect can be a more motivating and satisfying workplace. Self-managing teams are particularly prevalent today in such process-production industries as food, chemicals, and paper, and they are becoming increasingly popular in financial and other service organizations. In many cases they are being installed as part of a total change to a high-performance work organization (Lawler, 1992).

A critical influence on the effectiveness of a team is the behavior of the team's manager or supervisor. The traditional supervisory role disappears in this type of structure; what is needed is an individual who can help the team work on its internal operating processes and who can help with feedback, goal setting, and relations between the team and the rest of the organization. This is obviously a very different concept of the managerial role than the one that existed when *Motivation in Work Organizations* was published. At that time, the distinction was often made between the traditional supervisor, who controls subordinates by using extrinsic rewards and punishments, and the more participative supervisor, who involves individuals in decision making and responds to their suggestions in a supportive way. In the traditional organization, carefully written job descriptions, performance contracts, rules, and standard operating procedures were all used to establish accountability and supervisory control. Reward and discipline systems were put in place to reinforce the message that individuals were expected to perform according to the demands of the organization and the supervisor. Some research at that time showed that individuals were often more committed to decisions that they had a role in making, and that democratically led work teams were often more cohesive and satisfied. Missing from the research was an overall view of the distinction between managers and leaders, and an analysis of the role that leaders can play in motivating organizational behavior.

The last decade has seen a plethora of writings on the role of leaders, and a number of differences between leaders and managers have been identified (see, for example, Bennis & Nanus, 1985; Kotter, 1990). Leaders are typically seen as people who set direction, provide goals, and create a vision for the organization, while managers are seen as administrators who largely engage in traditional supervisory behaviors. There seems little question that motivation and satisfaction can be influenced by certain leadership behaviors. This point clearly ties back to the research on work design and motivational factors. To be motivating, tasks need to be meaningful and provide feedback about organizational success. Leaders can play a key role in establishing the meaningfulness and significance of the tasks that individuals and teams perform, and they can also help provide feedback from both internal and external customers.

In many ways, it is counterproductive to view managerial behaviors and leadership behaviors as necessarily competing. Most large, complex organizations need individuals who can be both leaders and managers. Managerial roles often require individuals who can define and measure performance and direct the operations of the organization. If that is all they do, however, the evidence suggests that they will do a poor job of creating a motivating and satisfying work setting; they also need to focus on the mission of the organization—its aims, goals, and agenda—and help others see how they can play a meaningful role in the organization.

High-Performance Work Organizations

At the time that *Motivation in Work Organizations* was written, very few organizations were willing to make a commitment to large-scale experimentation with new management approaches. Instead, they were happy to make small changes in pay systems, work design, or leadership behavior in order to improve organizational effectiveness. They were not willing to completely rethink the overall design of the organization and to create new approaches to organizing. Today the situation is much different.

There are a number of terms currently being used to describe the new work structures and management styles that organizations are implementing. "Total quality management," "reengineering," "the learning organization," "high-involvement management," and a host of other terms are being used to describe the types of organizational change processes and designs likely to be effective in today's competitive environment. Many of the change efforts popular today stress the reality that dramatic improvements in organizational effectiveness often require not just a change in reward systems, managerial behavior, or work design, but a total redesign of the way that organizations are managed.

There are a number of interesting examples of companies that have moved from a traditional to a high-involvement or high-performance work organization model. This organization-design approach is particularly interesting because it strives to create an organizational fit among the key elements covered in *Motivation in Work Organizations.* It emphasizes attracting individuals with the right need structures, designing work that is intrinsically motivating, extrinsically rewarding members of the organization for performance effectiveness, and having leaders who provide a participative-management environment and have a sense of vision and direction for the organization. In short, it does not simply represent a change in one of the many factors that influence motivation and satisfaction—it recasts all the key elements of the organization.

My work on organization design has been published in several books and has led me to distinguish among three different levels of employee involvement (see, for example, Lawler, 1992): (1) parallel suggestion involvement, (2) job involvement, and (3) high involvement. They differ in the degree to which they move the four key features of an organization to its lowest level. Briefly, the features are

1. *Information* about the performance, strategy, and mission of the organization.
2. *Rewards* that are based on the performance of the organization and the capabilities of individuals.
3. *Knowledge* that enables employees to understand and contribute to organizational performance.
4. *Power* to make decisions that influence organizational practices, policies, and directions.

When information, rewards, knowledge, and power are concentrated at the top, an organization is using traditional control-oriented management; when they are moved downward, it is practicing employee involvement in some form. Because the three approaches to involvement have different strategies for positioning power, information, knowledge, and rewards, these approaches tend to fit different situations and to produce different results. Let us consider how each of these three approaches operates, and the results each produces. Once we have reviewed them, we can discuss when and how they are best used.

Parallel Suggestion Involvement

In suggestion-involvement programs, employees are asked to solve problems and produce ideas that will influence how the organization operates. The programs are a parallel structure to the ongoing activities of the organization, because they take people out of their regular situations and put them in separate new situations that operate differently from the traditional organization.

Quality circles and other types of problem-solving groups are an extremely popular approach to suggestion involvement. They are often installed as one part of a total-quality program. Like written-suggestion programs, they ask employees to recommend ways that the operation of the organization can be improved. Suggestions are developed through a problem-solving group or quality circle. In quality circles, considerable training is done to enable the group to function effectively and to help individuals become efficient problem-solvers. The group does not have the power to implement their suggestions; instead, they depend on management to accept and implement their ideas.

Suggestion-involvement programs do not represent a major shift in the way control-oriented organizations deal with most issues. They rely instead on a special parallel structure to change the relationship between individuals and their organization. This structure gives people the chance to influence things that they would not normally influence and, in some cases, to share in the financial results of this new activity. It also usually leads to the communication of some additional information, and to greater knowledge among individuals. However, the change in knowledge, information, and rewards is limited to a small percentage of the work force. In addition, this change is encapsulated because individuals are expected to use it only when they are operating in special suggestion activities. During their regular work activities, it is business as usual.

Research on the parallel-structure or suggestion-involvement approach indicates that it can lead to improvements in organizational performance, particularly when used as part of a total-quality-management program (Lawler, 1986). Participants are often quite motivated to come up with new ideas — sometimes because they are given recognition rewards when they are successful, but mostly because they see a chance to make a difference, and this is the key reward. Case after case shows that individuals and groups often come up with suggestions that save considerable amounts of money. There also seems to be no doubt that most employees enjoy the opportunity to participate in problem-solving and, in the process, learn new skills and obtain new information. As a result, they are often more satisfied with their work situation, are absent less, and are less likely to quit while they are engaged in these activities.

Quality circles and other parallel structures are often easy to install and can be quickly implemented. The problem-solving groups can be small and do not need to disrupt the organization. They can be installed in a single plant or even in a department within a larger organization. However, they do not change the existing organization structure or affect the motivation of individuals in how they perform their regular jobs.

The European and American management literature contains well-documented studies showing the limitations of parallel suggestion involvement. The approach tends to have a "program character" about it that can make it seem temporary. Parallel structures are expensive to establish and operate. In some situations, they run out of suggestions because individuals do not have enough expertise to solve the more complex problems. Also, they are often resisted by the middle levels of management because parallel structures may threaten their power and force them to do extra work. Conflict can develop between those who are in parallel structures and those who are not; nonparticipants may resent being left out. Finally, suggestion-involvement approaches that are not supported by reward-system and other changes may simply lose their momentum and disappear, because they do not systematically change the way an organization operates or the way the total work force relates to the organization and its performance. In addition, individuals often feel dissatisfied if they cannot share in the financial savings realized from their suggestions. Overall, they are more supportive of continuous improvement change than transformational change, which produces new organizational structures and dramatic performance improvements.

Job Involvement

Job-involvement approaches focus on designing work in ways that will motivate better job performance. As discussed in Chapter 5, the job-enrichment approach focuses on creating individual tasks that give people feedback, increase their influence over how the work is done, require them to use a variety of skills, and give them a whole piece of work. Another job-involvement strategy calls for the creation of self-managing work groups or teams. As noted earlier, this is different from individual job enrichment in that the work group is the primary unit of involvement. It tries to create group tasks and group-performance measures and to make all members feel responsible for their group's performance. Groups designed according to this approach are often called autonomous work groups, self-managing groups, semiautonomous work groups, or work teams.

     Job involvement has significant implications for how an organization is structured and managed. In essence, individuals are given new skills and knowledge, new feedback, an additional set of decisions to make, and possibly a different reward system. Both the individual and the team approach have these effects, although the fully realized team approach has them to a greater degree. With the team approach, interpersonal skills and group decision-making skills need to be developed. The reward system is also changed more dramatically with groups or teams, since pay is often based on skills. Finally, teams can make certain decisions that individuals usually cannot. Both individuals and teams can control the way the work is done, and perform quality management, inventory, and other task-related activities. Teams can also make personnel-management decisions about hiring and firing, and may select their own supervisors.

The choice between individual and team job enrichment should be based on the technology of the workplace as well as the comparative advantages and disadvantages of the two approaches. Teams are more complicated to build and maintain but may be necessary if the work is so complex that no individual can do a whole part of it and get adequate feedback. Teams are usually most appropriate in process-production facilities such as chemical plants, glass works, and oil refineries, and in complex service situations such as airlines. In these cases, no individual can provide an entire service or produce an entire product; indeed, it may take an entire team or several teams with carefully managed relationships among them to handle such a complex job. As part of their efforts to reduce layers of management, many corporate reengineering programs have created teams that are responsible for entire work processes.

One final difference between teams and the individual work-design approach is that individual job enrichment typically does not create a world in which social rewards are important motivators. Since individuals are essentially doing their own work activities, with little social interaction and interdependence, there is often a lack of social rewards — particularly social rewards that are tied to good performance. The situation is quite different with a cohesive interdependent team. Not only is there a greater chance for social interaction, so that individuals can fulfill their social needs in the workplace, but also praise, recognition, and other kinds of social rewards can often be tied to effective performance. This occurs because everyone on a team gains when a particular individual performs well and helps others in the team. Teammates typically respond to this by offering praise and support to the individual who has contributed to team success. For individuals who value social rewards, particularly peer-based recognition, this can be a powerful motivator of performance and an important feature of teams.

Where the technology allows an individual to produce a whole product or offer a whole service, individual designs may be preferred because they are simple to install and can give the individual more direct feedback. As I mentioned earlier, this is increasingly possible because of the capabilities provided by computers and information technology. Even with individually enriched work, individuals can still come together as a team to engage in certain team activities, such as deciding which applicants to hire and how the workplace will be laid out and structured.

Overall, job involvement represents a significant change in the fundamental operations of an organization. Individuals at the lowest levels of an organization get new information, power, and skills, and may be evaluated and rewarded in new ways. The changes relate to particular work processes and activities and typically do not involve the structure and operation of the whole organization, nor the development of its strategic direction. Unlike parallel-suggestion approaches, job involvement affects the day-to-day work activities of all individuals. Involvement is not a special activity; it is the way in which work is done. Unlike suggestion programs, job involvement seems to be reasonably stable, particularly when teams are used, since they represent cohesive units that are difficult to dissolve.

The limitations of the job-involvement approach come primarily from lost opportunities. Because they limit employee involvement to immediate work decisions, they do not capture the contributions that individuals can make to strategic decisions and to higher-level management work. This can lead to a tendency for individuals in work teams to optimize their own performance without paying much attention to the overall performance of the organization. Job-involvement approaches may be canceled if they do not influence higher-level strategic decisions. Unless major restructuring is done to support the program, supervisors may be able to unilaterally make changes to jobs that take away critical decision-making power. Job-involvement efforts are most likely to be canceled when they affect only small parts of an organization. Like parallel structures, they can be installed on a limited basis and, as a result, can create friction between participants and nonparticipants.

Job-involvement efforts do have significant start-up costs. They always require training and often require new layouts of equipment and new information systems. Often overlooked is the need for supervisor training and for dramatically changing the supervisor's role. Job-involvement efforts are often resisted by middle managers, who may feel threatened by others' newly acquired power and who may be unable to learn the new skills required to manage successfully.

Job involvement essentially alters the intrinsic-reward situation in an organization. Because working effectively provides feelings of accomplishment, achievement, and efficacy, individuals usually become more motivated. The approach can also lead to higher levels of intrinsic satisfaction because of both the rewards received from working effectively and the development of new skills and competencies required for the more complex work. Although the extrinsic-reward situation may change as a result of installing a skills-based pay system, job involvement does not use extrinsic rewards to motivate performance. This is obviously a major omission in the approach, since extrinsic rewards such as pay can have a powerful impact on performance and can potentially contribute to the more effective performance of teams and individuals.

Critical to the effectiveness of the job-involvement approach is behavioral change on the part of the supervisor. Such change may be accomplished by training the manager to act in a more participative manner and demonstrate more leadership behavior. However, it may take a much more substantial change. Many of the gains that can be achieved through the job-involvement approach come from reducing the number of supervisors and the amount of overhead in the organization. Realizing these gains often requires a larger restructuring of the organization and the creation of a virtually new organizational architecture. All too often, the job-involvement approach fails to address these issues; as a result, perhaps a few more motivating jobs are created, but few gains are achieved by reducing overhead.

Overall, the job-involvement approach runs the risk of

failing to deal with the important role that extrinsic rewards can play in motivating performance. It also can fail to substantially change the overall operations of the organization so that all the gains that are possible from having a more intrinsically motivated work force are achieved.

High Involvement

The high-involvement approach has also been called the "commitment approach," "total employee involvement," and, perhaps more descriptively, "business involvement." This approach builds upon what has been learned from the suggestion-involvement and job-involvement approaches in an effort to produce high-performance organizations. It structures an organization so that people at the lowest level will have a sense of involvement, not just in how effectively they perform as individuals or in groups, but also in the performance of the total organization. High involvement goes considerably further than either of the other two approaches toward moving power, information, knowledge, and rewards to the lowest level. It creates an environment in which individuals care about the performance of the organization — because they know about it, are able to influence it, are rewarded for it, and have the knowledge and skills to contribute to it. To have high-involvement management, virtually every major feature of the organization needs to be designed differently than when the control approach is used (Lawler, 1992).

In the case of decision-making power, employees need to be involved in decisions about their work activities, and to play a role in organization-level decisions about strategy, organization design and other major issues. To make this happen, organizations need to be designed around business- or customer-based units, rather than divided into functional areas. Staff groups need to be kept small and placed in a service role. Task forces need to be used to involve cross-sections of the employee base in making important decisions about organization design and strategy. Perhaps most important, organizations need to have a flat structure with relatively wide spans of management.

In a high-involvement organization, everyone's rewards

should be based on the performance of the organization; hence, profit sharing, gainsharing, and some type of employee ownership are appropriate. In addition, individuals should be rewarded for their contributions. This is best handled in most cases by using skills-based pay for all employees. Pay information should also be disclosed, so that employees can understand how the pay system operates and participate in making decisions about other employees' pay. Finally, where practical, a policy of employment stability for all individuals can help reinforce the organization's stated commitment to its employees.

As with the other approaches, high involvement requires that employees have expertise in problem analysis, decision making, group process, and self-management. They also need cross-training to understand the entire work process in their work area. To understand their organization's pay-for-performance system and to participate in higher-level decision making, they must be trained in business economics and basic business strategy.

Getting relevant business information to all employees is a key to success in a high-involvement organization. Modern information technology is a valuable tool: it can potentially give employees throughout an organization the kind of operating data that will both inform them of how the business is performing and allow them to make business decisions, even though they are not at the senior management level. Information systems must also be designed to provide a good upward flow of information about how the organization is operating from a process point of view. Attitude-survey data, sensing sessions, and grievance information channels can be used for this. Finally, lateral communication must be supported by using cross-functional task forces, encouraging horizontal career moves, and, where possible, creating channels in the information-technology system that will encourage such communication.

The behavior of managers is critical to the success of a high-involvement organization. Earlier, the distinction was made between management behavior and leadership behavior. In high-involvement organizations, managers need to demonstrate substantial leadership behavior. In the absence of traditional control structures, substitute structures must be found. A sense of organizational direction, vision, goals, and purpose can be a powerful replacement for traditional controls. The responsibility for developing these substitutes should be taken by the senior management group. Without a clear sense of purpose and vision for the organization, there is a great danger that individual work units and teams may pursue their own objectives and agenda at the expense of the organization. In addition, it is quite possible that managers will revert to traditional, control-oriented reward-and-punishment behavior; this could eliminate the intrinsic motivation that is critical to the success of enriched jobs and self-managing work teams.

Creating a high-involvement organization is clearly a much different and more complex task than implementing job involvement or parallel-suggestion involvement. Virtually every feature of a control-oriented organization must be redesigned; in some cases, design innovation is necessary because the right approaches simply may not be developed or available.

There is relatively little data on the effectiveness of high-involvement organizations. The admittedly sketchy testimonial evidence that does exist generally indicates superior operating results; such organizations tend to be low-cost, low-overhead, relatively flexible, adaptive, and highly quality oriented and customer oriented (Lawler, 1992).

Much of the success of high-involvement organizations seems due to their ability to motivate and satisfy employees. Their very low turnover rates seem to be the product of a desirable mix of intrinsic and extrinsic rewards. Perhaps their most outstanding feature is their ability to motivate performance with both intrinsic and extrinsic rewards. The key to this is the combination of moving information, knowledge, power, and rewards to all members of the organization. In a traditional organization, reward systems based on plant or unit performance are not motivating: there is simply no line of sight between individual or team performance and organizational performance. In situations where individuals are informed about organization results — and have the chance to influence them — these reward systems can be quite motivating. There may be some loss of extrinsic motivation compared with a traditional organization;

such a loss is caused by the lack of strong individual-performance incentives but is usually offset by the effects of peer behavior on the motivation of individuals.

In a collective-reward system, peers will recognize and reward individuals for their outstanding performance in ways that simply do not occur with individual-reward systems. The reason for this, of course, is that in individual-reward systems, there is little gain for an individual if someone else performs well; indeed, it may be to the individual's disadvantage. The situation changes dramatically with group and organizationwide rewards. In these situations, it is to everyone's collective advantage that individuals and teams perform well. Thus, norms develop that support and recognize individuals who perform well. In fact, these norms may *demand* that individuals perform well.

Part of the self-management process is the ability of teams to discipline and manage the performance of their individual members. Because they emphasize interesting and challenging work, high-involvement organizations also capitalize on the motivation that comes from accomplishment, achievement, and effectiveness. Particularly where the organization has an important social mission, individuals may also be motivated by a sense of contribution to a social value or purpose they believe in.

Overall, the high-involvement approach can potentially create a superior motivational environment within an organization — one that combines both intrinsic and extrinsic motivation. The job-enrichment approach emphasizes intrinsic motivation, while traditional-management systems rely predominantly on extrinsic motivation. Because of this, neither approach can successfully maximize the motivation of the entire work force. One approach or the other may appeal to individuals who are primarily motivated by either intrinsic or extrinsic rewards, but neither will appeal fully to those individuals who are motivated by both types of rewards. Appreciable gains are possible through the combination of intrinsic and extrinsic motivation that is present in a high-involvement organization. It is precisely this phenomenon that allows for lateral integration and flattening of the organization along with the reduction of supervisors, directors, and control systems. It can also produce tremendous savings if it reduces turnover and absenteeism, both of which can be very costly to organizations. Finally, research shows that involvement produces a greater focus on quality, because individuals who want to excel see quality as an intrinsically rewarding outcome. The evidence shows that an emphasis on quality produces savings in many areas, including materials, labor, and repeat customer business.

Even though the high-involvement or high-performance organization model appears to have the highest potential for improving organizational performance, its widespread acceptance is still far from complete. It seems to fit particularly well in those organizations concerned with speed to market, high-quality products, and superior cost-performance. High involvement is increasingly being used by companies in Western Europe and the United States that face tough international competition; these companies realize that the ultimate competitive advantage is their ability to organize, manage, and motivate individuals. In many organizations, the practical application of high involvement is possible partly because of the evolution of information technology, which can allow individuals to work on whole work processes and receive the information they need to make complex decisions quickly. It also allows individuals and teams to be linked together without the extensive use of hierarchy. It is this capability, along with the creation of a context in which employees are motivated to operate without a controlling supervisor, that allows organizations to operate with fewer levels of hierarchy and to achieve increasingly higher levels of performance.

Motivating Organizational Change

A major challenge in producing large-scale organizational change lies in motivating individuals to change. In many respects, effective change management is essentially a matter of managing the motivation to change. As indicated by the expectancy model, this means making clear the negative consequences of not changing, as well as the positive consequences of adopting a new approach to management. Some of the anxieties associated with the change process can often be reduced by involving people in making decisions, but it is still often difficult to get organizations to make major changes.

All too often, major organizational change occurs only when an organization is in serious trouble and is faced with complete failure. At this point, of course, the motivation for change is at a maximum, and traditional resistance to change often disappears. Getting an organization to change before it is in a crisis situation is a critical motivational issue. This often takes strong leaders who can describe a very positive vision of the outcomes associated with change as well as the negative consequences of maintaining the status quo. Sometimes this can be facilitated by bringing data into the organization that demonstrate the consequences of the failure to change, and by familiarizing members of the organization with how other organizations' positive outcomes are related to new ways of managing.

My research on high-involvement management has often involved working with start-up divisions of traditionally managed organizations. These are often the easiest places to install new work structures and practices and evaluate their effectiveness. It simply turns out to be much easier to create a new high-involvement organization than to change an existing organization to this way of operating. The reasons for this are essentially motivational. Most of the individuals in traditional organizations are comfortable with the way their organization operates and are there precisely because it is a reasonably satisfying environment for them. Individuals at the top level of traditional organizations often feel that they have a great deal to lose by moving to a new organizational approach. As indicated earlier, however, they are also the ones who should lead the change effort. Giving up old practices to adopt new ones, particularly when the old ones are well established, is seen as quite a threat. Thus, it seems inevitable that any change in management will be easier and more frequent in new situations than in existing organizations. Nevertheless, there are increasing numbers of examples of existing organizations that have changed because of exceptional leadership by a management team or an individual manager that sees the need to change and is able to lead the rest of the organization in the change process.

As I write this introduction, I am struck by how rapidly management practices are changing and by the fact that this rate of change is likely to continue. Increasingly, organizations are realizing that their methods of organizing and managing can give them a critical competitive advantage; as a result, innovation and creativity are occurring in organization design. New developments are constantly appearing and new terminology is constantly being introduced. Even the work force itself has changed — readers will note that the language of *Motivation in Work Organizations* does not reflect the influx of women into those organizations which has occurred since it was written.

I am also struck, however, by the fact that, in order to be effective, every approach to management must deal with the issue of work motivation. No organization design or approach can succeed if it cannot motivate employees to perform well. To be motivating, a work system must confront the questions of why an individual should work for an organization, and why that individual should make an effort to improve the organization's performance. This was true in 1973, when *Motivation in Work Organizations* was first published, and is still true today. As was also true in 1973, it is clear that for individuals to be committed to joining and performing well in an organization, they must receive important rewards associated with their membership and performance. One thing has not changed: individuals are motivated by rewards.

References

Bandura, A. *Social Foundations of Thought and Action: A Social-Cognitive View.* Englewood Cliffs, N.J.: Prentice-Hall, 1986.

Bennis, W. and Nanus, B. *Leaders.* New York: HarperCollins, 1985.

Galbraith, J. R., Lawler, E. E., and Associates. *Organizing for the Future: The New Logic for Managing Complex Organizations.* San Francisco: Jossey-Bass, 1993.

Griffin, R. W. "Toward an Integrated Theory of Task Design." In Staw, B. and Cummings, L. L. (Eds.), *Research in Organizational Behavior,* Vol. 9, pp. 79–120. Greenwich, Conn.: JAI Press, 1987.

Hackman, J. R. "The Design of Work Teams." *In J. Lorsch (ed.), Handbook of Organizational Behavior,* pp. 315–342, Englewood, N.J.: Prentice-Hall, 1987.

Hackman, J. R. and Oldham, G. R. *Work Redesign.* Reading, Mass.: Addison-Wesley, 1980.

Kotter, J. P. *A Force for Change.* New York: Free Press, 1990.

Lawler, E. E. *High-Involvement Management: Participative Strategies for Improving Organizational Performance.* San Francisco: Jossey-Bass, 1986.

Lawler, E. E. *Strategic Pay: Aligning Organizational Strategies and Pay Systems.* San Francisco: Jossey-Bass, 1990.

Lawler, E. E. *The Ultimate Advantage: Creating the High Involvement Organization.* San Francisco: Jossey-Bass, 1992.

Lawler, E. E., Mohrman, S. A., and Ledford, G. E. *Employee Involvement and Total Quality Management: Practices and Results in Fortune 1000 Companies.* San Francisco: Jossey-Bass, 1992.

Locke, E. A. and Latham, G. P. *A Theory of Goal Setting and Task Performance.* Englewood Cliffs, N.J.: Prentice-Hall, 1990.

Mohrman, A. M., Resnick-West, S. M., and Lawler, E. E. *Designing Performance Appraisal Systems: Aligning Appraisals and Organizational Realities.* San Francisco: Jossey-Bass, 1989.

Mohrman, S. A., and Cummings, T. G. *Self-Designing Organizations.* Reading, Mass.: Addison-Wesley, 1989.

Zubhoff, S. *In the Age of the Smart Machine.* New York: Basic, 1988.

Preface

This book is about the motivational determinants of behavior in organizations. It is written for undergraduate and graduate students interested in behavior in organizations as well as for practitioners who must deal with the day-to-day motivational problems that occur in organizations. Partially because it is written with a student audience in mind, Chapters 2, 3, and 4 deal rather extensively with motivation theory. It is my belief that, in the area of motivation, students should be exposed to theory because, if they understand theory, they can think analytically about any of the motivational issues that occur in organizations. Chapters 5, 6, 7, 8, and 9 emphasize research and practice and translate theory into action by discussing topics such as how job design, leadership style, and pay systems affect motivation.

Practicing managers may wish to approach the book by concentrating their attention on Chapters 5 through 9, since this material is most directly relevant to their problems. Managers should also find the beginning chapters helpful in providing the kind of conceptual framework that will allow them to deal effectively with situations and people not specifically discussed in the book. The ability to analyze situations from the perspective of what influences motivation is a skill that managers must have

if they are to deal with the many complex motivational problems they confront. No book can offer solutions to all the specific problems that arise in organizations; thus, an understanding of what influences motivation is vital.

For me, this book represents the summation and integration of a number of years of research. Many people helped with
my research and influenced my thinking during this time. I
received helpful comments on the manuscript from Cortlandt
Cammann, J. Richard Hackman, Terry Mitchell, Lyman
Porter, and Gerrit Wolf. I wish to thank the reviewers of the
manuscript: Mason Haire, Massachusetts Institute of Technology; Edgar H. Schein, Massachusetts Institute of Technology;
and Victor Vroom, Yale University. Jane Doberstyn, Maryellen
Holford, and Barbara Prittie all helped with the typing and edit-
ing of the manuscript. Special thanks go to Ginny Decker for
her editorial work on the manuscript.

Edward E. Lawler III

The Author

Edward E. Lawler III is professor of management and organization in the business school at the University of Southern California and founding director of the Center for Effective Organizations. He received his B.A. degree (1960) from Brown University in psychology and his Ph.D. degree (1964) from the University of California, Berkeley, also in psychology. He has consulted with more than one hundred organizations and with four national governments on employee involvement, organizational change, and compensation and has been honored as a top contributor to the fields of organizational development, organizational behavior, and compensation. He is the author of more than two hundred articles and twenty-two books, and his works have been translated into seven languages. His books include *High-Involvement Management* (1986), *Strategic Pay* (1990), and *The Ultimate Advantage* (1992). He is coauthor of *Employee Involvement and Total Quality Management: Practices and Results in Fortune 1000 Companies* (1992, with S. A. Mohrman and G. E. Ledford, Jr.), and *Organizing for the Future: The New Logic of Organizing* (1993, with J. Galbraith and associates).

Motivation in
Work Organizations

one

Motivated Behavior in Work Organizations

In most manufacturing jobs the best worker produces two to three times as much as the worst worker. In other jobs, differences of even greater magnitude exist. This book is about one of the major reasons why workers produce at different rates: motivation. Motivation is certainly not the only factor that causes people to produce at different rates, since the performance level of an individual is influenced by many factors. In addition to being influenced by motivation, performance is affected by a worker's ability and by a number of situational and environmental factors. Mechanical breakdowns, low-quality materials, an inadequate supply of materials, and so on can severely limit production. Still, particularly in the case of lower-level jobs where little ability is required, motivation seems to be the single most important determinant of performance.

The important role of motivation in determining performance is graphically illustrated by Whyte's (1955) study of two workers in a machine shop. The workers in this shop were subject to a pay-incentive system that made them eligible for a bonus when their production exceeded 66 percent of what had been determined to be "normal" or standard production. One worker had an average productivity of only 52 percent of standard. Why

was he such a low producer? Was it because he did not have
the ability to do the work? Apparently not, since at one time
he had earned a substantial bonus. According to him, he didn't
produce more because he simply didn't want to work any harder;
or as he put it:

> You've got to keep your nose to the wheel. You
> can't stop for a visit, or you'll lose everything you've
> made . . . And even if things was fixed so you would
> make your regular bonus by working like hell—I
> still wouldn't want it if I had to make somebody
> sore to get it or have the whole shop down on me.
> Don't misunderstand me. I'd like a little bonus. But
> they don't give it away, and I won't pay the price
> they want—be a _____ [p. 41].

Not everyone in the machine shop felt this way about high
productivity, however. The second worker who was studied produced over 150 percent of standard and was highly motivated
by the bonus system. According to him:

> I'm out here to make money. If any of these damn
> loafers think they can stop me, let them try it. I
> keep my bills paid an' don't owe anybody a damn
> cent. I mind my own business and look after my
> job. I'm always on time. I never lay off an' I don't
> sneak out early. The company can count on me,
> so why the hell should I care what a bunch of damn
> snoopy bums think of me [p.41]?

The snoopy bums he refers to are his co-workers who reject
highly productive workers.

   The very different motivation levels of these two workers
did not come about by accident, nor is the discrepancy beyond
our ability to explain. It is a direct function of a number of factors, among which are the goals of the two workers, their perception of the situation, and the actual functioning of the particular reward system. But before we look in depth at what

determines a person's motivation in a work situation, we need to consider how the term "motivation" has been used by psychologists, and we need to look at the basic approaches to motivation that have been dominant in the field of psychology.

The Concept of Motivation

Psychologists have used the term "motivation" in a variety of ways. Because of this, they have not always agreed on exactly which types of behavior should be classified as motivated behavior. At the present time, there seems to be some agreement that the distinguishing characteristic of motivated behavior is that it is goal-directed. Bindra (1959) has said that the core of what is usually called the problem of motivation lies in the "purposive" or goal-directed aspect of behavior. The concept of motivation is not needed to explain or predict all behavior. No concept of motivation is necessary to explain the contraction of the pupil of the eye in response to light or the jerk of the knee in response to a blow. Some behavior is reflexive rather than purposive or goal-directed. We will follow the common practice of defining motivated behavior as behavior that is under central or voluntary control. Thus, reflexive behavior, which is strictly determined by the reaction of nerves to external stimuli, will not be dealt with.

It is generally accepted that, in examining goal-directed behavior, one must consider both what energizes the behavior and what directs the behavior toward the goal. Atkinson (1964) maintains that "the study of motivation has to do with the analysis of the various factors which incite and direct an individual's actions" (p. 1). M. R. Jones (1955) has stated that motivation is concerned with "how behavior gets started, is energized, is sustained, is directed, is stopped, and what kind of subjective reaction is present in the organism while all this is going on" (p. vii). Clearly, Jones' definition is more detailed and inclusive than Bindra's or Atkinson's. As we shall see, the research on motivation in organizations has, in fact, touched all the issues raised by Jones's definition, and suggests that they must all be considered if we are to understand motivation in organizations. Thus, we shall accept his definition, since it will produce the most comprehensive and valid coverage of the literature on motivation in organizations.

Common Sense and Motivation

"Common-sense explanations" of motivational phenomena generally consist of verbally linking a given activity with one or another of certain states or events that are culturally recognized as goals or desirable outcomes. Any given behavior is made intelligible to common sense when the sentence "X does Y in order to . . ." is completed. Thus, a satisfactory common-sense explanation of why someone works hard can take the form "X is working hard in order to earn more money." However, as a scientific explanation of why X is behaving as he is, this is hardly satisfactory. It does not say why X wants to earn more money or why X does Y rather than Z in order to obtain the money. Further, it does not say why X seeks money rather than some other goal or outcome. An acceptable scientific explanation of X's behavior must specify all these things. It must say why money is the goal, why money is sought rather than some other goal, and why X pursues the goal in the manner he does.

At this point it is important to distinguish between theories of motivation and theories that concern themselves with specifying the nature of human needs or drives. Acceptable theories of human needs or drives have to deal only with why outcomes such as pay, promotion, and job security are sought while other outcomes are avoided. This kind of theory should not be confused with a theory of motivation that tries to fully explain and predict behavior. To explain and predict behavior, a theory must state not only why some outcomes are sought while others are avoided but also the factors that influence how they are sought.

Many psychologists and managers do, however, confuse these two. They assume that, because they have theories that make statements about the attractiveness of objects or outcomes, they somehow have theories of motivation that can explain and predict behavior. This is a misleading assumption. Because of the nature of their theories, they are limited to saying why something is a goal and to predicting what kind of objects or outcomes will be sought. They cannot predict how a person will behave in order to obtain or avoid a particular outcome.

Motivation and the Nature of Man

The work on motivation in the field of psychology has been dominated by two different views of the nature of man. One represents man as being driven by inherited, conflicting, unconscious drives that cause him to behave in instinctual and, at times, self-destructive ways. The second view represents man as rational and aware of his goals and as behaving in those ways that he feels will help him achieve his goals. The first view had its origin in the writings of Freud and the neo-Freudians and has continued to develop during the last fifty years. The second view can be traced to the work of Plato and Aristotle and more recently to the work of Descartes, Hobbes, and Spinoza. A number of learning theories in psychology stem from the views of these philosophers. For example, the expectancy theories of Tolman and Lewin picture behavior as being determined by people's goals and the expectancies people have that various behaviors will lead to the goals. The drive theories of Hull and Spence emphasize that behavior is determined by drives and by learned associations between situation and behavior.

The distinction between man as a rational, goal-oriented being and man as a being governed by unconscious drives is a very important one. If we accept a view of man as a rational being, then the very design of organizations needs to be different from what it would be if we accept the instinctual model of man. The instinctual model calls for an organization dominated by controls by which the organization tries to monitor and direct the behavior of people. The rational model suggests that motivation can be influenced by the use of goals and that self-control is possible.

These models also suggest very different ways of approaching the study of motivation. One argues for trying to understand how people's goals develop and how people learn to obtain their goals. The other suggests trying to understand instincts and the analysis of individuals' fantasies, thoughts, and actions in order to understand what unconscious motives may be in operation.

At this point in the history of research on human motivation there is no doubt that at times people do behave in irrational ways and that their behavior is influenced by goals that are not conscious. The work of Freud and his successors has clearly shown this. The concepts of Freudian psychology have proved very helpful in the treatment of mentally ill people, who are often characterized by a low awareness of motives and by behavior that appears to be irrational.

It also seems clear, however, that the vast majority of human behavior is goal directed and is at least rational in the eyes of the behaver. Apparently, most people are aware of their goals and try to achieve them in what they think is the best way. Objectively, their way may not be the best, but at least in their eyes it appears to be the best. Research also shows that people have strong affective reactions to the results of their behavior. They have different feelings when they achieve their goals and when they don't. Their reactions are both predictable and important in understanding human behavior. Thus, in our discussion of motivation we are going to assume that:

1. People have many conscious, often complex and competing goals.
2. Most behavior is consciously goal directed.
3. People have affective reactions to the outcomes they obtain as a result of their behavior.

In summary, then, the principal task of any motivation theory should be to explain the voluntary choices people make among different behaviors. Our assumption is that this can best be accomplished by understanding the goals people have and how they feel these goals can be obtained. Admittedly, this view of motivation omits some behavior—specifically that which is not under voluntary control—but it probably includes a large proportion of the total behavior of adult human beings. It certainly includes almost all the crucial behaviors that individuals exhibit in the context of work organizations.

Why Motivation in Work Organizations?

Work organizations represent an important and challenging place in which to study human motivation. We live in a society that is dominated by organizations. Four out of five people work in organizations at one time or another during their lives; many people spend half their waking hours in work organizations. It is hard to deny the importance of understanding how motivation affects so much of the behavior that takes place in our society. It is also hard to deny that a work environment is highly conducive to the study of motivation. Work organizations control much of what happens to employees for eight or more hours a day. During this time, organizations try a number of different approaches designed to motivate employees to behave in certain ways. By studying the results of these organizational efforts, we can learn how people react to different motivational actions. Since employees within any work organization usually come from diverse educational, ethnic, and socioeconomic backgrounds, the opportunity also exists to focus on individual differences in motivation and behavior (Dubin, 1958).

It is precisely because we live in a society that is so dominated by organizations that we need to learn more about the determinants of organizational effectiveness. At times everyone has poked fun at the inefficiency of the large bureaucratic organizations that have evolved in our society. There is a serious side to this inefficiency, however. A complex interdependent society must have effective organizations if it is to provide a high quality of life for its members.

Those individual behaviors that are crucial in determining the effectiveness of organizations are, almost without exception, voluntary, motivated behaviors. Therefore, it is important that we understand how organizations influence the motivation of their individual members. If we are ever to have effective organizations we must understand how to encourage effective individual performance. We must understand why one employee works at less than 60 percent of standard and another works at over 150 percent of standard.

Studying motivation in organizations is challenging because of the enormity and complexity of the problem. Part of

the complexity is that work organizations come in different sizes,
shapes, and forms. They vary in the kinds of products they
produce, the kinds of customers they serve, and the kinds of
financial structures they have. However, they do have some common elements, and by understanding these elements we can go
a long way toward understanding how organizations can influence motivation. What are these common elements? As is
often observed, organizations are made up of two or more people, are goal oriented, and are designed to exist over some length
of time. These factors lead to the following characteristics, which
are important in studying motivation:

1. *Money plays an important role.* It plays a role because, to
attract and retain people, work organizations have to pay people.
Further, to survive, work organizations have to be financially
viable. Thus, in all work organizations the obtaining, allocating, and spending of money is a crucial issue. Since it is important to many people, money obviously can influence motivation.
Thus, any discussion of motivation in work organizations must
consider how the way an organization handles its money influences the motivation of its employees.

2. *Some type of hierarchy exists.* The structures of most work
organizations are characterized by superior/subordinate relationships. The reason for this is simple: as organizations grow
they develop coordination problems, and someone or something
is needed to see that the activities of the employees represent
a coordinated effort toward whatever the goals of the organization are. Organizations try to solve this problem by making some
people responsible for coordinating the work of others and by
creating information and control systems to monitor the work
of employees. Admittedly, at times it is hard to believe that the
extensive hierarchies that are developed (some organizations
have as many as 20 levels) actually contribute to coordination.
There is no doubt that in our society the superior/subordinate
relationship — the hierarchy itself — is crucial in terms of motivation. The essence of supervision is in influencing the behavior
of those being supervised — for example, by influencing motivation. The hierarchal structure of organizations also means that
some people have more status and power than others. Because

of this, the possibility of promotion within the structure is often important to people and thus exerts a significant influence on motivation.

3. *People are given assigned tasks to perform.* Taken together, all the tasks a person does are called his job. Large organizations have literally thousands of different jobs. The reason for this division of labor is simple: no one person can perform all the functions that are necessary to do such things as manufacture and sell a car. Thus, people are given responsibility for different parts of the manufacturing and sales process. Recent research has shown that how tasks are grouped to form jobs has a crucial influence on motivation. This connection should not be surprising. The person who works on an assembly line and does the same task over and over again every 15 seconds is obviously in a different environment from that of the person who does a less repetitious task, just as a salesman is in a different position from that of a corporation president.

Probably as many approaches to motivating employees have been tried as there are kinds of work organizations. Some organizations successfully motivate their employees by giving them interesting jobs, others use the principles of democratic management, while others use pay-incentive plans. This variety of approaches is not surprising, since — due to basic differences — some organizations are better equipped to motivate people in certain ways than are other organizations. For example, the type of product influences the way in which the organization can design jobs; thus, the product influences how much the organization can use job design to motivate behavior.

Just as organizations differ in what they can do to influence motivation, people differ in what motivates them to work. Some people work primarily because of the companionship it offers; others work for the money. Some work hard because there is a pay-incentive plan. Although in some ways these differences make it more difficult to understand motivation, they are comprehensible. As we shall see, motivational differences among employees stem from many different factors, including how they were raised and how they are treated at work. In some ways motivation would be even more difficult to understand if someone from the ghetto, without a high school education, could walk into the executive office of a large corporation and respond to organizational policies in the same manner as the college-educated son of the corporation's president. Because this possibility is very unlikely, we will continue to focus on the ways individuals differ in their motivation. In summary, adequate understanding of motivation requires that we be able to predict how specific individuals will react to specific organizational practices. We need to be able to predict how specific employees will react to pay-incentive plans, to democratic leadership, to routine jobs, and so on. As we shall see, this can be done with some accuracy if we understand how organizational practices affect people's goals and their views of how these goals can be obtained.

Performance $= f$(Ability $\times$ Motivation)

As stated at the beginning of this chapter, job behavior is influenced by factors other than motivation. One of the most important factors is ability. No matter how motivated a person is to perform well, good performance is not possible if the person lacks the necessary ability. Many theorists have suggested that the following equation expresses the relationship of ability and motivation to performance:

$$\text{Performance} = f(\text{Ability} \times \text{Motivation}).$$

For their purpose in this equation, both ability and motivation are thought of as varying from 0 to 1. Because the equation calls for a multiplicative combination of ability and motivation, if either is low, then performance must be low. In other words, high motivation can make up for low ability only to a limited extent, which also applies to high ability and low motivation.

Much evidence supports the fact that ability and motivation do combine multiplicatively to determine performance (Lawler, 1971). It is clear that people are limited in their response capabilities and that this limitation does influence performance. Some people simply don't have the ability to be professional baseball players or sopranos. Therefore, no matter how motivated some people are, they will never be successful in these occupations.

One very important further point needs to be made about the (Ability × Motivation) formulation. The most commonly used definition of the term "ability" includes all of the training, experience, talent, and aptitude that are necessary to perform well in a given situation. In other words, ability refers to how well the person can perform at the present time. The concept of ability is differentiated from the concept of aptitude, which refers to whether an individual can be brought through training and experience to a specified level of ability. Therefore, aptitude refers to how much the person's response capabilities can be developed. In line with this distinction between ability and aptitude, the equation presented earlier is best stated:

$$\text{Performance} = f(\text{Ability} \times \text{Motivation}),$$

where

$$\text{Ability} = f[\text{Aptitude} \times (\text{Training} + \text{Experience})].$$

This elaboration is necessary, since we are interested in present performance, which is most directly influenced by developed response capability.

One important implication of this point is that not all performance problems that occur in organizations are caused by low motivation. Often, particularly in higher-level jobs, performance problems are caused by low ability. Thus, in diagnosing the performance problems of individuals in organizations, it is crucial to try to find out how much of the problem is due to poor ability and how much of it is due to low motivation. Poor performance caused by low motivation clearly requires different kinds of corrective action from that required by poor performance caused by low ability. As we shall see, those problems that are caused by low motivation can often be solved by a change in the job design, the manner of leadership, or the type of reward system. Problems that are caused by low ability levels may be more difficult to solve. First, it is necessary to determine whether the problem can be overcome by training. Often the problem is not that the person lacks the aptitude or talent to perform well but that he or she lacks the training and experience needed to perform well. If this deficiency is the case, then training can solve the problem, but if aptitude is low, then there is no way to improve performance.

Plan of This Book

The first step in explaining motivated behavior is to understand how objects or outcomes become goals for people. Thus, in Chapter 2 we will consider a number of different theories that specify why certain outcomes are valued by people and what factors influence the values people assign to their goals. Most of these theories can be classified as content theories because they describe the needs, motives, and goals of people. In Chapter 3 we will consider some process theories of motivation that try to explain how behavior is directed and why people choose a particular way of behaving in order to reach a particular goal. As stressed so far, in order to understand motivated behavior we need to know both what the goals of people are and how people decide which way to try to achieve them. Thus, Chapters 2 and 3 present complementary rather than competing views of motivation. Chapter 4 will complete our look at the different theories that are relevant to the study of motivation. There we will look at different theories of satisfaction that deal with the issue of how people react to the results of their behavior.

Chapter 5 is concerned with the membership and attendance decisions people make. It will look at the research evidence of why people work, how they choose where to work, and how motivation influences absenteeism. Chapters 6, 7, and 8 deal with organizational factors that influence the motivation of employees to perform effectively. Chapter 6 is concerned with rewards such as pay and promotion, Chapter 7 with job design, and Chapter 8 with interpersonal influences. As we shall see, each of these factors can have a strong influence on both employee satisfaction and motivation. Finally, Chapter 9 presents a summary and integration of several views of how people are motivated in work organizations and relates these views to the evidence that has been presented.

two

Drives, Needs, and Outcomes

For centuries, psychologists and philosophers have tried to explain why some objects or outcomes seem to be desired by people while others are not. The concepts of instinct, drive, intrinsic motives, functional autonomy, derived motives, and many others have been used to explain this phenomenon. This chapter will review many of these concepts and present an integrated view of present knowledge about why certain outcomes are desirable or attractive to people.

An adequate explanation of why certain outcomes are desirable must deal with three separate but interrelated questions:

1. What is it about the nature of individuals that causes outcomes to become desirable to them?
2. What general classes or groups of outcomes do people find desirable or undesirable?
3. What factors influence the desirability of outcomes; that is, how does the desirability of outcomes change over time and why do individuals differ in the importance they attach to various outcomes?

Unless the second and third questions are answered, it is impossible to predict the kind of behavior choices a person will

make. Although the answer to the first question is not needed
in order to predict behavior, most theorists have found that answering it is a prerequisite to answering questions two and three.
That is, these theorists have found it necessary to make assumptions about what causes outcomes to be important in the first
place in order to make statements about the kinds of outcomes
people value and the things that are likely to influence the attractiveness of outcomes.

Our first question has typically been answered by a set
of assumptions about man's internal state. For example, some
theorists have assumed that man has homeostatic drives, others
have talked of instincts, while still others have talked of learned
drives. The second question has been answered by the development of a number of need or outcome classification systems.
Some of these systems assume only two classes of needs while
others assume more than 20. The third question has been answered in many different ways. Maslow (1943), for example,
has theorized that needs are arrayed in a hierarchy such that
the lower-level needs have to be satisfied before the higher-level
needs come into play. Other psychologists have stressed that
learned associations can cause changes in the attractiveness of
outcomes.

Not every theory that has dealt with the attractiveness of
outcomes has attempted to answer all of these questions. In fact,
some theories have dealt essentially with only one of the questions. For example, in his discussion of the competence motive,
White (1959) is concerned with establishing the existence of that
motive. He does not present a general classification of motives,
nor does he make statements about what influences the importance of other motives. As we discuss the various theories dealing with the attractiveness of outcomes, it is important to note
which of the three questions are answered and which are ignored.

Let us now turn to a consideration of some of the more
prominent theories.

Historical Approaches

Prior to the 1940s three theoretical approaches to explaining why
outcomes are valued dominated the thinking in psychology. The

first two, instinct theory and hedonism, do not make scientifically testable predictions of what outcomes people will seek. The third, drive theory, represents an attempt to develop a theory that does make testable predictions.

Instinct Theory

Charles Darwin was the first to call the attention of the scientific world to the possibility that much of human and animal behavior may be determined by instincts. He thought that many "intelligent" actions were inherited, and he provided a number of examples from his research on animals to support this view. William James, Sigmund Freud, and William McDougall developed the instinct doctrine as an important concept in their psychological theories. Some theorists thought of instincts as mechanical and automatic rather than as conscious motivators of behavior, but McDougall, who developed the most exhaustive taxonomy of instincts, thought of them as purposive, inherited, goal-seeking tendencies.

McDougall (1908) wrote that "we may then define an instinct as an inherited or innate psycho-physical disposition that determines the possessor to perceive and pay attention to objects of a certain class, to experience an emotional excitement of a particular quality on perceiving such an object, and to act in regard to it in a particular manner, or at least to experience an impulse to such action" (p. 39). Thus, the "pugnacity instinct" was an instinct that manifested itself in fighting when the organism was exposed to appropriate stimuli. At first McDougall thought he could account for all behavior in terms of about a dozen instincts. However, as time progressed he added more and more instincts to his list so that by 1932 his list included 19 instincts. Other psychologists added more, so that by the 1920s the list of instincts totaled nearly 6000, including the "instinct to avoid eating apples in one's own orchard" (Murray, 1964, p. 6).

In a sense, instinct theory died of its own weight. As more and more instincts were stated, psychologists began to question the explanatory usefulness of the approach. To say that an animal fights because of the instinct of pugnacity or

that an individual takes a job because he has an instinct to work
is merely to give a redundant description of the observed behavior that adds nothing to our understanding of why the behavior took place. The tendency of some psychologists to add a new
instinct to explain each new behavior that was observed also
weakened the theory. As instinct theory developed, it seemed
to provide unsatisfactory answers to all of our questions. It said
that heredity determined which goals or outcomes organisms
would seek (which was incomplete and misleading) and that people's goals consisted of the objects they sought (a circular definition). Thus, instinct theory did not allow for the prediction of
which outcomes would be sought, it allowed only for the *post
hoc* explanation of why certain goals were sought. Instinct theory
also failed to provide a useful classification of the type of outcomes people sought. The original list of instincts was too short
and the later ones were so long that they proved useless.

Hedonism

The origins of most contemporary conceptions of motivation
can be traced to the principle of hedonism (Atkinson, 1964).
In turn, hedonism can be traced to the original writings of the
English utilitarians. The central assumption is that behavior is
directed toward outcomes that provide pleasure and away from
those that produce pain. In every situation people strive to obtain those goals or outcomes that provide the most pleasure.
Despite its simplicity and popularity, the principle of hedonism
fails to answer any of our three questions adequately. Nothing
is said about why certain things give pleasure while others don't.
There is no specification of the types of outcomes that are pleasurable or painful or even how these outcomes can be determined
in advance for a particular individual. Any kind of behavior
can be explained after the fact by postulating that particular outcomes were sources of either pain or pleasure. Finally, nothing
is said about how the attractiveness of outcomes may be modified by experience or environmental circumstances. In short,
the hedonistic assumption has no real empirical content leading to predictions of behavior and, thus, it is untestable.

Despite the fact that hedonism can be described as circular and lacking in content, its influence on psychology has been extensive. As one psychologist stated, "the study of motivation by psychologists has largely been directed toward filling in the missing empirical content in hedonism" (Vroom, 1964, p. 10). It is certainly true that almost all modern theories assume that people direct their behavior toward outcomes that they find pleasurable and away from those that they find unattractive. However, most modern theories do attempt to overcome the circularity of hedonism. They specify in advance how attractive specific outcomes will be to particular individuals and they develop models that predict when the attractiveness of outcomes will change.

Drive Theory

Drive theory developed partially as a reaction to instinct theory and hedonism. It is in the tradition of hedonism, but it is more closely tied to empirical events and therefore more testable. In 1918, R. S. Woodworth published a little book entitled *Dynamic Psychology* in which he advanced the view that psychologists should study what induces people to behave in particular ways. He referred to this inducement as drive, and the concept of drive soon replaced the concept of instinct in the psychologist's glossary of important terms. Later, the term "drive" took on a very precise meaning in the writings of C. L. Hull (1943). He assumed that all behavior is motivated by either primary or secondary drives. According to Hull, the primary drives were biologically based; they represented states of homeostatic imbalance. Hull's position was that:

> The major primary needs or drives are so ubiquitous that they require little more than to be mentioned. They include the need for foods of various sorts (hunger), the need for water (thirst), the need for air, the need to avoid tissue injury (pain), the need to maintain an optimal temperature, the need to defecate, the need to micturate, the need for rest

(after protracted exertion), the need for sleep (after protracted wakefulness), and the need for activity (after protracted inaction). The drives concerned with the maintenance of the species are those which lead to sexual intercourse and the need represented by nest building and care of the young [pp. 59–60].

In Hull's theory, outcomes become rewards when they are able to reduce primary drives and thereby reduce homeostatic imbalance and the tension that occurs when organisms are in a state of ecological deprivation. Thus, food is a reward to a hungry person and water is a reward to a thirsty person. Hull also stressed that drive strength can be increased by deprivation and reduced as needs become satisfied. Thus, the hungrier a person gets, the more he desires food; but as he eats food, he becomes less hungry and his desire diminishes. Although Hull assumed that all rewards and drives are ultimately based on the reduction of primary drives, he recognized that certain secondary drives and rewards could develop — or be "learned" — if in the past they were associated with food or other primary rewards. Thus, money is a secondary reward because it is often associated with food and other primary rewards. Social approval becomes a reward for children who are praised for eating well, or dressing themselves, and so on. According to Hull's view, most of the rewards used by work organizations would be considered secondary rewards.

Hull's theory represents a significant advance over the previous theories of motivation. It gives a clear-cut answer to the question of what objects or outcomes have value — that is, objects or outcomes that either reduce primary, biologically based drives or have been related to outcomes that do. It also provides a classification of drives that is still commonly used (it divides them into primary and secondary drives, and it specifies what the primary drives are). Finally, it says that deprivation increases drive strength, whereas obtaining the desired outcomes reduces drive strength. Thus, Hull's theory has answers to all three of our questions. But the real significance of Hull's theory rests in the fact that it is empirically testable. Since it specifies in detail the relationship between such measurable things as deprivation, drive, and learning, the theory can be tested, and it has spawned a large number of research studies.

At this point it is safe to say that these studies have found Hull's theory to be inadequate in a number of important respects. The most important shortcomings have to do with the ability of the theory to explain motivation that is not based on primary drives. Hull's basic point about organisms' possessing certain primary drives that become stronger with deprivation and weaker with satisfaction still seems valid. What does not seem valid is his argument that all secondary motives are learned on the basis of primary physiological or homeostatic drives.

There is no solid evidence that drives can be learned on the basis of their association with positive drives such as hunger and thirst (Cravens and Renner, 1970). There is evidence that organisms will work for rewards that have been associated with the reduction of a primary drive if the primary drive is present. However, when the primary drive is not present, there seems to be no "acquired" drive to obtain the reward. For example, in the classic experiments of Wolfe (1936) and Cowles (1937), chimpanzees learned to associate tokens with the acquisition of food. Initially, the chimps learned to operate an apparatus that required lifting a weight to obtain grapes. They continued to operate it when the only visible reward was a token that had been associated with the grapes. However, they didn't seem to develop an acquired need for tokens, since they were willing to work to obtain the tokens only as long as they were hungry and the tokens led to something they desired—that is, food. Hence, it is difficult to see how Hull's explanation can help us understand why workers continue to work for more money even when their basic needs are satisfied.

More damaging to Hull's view than the evidence on the failure of animals to acquire learned drives is the great amount of evidence indicating that people and animals are attracted to many outcomes that do not seem to be directly related to primary needs. Rats will learn mazes in order to explore novel environments, monkeys will solve puzzles even though they receive no extrinsic rewards, and people will work simply in order to develop their skills and abilities and to increase their competence. These and many other phenomena cannot be explained easily by drive theory.

Contemporary Approaches

Recently, many psychologists have rejected the emphasis of drive theory on primary drives and have argued that people have many needs. This argument has come particularly from those psychologists who are interested in studying human behavior. As we shall see, they have proposed a number of needs that do not seem to be directly related to homeostatic imbalance, organism survival, or species survival. This recent work on motivation has produced two somewhat different approaches.

Researchers in one group have focused on establishing the existence of one or two human motives that they consider to be particularly important. Thus, McClelland has focused on the achievement motive and White has focused on the competence motive. They have not tried to develop complex need, or motive, classification systems. In other words, they have not tried to answer our second question. They have contented themselves with trying to understand why one set or type of outcomes is attractive to people. Other researchers have tried to develop need, or motive, classification systems in an attempt to predict which kinds of outcomes will be attractive to people. Murray's (1938) list of needs and Maslow's (1943) statement of a need hierarchy are examples of this approach. But before we consider these classification systems, we need to look at some of the needs that have been proposed as necessary additions to the primary drives observed by Hull.

The Affiliation Motive

A number of researchers have presented evidence to show that an affiliation motive exists. They have shown that social interaction is attractive to people and that it is particularly likely to occur under certain conditions. For example, Schachter (1959) has shown that people seek the companionship of others when they are anxious and confused about their motives. In Schachter's work, college students faced with the prospect of being shocked were given the opportunity to be with another person. The subjects under such anxiety were more likely to accept invitations to be with others than were subjects who were not under such anxiety. This result occurred even when the subjects were not permitted to talk to the person they were to be with. Other research suggests that people are likely to seek social interaction at times when they are doubting their self-esteem.

Harlow (1958) has presented some interesting evidence suggesting that the social motive may be innate. As part of his work with monkeys he raised some infant monkeys, providing them with two surrogate mothers in place of their natural mothers. One surrogate mother consisted of a cylinder of wire mesh with an opening in the center of the "breast" for a bottle. The other was similarly shaped but was covered with cotton terry cloth. In the experiment, baby monkeys were placed in cages containing two "mothers." Half were fed from the cloth mother, the other half from the wire mother. According to drive theory, the monkeys who were fed by the wire mother should have become attached to the wire mother because it provided the drive reduction — that is, the milk. However, it did not work out that way. The monkeys who were fed on the wire mother spent most of their time clinging to the cloth mother. Thus, it appears that monkeys develop their attachment to their mothers based on contact comfort rather than on primary-drive reduction.

However, the important point for us about the research on the need for social contact is not whether this need is innate or acquired but that it exists in most adult human beings. It clearly is an important motivation — one that has a significant impact on behavior in organizations. Many organizations have discovered — to their sorrow — that jobs that do not provide opportunities for social contact have higher turnover and absenteeism rates because employees simply cannot stand the isolation. Frequently, unnecessary social isolation results from mechanical and architectural designs that do not consider employees' needs for social relationships.

Need for Equity

People want to be treated fairly. They observe what happens to other people and if they receive either "too much" or "too little" in comparison to other people it makes them uncomfortable. For example, one study showed that dissatisfaction with promotion was highest in Army units where promotion rates were high. Why? Because the individuals who weren't promoted in these units felt unfairly treated. Adams (1963, 1965) has developed a theory that makes a number of interesting predictions about the effects of wage inequity on work output, work quality, and attitudes toward work. Although this theory is a general theory of social inequity, it has been tested largely with respect to the effects of wage inequity, and it has some interesting things to say about how equity may affect the attractiveness of rewards. Its predictions seem to be particularly relevant to understanding the effects of offering various sizes of pay increases and the effects of paying different wage rates.

Adams (1965) defines inequity as follows:

> Inequity exists for Person when he perceives that
> the ratio of his outcomes to inputs and the ratio of
> Other's outcomes to Other's inputs are unequal.
> This may happen either (a) when he and Other are
> in a direct exchange relationship or (b) when both
> are in an exchange relationship with a third party,
> and Person compares himself to Other [p. 280].

Outcomes in the job situation include pay, fringe benefits, status, the intrinsic interest of the job, and so on. Inputs include how hard the person works, his education level, his general qualifications for the job, and so on. It must be remembered that what determines the equity of a particular input-outcome balance is the individual's perception of what he is giving and receiving; this cognition may or may not correspond to an observer's perception or to reality.

Equity theory states that the presence of inequity will motivate an individual to reduce inequity and that the strength of the motivation to reduce inequity varies directly with the perceived magnitude of the imbalance experienced between inputs and outcomes. Feelings of inequity can be produced in a variety of ways and in a variety of situations. Adams has studied inequity produced by overpayment. His research suggests that overpayment is less attractive to employees than equitable payment is. There is evidence, for example, that when a person is paid on a piece rate and feels overpaid, he will reduce his productivity in order to reduce the amount of pay he receives. The important thing for this discussion about the research on equity theory is that people tend to seek equity in their work activities, which can affect their job behavior.

Activity and Exploration

Too little stimulation is very uncomfortable for humans. In one study, college students were employed at $20 a day to stay in a low-stimulation environment (Bexton, Heron, & Scott, 1954). They were asked to remain for as many days as they could, lying on a cot in a lighted, partially sound-deadened room. They wore translucent goggles, gloves, and cardboard cuffs that minimized tactile stimulation. An air conditioner provided a noise that blocked out other sounds, and the students rested their heads on a U-shaped pillow. After a certain period—usually filled with sleeping—the subjects found this situation impossible to tolerate and asked to leave the experiment. Rarely did a subject endure it for as long as two days despite the fact that the pay was relatively high. Other studies have reported similar results, stressing that under these conditions people seem to develop a hunger for stimulation and action leading to such responses as touching the fingers together and twitching the muscles.

Research by Scott (1969) has shown that the results are very similar when people are given repetitive tasks to perform. They develop a negative attitude toward the task, and, as time goes on, they take more breaks and try in many ways to vary their behavior. As we shall see, this finding has direct implications for the design of jobs in organizations.

Other studies have shown that both people and animals

seek out opportunities to experience novel situations. Butler (1953) has shown that monkeys will learn to push open a window for no reward other than being able to see what is going on in a room, and they will keep doing it. Butler has also shown that the strength of the drive for novel stimulation can be increased by deprivation. An experiment by Smock and Holt (1962) has shown that if children are given a chance to control what they see on a television screen, they will look at objects that offer complex stimuli rather than unconflicting, simple stimuli.

Many studies of rats have shown that they will learn certain behaviors in order to experience novel stimuli. In one experiment, rats preferred a goal box that contained objects to an empty goal box. Miles (1958) found that kittens would learn things when the reward was simply the opportunity to explore a room. There is much evidence that humans and animals will try to solve puzzles simply because of the stimulation provided by working on them. Harlow (1953) has shown that monkeys will persist in solving puzzles for many days. One monkey, who was presented with a square peg and a round hole, persisted for months in trying to get the two to fit together. (The monkey finally died of perforated ulcers.)

Several theorists have suggested that the results of both the stimulus-deprivation studies and the studies of novel-stimulus environments can be explained by considering how novelty affects stimulus attractiveness (Berlyne, 1967). According to activation theory, people become used to a certain level and pattern of stimulation from the environment. For some people this adaptation level may be a relatively low level of stimulation; for others it may be a rather high level. Regardless of where a person's level of adaptation is, however, psychologists hypothesize that deviation from it will have a strong impact on the person. Slight deviations will be experienced as pleasurable and rewarding while large deviations will be experienced as noxious and dissatisfying. Figure 2.1 illustrates this point graphically. According to this approach, the subjects in the stimulus-deprivation experiment were uncomfortable because the situation fell too far below the adaptation level. The animals who wanted to explore new things were attracted to them because

Figure 2.1. The Butterfly Curve.

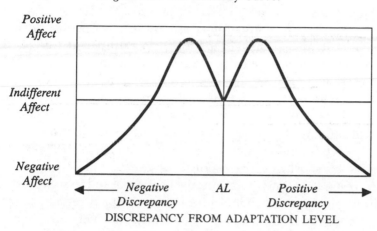

DISCREPANCY FROM ADAPTATION LEVEL

Source: From Haber, R. N. Discrepancy from adaptation level as a source of affect. *Journal of Experimental Psychology,* 1958, *56,* 370–375. Copyright © 1958 by the American Psychological Association, and reproduced by permission.

these new things represented stimulus situations that were somewhat above their adaptation levels. Presumably if the stimulus situations had been too far above their adaptation levels, the animals would have avoided them, and indeed there is evidence that both animals and people fear situations that are very unfamiliar to them.

One of the problems with activation theory is that it can be very difficult to measure in advance what a person's adaptation level is. Still, the theory and its related research provide some interesting evidence to support the point that not all drives or needs are either primary or learned on the basis of primary drives. It is hard to see how people's reactions to different levels of stimulation can be explained by reference to a drive that has been learned on the basis of a primary drive.

Achievement

The achievement motive has been extensively studied by D. C. McClelland. It is defined by McClelland (1951, 1961) as a desire

to perform in terms of a standard of excellence or as a desire
to be successful in competitive situations. McClelland stresses
that achievement motivation is present in most people but that
the amount people have depends on a number of things, including how they were treated during childhood. One study has
shown that high-need-achievement people tend to come from
families where high demands were made for independence and
performance at an early age. Their mothers evaluated their accomplishments favorably and rewarded them liberally.

McClelland measures the strength of people's achievement
motive by scoring their responses to a series of pictures. The
pictures are shown to individuals who are asked to write a five-
minute story about what is going on in the picture. The stories
are scored on the basis of how frequently achievement-oriented
themes are mentioned (for example, "He will try his best to succeed"). The following is an example of a story showing a strong
achievement theme. It was written in response to a picture showing a young boy in the foreground and a hazy representation
of an operation in the background.

> A boy is dreaming of being a doctor. He can see
> himself in the future. He is hoping that he can make
> the grade. It is more or less a fantasy. The boy has
> seen many pictures of doctors in books, and it has
> inspired him. *He will try his best* and hopes to be-
> come the best doctor in the country. He can see
> himself as a very important doctor. He is perform-
> ing a very dangerous operation. He can see him-
> self victorious and is proud of it. He gets world
> renown for it. He will become the *best doctor in the
> U.S.* He will be an honest man, too. His name will
> go down in medical history as one of the *greatest men*
> [Atkinson, 1958, p. 193].

McClelland's research has shown that under certain conditions achievement motivation can be an important motivator
of good performance in work organizations. When achievement
motivation is operating, good job performance becomes very

attractive to people; as a result, the motivation to perform well is higher. Achievement motivation typically does not operate when people are performing routine or boring tasks where no competition is involved. However, when challenge and competition are involved, achievement motivation can stimulate good performance. A study by French (1955) clearly illustrates this point. In French's study, Officer Candidate School cadets performed a simple task under three different sets of instructions. Under the "relaxed" instructions the subjects were told that the experimenter was merely interested in determining what kinds of scores people make on the test. The "task-motivated" instructions said that the task was a measure of people's ability to deal rapidly with new materials. The "extrinsically motivated" instructions said that the best performers could leave while the others had to continue performing. Performance was highest under the "task-motivated" instructions and lowest under the "relaxed" instructions. Subjects with high need for achievement performed better on the "task-motivated" instructions but not under the two other kinds of instructions.

Other studies also support the view that people can be motivated simply by a drive to achieve. For example, Alper (1946) gave two groups of subjects a list of nonsense syllables to learn. Only one group was told it was an intelligence test. A test given 24 hours later showed that the "intelligence test" group remembered more of what they had learned. McClelland (1961) showed that successful people in competitive occupations tend to be universally high in achievement motivation. For example, he showed that successful managers from countries such as the United States, Italy, and India tend to be high in achievement motivation.

Overall, the research on achievement motivation suggests that such motivation is most likely to be present when moderately challenging tasks have to be performed (where about a 50-50 chance of success exists), in competitive situations, in situations where performance is perceived to depend upon some important or valued skill, and in situations where performance feedback is given. The research also suggests that people with a high need for achievement tend to seek out situations in which they can achieve, and they tend to find successful performance attractive once they are in these situations. These points have important implications for the design of jobs in organizations and for the kinds of people that are attracted to jobs in different types of work situations.

Judging from the research cited earlier on the effects of child rearing on the strength of need for achievement, it seems certain that achievement motivation is a partly learned drive. McClelland in fact argues that it is differentially present in certain cultures precisely because child-rearing practices differ. However, even though achievement motivation is a learned drive, it is hard to see how it could develop because of the primary drives. There may be some relationship here, since success often helps people to obtain primary rewards, such as food; but it is hard to see how the primary drive approach can explain the fact that early independence training leads to a strong need for achievement. Thus, even though achievement is a learned drive, it seems that it is only partially learned on the basis of primary drives.

Competence

Robert W. White (1959) has argued for the existence of a competence motive. He uses competence to refer to an organism's capacity to interact effectively with its environment. In organisms capable of little learning, competence is considered to be innate; however, competence in man — that is, his fitness to interact with the environment — is slowly attained through prolonged feats of learning. The human learning that is needed to gain competence is characterized by high persistence and a strong goal orientation. Because of this dedication to learning, White argues that it is necessary to treat competence as having a motivation aspect that is separate from motivation derived from primary drives or instincts. He presents considerable evidence of organisms trying to cope with their environment seemingly for no other reason than that they want to master it. As White notes, there are repeated references in psychological literature

> . . . to the familiar series of learned skills which
> starts with sucking, grasping, and visual explora-
> tion and continues with crawling and walking, acts
> of focal attention and perception, memory, lan-
> guage and thinking, anticipation, the exploring of
> novel places and objects, effecting stimulus changes
> in the environment, manipulating and exploiting
> the surroundings, and achieving higher levels of
> motor and mental coordination. . . . Collectively
> they are sometimes referred to as mechanisms . . .
> but on the whole we are not accustomed to cast a
> single name over the diverse feats whereby we learn
> to deal with the environment. . . . I now propose
> that we gather the various kinds of behavior just
> mentioned, all of which had to do with effective in-
> teraction with the environment, under the general
> heading of competence . . . it is necessary to make
> competence a motivational concept; there is a com-
> petence motivation [1959, pp. 317–318].

White argues that competence motivation is aroused when people are faced with somewhat new situations, and wanes when
a situation has been explored and mastered to the point at which
it no longer presents a challenge.

There is an obvious similarity between White's view of
when competence motivation is aroused and the activation theorists' view of how stimulus novelty affects motivation. Both argue for high motivation when somewhat novel situations are
encountered. White's theory is also very closely related to the
theory of achievement motivation, since both talk of man's need
to perform adequately. In fact, White says that achievement
may be one outcome of competence motivation. White's theory
has some interesting implications for the design of jobs in organizations. It suggests that if presented with the right task, people
can be motivated to perform effectively without the use of extrinsic rewards such as pay and promotion. However, once the
task is mastered, competence motivation will disappear. It is

also interesting to note that White, like other recent theorists, argues that the competence motive is not based on any primary drive. Although he does not say exactly where it comes from, he does imply that man's desire to be competent is innate.

Self-Actualization

In the last thirty years a number of psychologists have introduced concepts into their theories that have to do with people's need to grow and develop. Table 2.1 lists some of these theorists and their concepts. The work of Maslow has had by far the greatest impact on the thinking concerned with motivation in organizations. Maslow uses the term "self-actualization" to describe the need people have to grow and develop. According to him, it is the "desire for self-fulfillment, namely . . . the tendency [for a person] to become actualized in what he is potentially . . . the desire to become more and more of what one is, to become everything that one is capable of becoming . . ." (1954, pp. 91–92). Maslow stresses that not all people function on the self-actualization level. He then goes on to describe the characteristics of people who are motivated by self-actualization. According to him, much of the self-actualizing person's behavior is motivated solely by the sheer enjoyment he obtains from using and developing his capacities. He does not necessarily behave in accordance with extrinsic goals or rewards. For him, the goal is simply to behave in a certain way or experience a certain feeling. Maslow makes the point like this:

> . . . we must construct a profoundly different psychology of motivation for self-actualizing people, e.g., expression motivation or growth motivation, rather than deficiency motivation. Perhaps it will be useful to make a distinction between living and *preparing* to live. Perhaps the concept of motivation should apply *only* to non-self-actualizers. Our subjects no longer strive in the ordinary sense, but rather develop. They attempt to grow to perfection

Table 2.1. List of Theorists Classified as
Emphasizing Self-Actualization, and the Term Each Uses.

Kurt Goldstein (1939)	Self-actualization
Erich Fromm (1941)	The productive orientation
Prescott Lecky (1945)	The unified personality; self-consistency
Donald Snygg and Arthur Combs (1949)	The preservation and enhancement of the phenomenal self
Karen Horney (1950)	The real self and its realization
David Riesman (1950)	The autonomous person
Carl Rogers (1951)	Actualization, maintenance, and enhancement of the experiencing organism
Rollo May (1953)	Existential being
Abraham Maslow (1954)	Self-actualization
Gordon W. Allport (1955)	Creative becoming

Source: Adapted from C. N. Cofer and M. H. Appley, *Motivation: Theory and Research.* Copyright © 1964 by John Wiley & Sons, Inc. Reprinted by permission.

and to develop more and more fully in their own style. The motivation of ordinary men is a striving for the basic need gratifications that they lack. But self-actualizing people in fact lack none of these gratifications; and yet they have impulses. They work, they try, and they are ambitious, even though in an unusual sense. For them motivation is just character growth, character expression, maturation, and development; in a word, self-actualization [p. 211].*

Thus, like White and others, Maslow is careful to say that all motivation is not tied to the primary drives. Maslow also stresses that people will work to obtain outcomes that are intrinsic, such as feelings of growth. He completely rejects the view that valued outcomes have to be related to such extrinsic rewards as food and water. Maslow probably goes further than any of the other theorists we have reviewed in stressing the differences between motivation based on primary drives and motiva-

*From *Motivation and Personality* (2nd ed.) by A. H. Maslow. Copyright © 1970 by Harper & Row, Publishers, Inc. Reprinted by permission of the publishers.

tion that is independent of primary drives. He says that, unlike motivation based on primary drives, motivation based on growth needs does not decrease as the needs become satisfied. Quite to the contrary, Maslow argues that as people experience growth and self-actualization they simply want more. In his view, obtaining growth creates a desire for more growth, whereas obtaining food decreases one's desire for food.

Maslow argues that the concept of self-actualization can explain a significant amount of the motivation in organizations. He states that, particularly at the managerial level, many people are motivated by a desire to self-actualize. There is a considerable amount of evidence to support this point. In one study, managers rated the need for self-actualization as their most important need (Porter, 1964). In addition, most large organizations abound with training and development programs designed to help people develop their skills and abilities. Sometimes people do enter these programs in the hope of obtaining a raise or promotion, but on other occasions they do it only because it contributes to their self-development. There is also evidence of people seeking more challenging jobs for no other reason than to develop themselves.

An interesting contrast to Maslow's work on self-actualization is provided by the work of existential psychologists such as Allport (1955) and Rogers (1961). They too talk of people being motivated by desires that are not related to obtaining rewards such as money and status. However, they give less emphasis to the development of skills and abilities and the achievement of goals than does Maslow, and they give more emphasis to new experiences as a way of learning about one's self. Rogers, for example, talks of people being motivated "to be that self which one truly is." He emphasizes self-discovery and the importance of being open to experience. Perhaps because they don't emphasize skill development and accomplishments as much as Maslow, the existential psychologists have not had much impact on the research of psychologists interested in work organizations. This is unfortunate, and it is important to remember that at times people may be motivated by nothing more than self-discovery and a desire to experience.

Need-Classification Theories

Numerous lists and classifications of needs have been presented by psychologists. One of the most important is Henry A. Murray's (1938) list of "psychogenic" or "social" needs. This list, which contains more than 20 motives, was arrived at on the basis of the study of a number of "normal" people. Although Murray's list has been very influential in the field of psychology, it has not been applied very much to the study of motivation in organizations, probably because its length greatly reduces its usefulness. Like the early lists of instincts, it is so long that there is almost a separate need for each behavior people demonstrate. A look at Table 2.2, which lists some of Murray's needs, may help the reader gain an impression of the nature of the problem. The issue is not whether Murray has identified separate kinds of behavior (he has) but whether these behaviors might not be better dealt with by a more parsimonious list of needs.

Maslow's hierarchical classification of needs has been by far the most widely used classification system in the study of motivation in organizations. Maslow differs from Murray in two important ways: first, his list is shorter; second, he argues that needs are arranged in a hierarchy.

Maslow's (1943, 1954, 1970) hierarchical model is composed of a five-level classification of human needs and a set of hypotheses about how the satisfaction of these needs affects their importance.

The five need categories are as follows:

1. *Physiological needs,* including the need for food, water, air, and so on.
2. *Safety needs,* or the need for security, stability, and the absence of pain, threat, or illness.
3. *Belongingness and love needs,* which include a need for affection, belongingness, love, and so on.
4. *Esteem needs,* including a need for both personal feelings of achievement or self-esteem and for recognition or respect from others.
5. *The need for self-actualization,* a feeling of self-fulfillment or the realization of one's potential.

Table 2.2. Some Items from Murray's List of Needs.

Social Motive	Brief Definition
Abasement	To submit passively to external force. To accept injury, blame, criticism, punishment. To surrender. To become resigned to fate. To admit inferiority, error, wrongdoing, or defeat. To confess and atone. To blame, belittle, or mutilate the self. To seek and enjoy pain, punishment, illness, and misfortune.
Achievement	To accomplish something difficult. To master, manipulate, or organize physical objects, human beings, or ideas. To do this as rapidly and as independently as possible. To overcome obstacles and attain a high standard. To excel oneself. To rival and surpass others. To increase self-regard by the successful exercise of talent.
Affiliation	To draw near and enjoyably cooperate or reciprocate with an allied other (an other who resembles the subject or who likes the subject). To please and win affection of a cathected object. To adhere and remain loyal to a friend.
Aggression	To overcome opposition forcefully. To fight. To revenge an injury. To attack, injure, or kill another. To oppose forcefully or punish another.
Autonomy	To get free, shake off restraint, break out of confinement. To resist coercion and restriction. To avoid or quit activities prescribed by domineering authorities. To be independent and free to act according to impulse. To be unattached, irresponsible. To defy convention.
Counteraction	To master or make up for a failure by restriving. To obliterate a humiliation by resumed action. To overcome weaknesses, to repress fear. To efface a dishonor by action. To search for obstacles and difficulties to overcome. To maintain self-respect and pride on a high level.
Defendance	To defend the self against assault, criticism, and blame. To conceal or justify a misdeed, failure, or humiliation. To vindicate the ego.
Deference	To admire and support a superior. To praise, honor, or eulogize. To yield eagerly to the influence of an allied other. To emulate an exemplar. To conform to custom.
Dominance	To control one's human environment. To influence or direct the behavior of others by suggestion, seduction, persuasion, or command. To dissuade, restrain, or prohibit.

Table 2.2. Some Items from Murray's List of Needs, Cont'd.

Social Motive	Brief Definition
Exhibition	To make an impression. To be seen and heard. To excite, amaze, fascinate, entertain, shock, intrigue, amuse, or entice others.
Harmavoidance	To avoid pain, physical injury, illness, and death. To escape from a dangerous situation. To take precautionary measures.
Infavoidance	To avoid humiliation. To quit embarrassing situations or to avoid conditions that may lead to belittlement, scorn, derision, or indifference from others. To refrain from action because of the fear of failure.
Nurturance	To give sympathy and gratify the needs of a helpless object: an infant or any object that is weak, disabled, tired, inexperienced, infirm, defeated, humiliated, lonely, dejected, sick, mentally confused. To assist an object in danger. To feed, help, support, console, protect, comfort, nurse, heal.
Order	To put things in order. To achieve cleanliness, arrangement, organization, balance, neatness, tidiness, and precision.
Play	To act for "fun" without further purpose. To like to laugh and make jokes. To seek enjoyable relaxation from stress. To participate in games, sports, dancing, drinking parties, cards.
Rejection	To separate oneself from a negatively cathected object. To exclude, abandon, expel, or remain indifferent to an inferior object. To snub or jilt an object.
Sentience	To seek and enjoy sensuous impressions.
Sex	To form and further an erotic relationship. To have sexual intercourse.
Succorance	To have one's needs gratified by the sympathetic aid of an allied object. To be nursed, supported, sustained, surrounded, protected, loved, advised, guided, indulged, forgiven, consoled. To remain close to a devoted protector. To always have a supporter.
Understanding	To ask or answer general questions. To be interested in theory. To speculate, formulate, analyze, and generalize.

More important than the definition of these five need
groups, however, is the *process* by which each class of needs becomes important or active. According to Maslow, the five need
categories exist in a hierarchy of prepotency such that the lower
or more basic needs are inherently more important (prepotent)
than the higher or less basic needs. This means that before any
of the higher-level needs will become important, a person's physiological needs must be satisfied. Once the physiological needs
have been satisfied, however, their strength or importance decreases, and the next-higher-level need becomes the strongest
motivator of behavior. This process of "increased satisfaction/
decreased importance/increased importance of the next higher
need" repeats itself until the highest level of the hierarchy is
reached. Maslow has proposed in later revisions of his theory
(1968, 1970) that at the highest level of the hierarchy a reversal
occurs in the satisfaction-importance relationship. He states
that for self-actualization, increased satisfaction leads to *increased*
need strength. "Gratification breeds increased rather than decreased motivation, heightened rather than lessened excitement"
(1968, p. 30).

In short, individual behavior is motivated by an attempt
to satisfy the need that is *most important* at that point in time.
Further, the strength of any need is determined by its position
in the hierarchy and by the degree to which it and all lower needs
have been satisfied. Maslow's theory predicts a dynamic, step-
by-step, causal process of human motivation in which behavior
is governed by a continuously changing (though predictable)
set of "important" needs. An increase (change) in the satisfaction of the needs in one category *causes* the strength of these needs
to decrease, which results in an increase in the importance of
the needs at the next-higher level. Maslow does say that the hierarchy of needs is not a rigidly fixed order that is the same for
all individuals. Especially in the case of needs in the middle of
the hierarchy, the order varies somewhat from person to person. However, this view clearly states that physiological needs
are the most prepotent and that self-actualization needs are
usually the least.

Two other need-hierarchy theories have been stated. One

is by Langer (1937) — predating Maslow's — and another by Alderfer (1969). Alderfer's (1972) theory is the best developed of these two theories. Alderfer argues for three levels of needs: existence, relatedness, and growth. Like Maslow, he argues that the satisfaction of a need influences its importance and the importance of higher-level needs. He agrees with Maslow's hypothesis that the satisfaction of growth needs makes them more important rather than less important to people; however, he also hypothesizes that the lack of satisfaction of higher-order needs can lead to lower-order needs becoming more important to people. He then argues that the importance of any need is influenced by the satisfaction/frustration of the needs above and below it in the hierarchy. He also assumes that all needs can be simultaneously active; thus, prepotency does not play as major a role in his theory as it does in Maslow's.

From the point of view of the three questions we asked at the beginning of the chapter, the hierarchical theories of Maslow and Alderfer provide rather complete answers to the last two questions. These theories make specific statements about what outcomes people will value (outcomes that satisfy whatever need or needs are active). They also make specific predictions about what will influence the attractiveness of various outcomes — for example, satisfaction of relevant needs, including those lower on the hierarchy. They provide less complete answers to our first question, since they are not clear on why needs originate. They do, however, imply that the lower-order needs are innate and that the higher-order needs are present in most people and will appear if not blocked from appearing.

The hierarchical concept has received a great deal of attention among those interested in organizations. This interest is undoubtedly because the concept, if valid, provides a powerful tool for predicting how the importance of various outcomes will change in response to certain actions by organizations. It also can provide some important clues concerning what is likely to be important to employees. It suggests, for example, that as people get promoted in organizations and their lower-level needs become satisfied, they will become concerned with self-actualization and growth. It also suggests that if a person's job security is threatened, he will abandon all else in order to protect it. Finally, it suggests that an organization can give an employee enough of the lower-level rewards, such as security, but that it cannot give him enough growth and development. Thus, as employees receive more valued outcomes from organizations, they will *want* more, although the nature of what they want may change from things that satisfy their lower-order needs to things that satisfy their higher-order needs. As more than one manager has noted, "We have given our employees good working conditions, high pay, and a secure future. Now they want more interesting jobs and a chance to make more decisions. Won't they ever be satisfied?" Need hierarchy suggests that they won't!

An Approach to Outcome Attractiveness

The approaches of Maslow, McClelland, and others are useful in thinking about motivation in organizations. They clearly indicate a number of important points that need to be included in any approach that tries to deal with the issue of why certain outcomes are attractive to people. However, there are still many questions. The rest of this chapter will be concerned with answering these questions and with developing an approach to explaining outcome attractiveness.

Drives, Needs, Motives, or Just Outcomes?

All of the theorists discussed so far have assumed that outcomes are attractive to a person because of some drive, motive, or need the person has. On the other hand, Vroom (1964) has taken a different approach. He does not use the terms "drive," "need," or "motive" in his theory. He simply says that outcomes have value if they lead to other valued outcomes. Nothing is said about what causes people to value those other outcomes nor about what other outcomes are likely to be valued. Although it does solve the problem of trying to understand why individual outcomes are attractive, a theory that deals with the problem as Vroom's does sacrifices predictive power, in contrast to a theory of needs that states in advance what outcomes are likely to be valued and what affects their value.

A theory of needs can make some predictions — such as when outcomes will be important and what will be the effects of certain events — that Vroom's theory cannot make. For example, if it is known that pay is important to an individual because it leads to prestige, Vroom's theory can only predict that, as prestige outcomes become less important, so will pay. On the other hand, a need theory such as Maslow's can make further predictions. It can predict what conditions will affect the importance of prestige outcomes — that is, satisfaction of esteem needs or lower-level needs — and can then predict what the effect of a number of factors, such as a promotion, will be on the importance of pay.

The issue of whether needs are innate or learned is an important one, but since we are dealing with adults whose need structures are already developed, it is not crucial for us. This issue is important for us only in the sense that it might provide information about how common it is for people to have a need. Innate needs should be present in a greater proportion of the society than learned needs. Of course, at this point no one seriously argues that any needs other than the basic ones are either purely learned or purely innate. Still, it does seem that the needs that are lower on Maslow's hierarchy are more innate and, therefore, more universally present than are those that are at the top of the hierarchy.

For our purposes a theory of needs does not have to specify why people have needs, since it can say something about the needs people have and the conditions under which certain needs operate without doing this. All it has to say is that certain outcomes can be grouped together because when one is sought the others are sought and when one is obtained the others are no longer sought. People often have several groups of such outcomes. The groups can be called "needs," and, if the same ones are sought by most people, then it is reasonable to speak of a "human need" for the group of outcomes. Perhaps it should be added that before a group of outcomes is called a need the outcomes should be sought as ends in themselves rather than as instruments for obtaining other outcomes. For example, food outcomes are sought as an end in themselves, and thus we speak of a *need* for food; a big office is not an end in itself, and thus cannot be called a need. Once it is decided that people have needs, the question is "how many needs?"

How Many Needs?

Interestingly, theorists defining different categories of human needs usually don't disagree over which specific outcomes are likely to be goals for people, but they do disagree on what kinds of needs lead to outcomes taking on goal characteristics. Psychologists have argued that people have from three to several hundred needs. Part of the reason for this variance rests in the way needs are defined. Originally, the criterion was simple; needs or drives were only said to exist when it could be established that a physiological basis could be found for the attractiveness of the outcomes sought by a person.

The recent research on higher-level needs has clearly shown this approach to be too restrictive. A suggested alternative is to use the term "need" to refer to clusters of outcomes that people seek as ends in themselves. This definition, however, does not solve the problem of how to determine what constitutes a valid cluster. Different foods provide a simple example of the problem. Various food objects can be grouped together in the sense that when a person wants one he often wants the others, and when he gets enough of one he may lose interest in the others. Thus, we can say that people have a need for meat rather than saying that people have a need for roast beef or steak. By thinking in terms of outcome clusters such as the one just described, we move to a more general level and begin to group outcomes more parsimoniously. The question that arises now, however, is where to stop. That is, at what level of abstraction or generality should we stop grouping outcomes. Should we, for example, stop at the level of meat or put all food outcomes together and speak of a need for food, since food objects are somewhat similar in attractiveness, as shown in Figure 2.2? The

Figure 2.2. An Outcome Cluster.

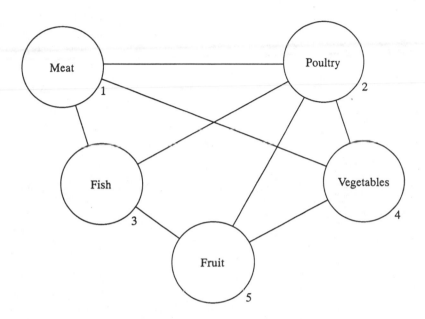

former is a tighter cluster in the sense that the attractiveness of different kinds of meat is probably more closely related than is the attractiveness of meat to the attractiveness of fruit. However, there are still tighter clusters (different kinds of steak), and thus there is no final answer to the question of how tight a cluster should be.

It is also possible to go to a higher level of abstraction and combine food outcomes with water and oxygen and call this combination an existence need (see Figure 2.3). This existence need includes all the outcomes that people need to sustain life. The criterion for grouping at this level is different from the criterion stated earlier (when one outcome is sought the other will be sought, and when one is obtained the attractiveness of the other is affected). The grouping in Figure 2.3 is based on the fact that all the outcomes have a common property: they are necessary for existence. Unlike the cluster shown in Figure 2.2, the attractiveness of one is not necessarily related to the

Figure 2.3. An Existence-Need Cluster.

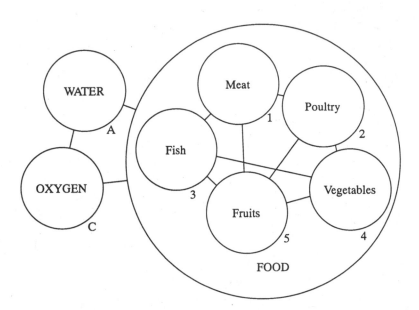

other. Using this system, we would say that people desire food objects because of a basic need to exist; whereas, if we operated at a lower level, we would say people desire food objects because of a need for nourishment. A somewhat similar grouping problem occurs with achievement, self-actualization, and competence. Although it is possible to say that these concepts each represent separate needs, they also overlap in many respects. They all focus on the attractiveness to people of dealing effectively with challenging problems. Thus, they can be grouped and labeled as "a need for competence and growth" or they can be treated separately.

Ultimately, the best approach to categorizing needs is that which allows the greatest prediction of behavior in organizations. Unfortunately, at the moment there is not enough research evidence to allow us to state conclusively which listing of needs leads to the greatest predictability. Because of this lack of evidence, the best approach would seem to be grouping only those outcomes that have a strong empirical relationship to each other. By this condition we mean those outcomes that can be observed to have common degrees of attractiveness to people. Using this criterion and thinking in terms of organizations, the following needs can be identified:

1. A number of existence needs — primarily sex, hunger, thirst, and oxygen.
2. A security need.
3. A social need.
4. A need for esteem and reputation.
5. An autonomy or freedom need.
6. A need for competence and self-actualization.

Is There a Need Hierarchy?

Now that we have identified a specific set of human needs, we must consider whether these needs should be arranged in a hierarchy. What does the evidence show about the existence of a need hierarchy?

There is strong evidence to support the view that unless existence needs are satisfied, none of the higher-order needs will come into play. There is also evidence that unless security needs are satisfied, people will not be concerned with higher-order needs. One report shows that subjects kept in a state of hunger think of little else than food (Keys, Brozek, Henschel, Mickelsen & Taylor, 1950). Similar data is available in the literature on brainwashing and concentration camps (Lawler & Suttle, 1972).

There is, however, very little evidence to support the view that a hierarchy exists above the security level. Thus, it probably is not safe to assume more than a two-step hierarchy with existence and security needs at the lowest level and all the higher-order needs at the next level. This line of thinking leads to the prediction that unless these lower-order needs are satisfied, the others will not come into play. However, which higher-order needs come into play after the lower ones are satisfied and in what order they will come into play cannot be predicted. If anything, it seems that most people are simultaneously motivated by several of the same-level needs. On the other hand, people do not seem to be simultaneously motivated by needs from the two different levels. One person might, for example, be motivated by social and autonomy needs, while another might be motivated by hunger and thirst. Once a need appears, it does seem to persist until it is satisfied or the satisfaction of the lower-order needs is threatened. The one exception to this rule is the need for self-actualization and competence. Unlike the other needs, evidence shows that this need does not appear to be satiable and, thus, is not likely to cease to be important unless the satisfaction of one of the lower-level needs is threatened.

Can Outcomes Satisfy More Than One Need?

There is a considerable amount of research evidence indicating that some outcomes are relevant to the satisfaction of more than one need. That is, when these outcomes are obtained they affect the attractiveness of more than one cluster of outcomes. A classic example is pay (Lawler, 1971). Pay appears to have the ability to satisfy not only existence needs but also security and esteem needs. For example, Lawler and Porter (1963) report that the more a manager is paid, the higher is his security- and esteem-need satisfaction. This statement means that when a person is trying to satisfy either security or esteem needs, pay will be important. It is not difficult to see why pay has the ability to satisfy a number of needs. Pay can be used to buy articles, such as food, that satisfy existence needs, and high pay also earns a certain amount of esteem and respect in our society.

How Important Are Different Needs?

Literally hundreds of studies have tried to measure the importance of different needs and outcomes to employees. Some idea of the importance of different needs can be obtained by looking at the data collected by Porter (1964), which appears in Figure 2.4. These data show that for over 1900 managers sampled, the higher-order needs are clearly the most important. Other data

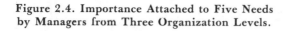

Figure 2.4. Importance Attached to Five Needs
by Managers from Three Organization Levels.

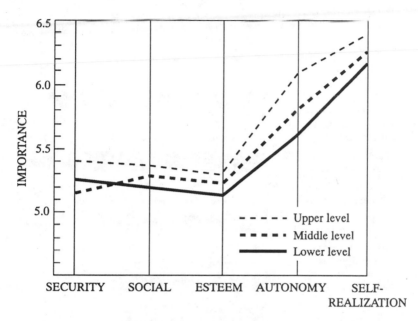

from the study show that the managers are most satisfied with
the lower-order needs. Thus, it follows that these lower-order
needs should be the least important. Whether this same concern with higher-order need satisfaction exists at the lower levels
in organizations is not clear. The data presented in Figure 2.4
show that higher-order needs do seem to be somewhat less important to lower-level managers than to higher-level managers.
Other data suggest that pay and certain lower-level needs are
rated as more important by workers than by managers (Porter
& Lawler, 1965). Dubin (1956), for example, argues that the
workplace is not a central part of the life of most industrial workers and that it is unwise to expect the workers to be concerned
with fulfilling their higher-order needs within the context of their
jobs.

Figure 2.5 shows the average ratings of the importance
of job factors in a large number of studies (16 studies and 11,000
employees). Most of these studies were done on nonmanagerial

Figure 2.5. Average Importance of Factors in Employee Attitudes (Compiled from 16 Studies, Including over 11,000 Employees).

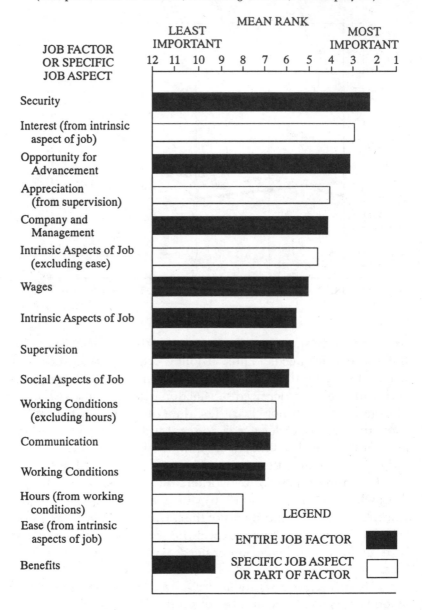

Source: From Herzberg et al., *Job Attitudes: Review of Research and Opinion.* Copyright © 1957 by the Psychological Service of Pittsburgh. Reprinted by permission.

employees. It shows job security and intrinsic job interest to be the most important factors to the employees. Lawler (1971) reviewed 43 studies in which pay was rated, and found that its average rating was third. This is an interesting finding, but, like other findings that are based on employee ratings of how important various needs and job characteristics are, it must be interpreted very cautiously. These ratings are difficult for people to make and are strongly influenced by how the questions are worded. Thus, it is impossible to reach any strong conclusions about which job factors are the most important. Perhaps the most significant thing to remember from these studies is that employees rate a number of factors as very important. Some of these factors seem to be most strongly related to lower-order needs, while others are related to higher-order needs.

Individual Differences in Need Strength

Large differences clearly exist in the goals and needs people have, and these differences must be considered when viewing individual motivation in organizations. For example, Lawler reports that in about ¼ of the cases he analyzed, pay was rated as first in importance. Because of these differences a pay system that will motivate one person is often seen as irrelevant by others. Porter's (1963) data show that managers at different organization levels differ in the degree to which they are motivated by higher-order needs. Other data show that managers are motivated by different needs: some managers are motivated by self-actualization, while others are motivated by autonomy. There is also evidence that some people seem to be fixated on such lower-order needs as security.

Many individual differences in need strength are understandable if we relate them to personal characteristics and situations. Hulin and Blood (1968), for example, point out that urban workers have different values from those of rural workers. Urban workers seem to be more alienated from work and apparently are less concerned with fulfilling higher-order needs on the job. For an interesting example of the type of individual profile that can be drawn from the research on need strength, consider the profile of a person to whom money is likely to be very important (Lawler, 1971).

The employee is a male, young (probably in his
twenties), his personality is characterized by low
self-assurance and high neuroticism; he comes from
a small town or farm background, he belongs to a
few clubs and social groups, and he owns his own
home and probably is a Republican and a Protes-
tant [p. 51].

In summary then, there are significant individual differences among employees in the importance of different needs and
outcomes. These differences are not surprising; in fact, many
are predictable from what has been said about how the importance of needs is affected by the satisfaction of needs and by
certain child-rearing experience. There is also evidence that these
individual differences are related in meaningful ways to a number of organizational factors, such as management level, and
to personal characteristics, such as age, sex, and education level.
This point has some interesting implications for the management of organizations, since it means that it is possible to identify those people for whom a particular reward is likely to be
important.

How Changeable Is the Importance of Needs?

There is evidence to indicate that some things can and do influence the importance of needs. Still, the evidence suggests that
organizations have relatively little influence over how important various outcomes will be to their members. The importance of needs is determined partly by hereditary factors and
partly by childhood experiences — things over which organizations have no control. Organizations can influence only two of
the factors that determine need importance: need satisfaction
and need arousal. Satisfaction influences importance, and organizational practices strongly influence satisfaction. Achievement motivation can be aroused by certain tasks and situations,
as can competence motivation. Since organizations do have partial control over the situation in which their employees work,
they can create conditions that will arouse certain needs. How-

ever, these needs must be present in the individual in order to be aroused, and whether the needs are present is a function of many things beyond the control of the organization.

Probably the best opportunity organizations have to influence the needs of their employees is provided by the selection process. Since need importance is relatively fixed and it is possible to identify people who are high on particular needs, organizations can select people who have the kinds of need-strength patterns they want. This would seem to be a much better approach than trying to change people's needs once they join the organization. This point also has some interesting implications for managers who have to motivate employees. It suggests that rather than trying to change the needs of their subordinates, managers should concentrate on placing people in jobs where their need structure is appropriate. The motivation system that is used must fit the needs of the person or it will not work. If pay is not important to an employee, he or she will never be motivated by a pay-incentive system.

Has There Been an Overall Change in the Relative Importance of Needs?

Many writers (for example, Roszak, 1969) have speculated that the strength of the various needs in the population has been changing over the past 60 years. They argue that only recently has a significant proportion of the population been concerned with needs such as self-actualization and autonomy. (And it is interesting to note that only recently have psychologists been concerned with needs such as self-actualization.) The concept of man as a self-actualizing organism is essentially a development of the 1960s.

Two reasons are generally advanced for the emergence of higher-order needs. First, there is the rising level of education in our society; approximately 40 percent of the high school graduates in the United States go to college. Second, the standard of living has constantly increased so that fewer and fewer people are concerned with satisfying their existence needs and, thus, can focus on satisfying their higher-order needs.

Unfortunately, there is very little evidence to either support or disprove the view that the strength of needs is changing. To test this view adequately we would have to compare need-strength data collected 60 years ago from a random population sample with data collected recently. Unfortunately, such data do not exist. There are, however, some data that can be said to support the view that higher-order needs have become more important. We've already seen that there is evidence to support a two-step hierarchy. If we accept the fact that the standard of living is higher, then, on the basis of a two-step hierarchy, this higher standard of living supports the view that higher-order needs probably are more important. In addition, Porter's (1962) data show that younger managers place greater importance on self-actualization than older managers do. This could, of course, be simply a function of age, but it could also be due to the higher education level of these younger managers and the fact that they never experienced a depression.

There is also some direct evidence that higher-educated people are more concerned with self-actualization. Finally, there is the fact that the idea of self-actualization has gained fairly wide attention in our society. It now seems "in" to talk about self-actualization; and, as we pointed out, the concept of "self-actualization" is now prominent in psychology. Although this evidence is only indirect, it does support the view that concern with self-actualization has increased recently. In summary, although there is little direct data to support the view, it probably is true that, in general, people are somewhat more concerned with satisfying higher-order needs than they used to be.

Summary and Conclusions

The following statements summarize the major points that have been made so far about human needs.

1. Needs can be thought of as groups of outcomes that people seek.
2. Man's needs are arranged in a two-level hierarchy. At the lowest level are existence and security needs; at the other level are social, esteem, autonomy, and self-actualization needs.

p.20 affiliation motive

p.30 SA
p.30 SA

p.36 need satisf

p.37 theory — statement of values
             — predict outcome

p.40 defn of needs

p.43 little evid to support
           hierarchy above security

p.44 study

p.50 —   higher-edu —
                ↑ concern for SA

MILWAUKEE LEAD WORKS

4715 North 27th Street
P.O. Box 09038
Milwaukee, WI 53209-0038
(414) 873-5710
1-800-236-0774
FAX NUMBER: (414) 873-8391

2210 Heldt Street
P.O. Box 633
Merrill, WI 54452
(715) 536-5518
1-000 236-0074
FAX NUMBER: (715) 536-485

Since 1926

MILWAUKEE LEAD WORKS

4715 North 27th Street
P.O. Box 09038
Milwaukee, WI 53209-0038
(414) 873-5710
1-800-236-0774
FAX NUMBER: (414) 873-8391

2210 Ileldt Street
P.O. Box 633
Merrill, WI 54452
(715) 536-5518
1-800-236-0074
FAX NUMBER: (715) 536-48

Since 1926

3. The higher-level needs will appear only when the lower-level ones are satisfied.
4. All needs except self-actualization are satiable, and as needs become satisfied they decrease in importance.
5. A person can be motivated by more than one need at a given point in time and will continue to be motivated by a need until either it is satisfied or satisfaction of the lower-order needs is threatened.

Thus, we have answered two of the three questions asked at the beginning of the chapter. A classification system for needs has been developed, and statements have been made about what influences the importance of needs. No conclusions have been reached about why people develop needs or about whether needs are innate or learned because these questions don't seem to be answerable at this time.

three

Motivation and Behavior

To predict an individual's behavior, it is necessary to know the attractiveness of outcomes to the individual; however, this knowledge is not sufficient. We must also know what factors other than outcome attractiveness influence people's choices about which outcomes to seek and why people choose to behave in a particular way to obtain the outcomes they seek. For example, evidence from the research on piece-rate pay plans shows that these plans produce different behavior among people who are equally motivated to earn money. Some people restrict their productivity while others produce as much as they can. In this chapter we will consider those motivation theories that are concerned with specifying:

1. What determines which outcomes a person will try to obtain?
2. What determines the behaviors a person will be motivated to perform in order to obtain desired outcomes?

A number of motivation theories suggest scientific explanations of why people choose particular behaviors to obtain their goals. Theories have been suggested by social psychologists to explain social behavior and by learning theorists to explain learning. Similarly, motivation theories with special relevance to clinical psychology, physiological psychology, and child psychology have been developed. Altogether, hundreds of different motivation theories have been stated.

However, we don't need to include all of these theories in our discussion for two reasons: first, many so-called theories of motivation simply are not sufficiently developed to take into account all the phenomena with which an acceptable theory must deal; second, there is a high degree of convergence among the more fully developed theories. The works of Lewin, Tolman, Rotter, and others converge into one stream of thinking that can be called "expectancy theory." A second clear stream of thinking about motivation is apparent in the work of theorists such as Hull and Spence. This approach has been labeled "drive theory."

Drive Theory

We have already discussed the aspect of drive theory dealing with why outcomes are attractive. However, probably the most important part of the theory has to do with its prediction of how people will behave in order to obtain the outcomes that attract them.

The first significant conceptual advance beyond hedonism was made by Thorndike (1911) in the law of effect:

> Of several responses made to the same situation, those which are accompanied or closely followed by satisfaction to the animal will, other things being equal, be more firmly connected with the situation, so that, when it recurs, they will be more likely to recur; those which are accompanied or closely followed by discomfort to the animal will, other things being equal, have their connections with that situation weakened, so that, when it recurs, they will be less likely to occur. The greater the satisfaction or discomfort, the greater the strengthening or weakening of the bond [p. 244].

The law of effect does not say why certain events are satisfying or dissatisfying, but it does introduce learning and past events into the concept of motivation. Thorndike's law uses learning and previous stimulus-response connections to explain how present behavior is directed toward satisfying events and away from painful events. Because it emphasizes the impact of learning, the law of effect has been recognized as an important step toward the development of a testable theory of motivation.

Modern thinking about drive theory really began with Hull's work. Hull recognized that, to explain behavior, both the "striving" for goals and the "strengthening of connections" related to goals had to be considered. In his major work, *Principles of Behavior* (1943), Hull developed the formula $_sE_R = {_sH_R} \times D$ to explain what he called the "impetus to respond," or $_sE_R$ (effective habit strength). The variable $_sH_R$ stands for habit strength and takes into account the learning of the organism. The variable D stands for drive. This formula suggests that behavior is influenced by a mulitplicative combination of drive strength and habit strength. The multiplicative relationship indicates that unless drive is present, there will be no impetus to respond.

In Hull's theory, drive essentially has two influences on behavior: an energizing influence and a partial directing influence. Drive is seen as a general exciter of all responses; this function of exerting an energizing influence is drive's most important role. The second aspect of drive is based on Hull's assumption that different biological needs produce qualitatively different patterns of internal stimulation. Hull argued that these drive stimuli have an important part in determining what kind of behavior a particular need will elicit, since the stimuli provide cues to what the "correct" behavior is — hence, the partial directing influence of drive. Hunger, for example, produces different cues than thirst; when hungry, the organism is "directed" to do whatever it did the last time to reduce hunger, rather than what it did to reduce thirst.

After developing the concept of drive, Hull turned his attention to the concept of habit strength ($_sH_R$), which he defined as the connection between a stimulus and a response. For Hull, habit strength is an associative connection that influences the kind of behavior the drive will energize. According to Hull, the strength of a habit depends on four factors:

1. The contiguity of the stimulus and response during training.
2. The closeness of the S-R event to a positively reinforcing state of affairs.
3. The number of positive reinforcements.
4. The magnitude of positive reinforcement during training.

Perhaps the best way to explain Hull's thinking is to look at the behavior of a rat in a maze. The animal will be stimulated to act only to the extent that some drive is present, since drive is required in order to sensitize habit strengths into action. The particular habit strength that is sensitized into action will depend on the rat's previous experience in a maze. If at the present time he is hungry and if in the past he found that turning to the right when he was hungry led to large quantities of food, he is likely to turn to the right. On the other hand, if the rat has only been in the maze when he was thirsty and on turning right he immediately found large amounts of water, he is not particularly likely to turn right now that he is hungry. The drive stimulus is different in the second situation, so a new S-R connection has to be established.

Along the same lines, if a hungry rat has been in a maze and on turning right found little food, or found food only later, he will not be particularly likely to turn right the next time he's in the maze. His $_sH_R$ for turning right will not be strong, since it has not been properly reinforced. In short, for Hull the probability of an organism's behaving in a particular way is influenced by two major factors: (1) the degree to which the organism's drive state is strong enough to energize behavior, and (2) the degree to which the behavior has been closely associated with large, appropriate rewards in similar situations.

The heavy emphasis of drive theory on the establishment of S-R connections has led some to call theories such as Hull's "hedonism of the past." The clear suggestion of Hull's work is that it is not the anticipation of a large pay raise or other reward that motivates someone, but the previous experiences he has had in similar situations. Thus, offering a large rather than a small raise will not immediately lead to stronger motivation — although in the long run stronger motivation may result, since receiving the raise will result in the gradual establishment of a stronger $_sH_R$.

Although Hull's initial statement of his theory represents a landmark in the development of modern drive theory, he and others have made significant changes in the theory since 1943 in response to certain criticisms. As originally stated, the theory did not account for the actual effects of changing the size of rewards. According to the theory, changes in size of reward can only gradually influence behavior, since size of reward influences $_sH_R$, which changes only gradually — hence, the prediction mentioned earlier that little immediate effect can be expected from giving a large rather than a small pay raise.

Studies by Crespi (1942, 1944) and Zeaman (1949) clearly showed that rats trained to run to a large reward showed abrupt decreases in speed of running when given a smaller reward. Rats trained to run to small rewards showed equally abrupt increases in running speed when a larger reward was given. These results did not support Hull's prediction of a gradual change in habit strength; instead, the studies showed that shifts in size of reward have an immediate effect on behavior.

To accommodate this experimental evidence, Hull (1952) revised his theory. He introduced "amount of incentive" as a separate motivational variable (K) in the equation for reaction potential; so that, instead of reading $_sE_R = D \times {_sH_R}$, Hull's equation read $_sE_R = D \times K \times {_sH_R}$. Hull used K to refer to anticipatory goal reactions that can change quickly in strength as changes take place in reward size. K is a motivational variable like D because K can also energize habits.

Perhaps the most striking point about this change in drive theory is that it sharply reduced the areas of disagreement between drive theory and the expectancy theories of Lewin and Tolman. For a considerable time the approaches were easily differentiated by the fact that one was very forward-looking and concerned with anticipated goals, while the other was not. With the change in Hull's theory, the difference greatly decreased.

However, drive theory still remains more oriented to the past than expectancy theory, which is much more oriented toward hedonism of the future than of the past.

Expectancy Theory

Like drive theory, expectancy theory can be traced back to hedonism and the work of the English utilitarians. In the 1930s, however, expectancy theory began to develop a different thrust. At this point, Tolman (1943) began to talk about expectations and to argue for an approach that was more cognitively oriented, and Kurt Lewin (1935) presented a cognitively oriented theory of behavior that contained terms such as "valence" and "force." Out of this early work by Tolman and Lewin, a number of very similar motivation theories have developed. All of these theories include a concept of valence — that is, the attractiveness of an outcome — and a concept of expectancy — that is, the likelihood that an action will lead to a certain outcome or goal. The theories also converge in that they see valence and expectancy combining multiplicatively to determine behavior; hence, these theories can be referred to as expectancy × valence theories of motivation.

A number of theorists have picked up the main points of the early work of Tolman and Lewin and have built their own motivation theories within the expectancy × valence framework. The more prominent of these theorists are listed in Table 3.1. All of the theorists maintain that the strength of a tendency to act in a certain way depends on the strength of an expectancy that the act will be followed by a given consequence (or outcome) and on the value or attractiveness of that consequence (or outcome) to the actor.

Vroom's theory (1964) is the only one listed in Table 3.1 that was stated specifically for the purpose of dealing with motivation in the work environment. Thus, his theory is the logical one to examine to see how expectancy theory can be applied to work motivation. For Vroom, valence (V) refers to affective orientations toward particular outcomes. An outcome is positive if a person prefers attaining it to not attaining it, neutral if the person is indifferent to it, and negative if the person prefers

Table 3.1. Expectancy Theories of Motivation.

Theorist	Determinants of Impulse to Action
Tolman	Expectancy of goal, demand for goal
Lewin	Potency × valence
Edwards	Subjective probability × utility
Atkinson	Expectancy × (motive × incentive)
Rotter	Expectancy, reinforcement value
Vroom	Expectancy × valence; where valence is (instrumentality × valence)
Peak	Instrumentality × attitude (affect)

Source: From *Pay and Organizational Effectiveness: A Psychological View* by E. E. Lawler. Copyright © 1971 by McGraw-Hill Book Company. Used by permission of the publisher.

not attaining it. Valence can vary from +1 to −1; neutral outcomes are 0. Vroom emphasizes that valence refers to an outcome's anticipated reward value rather than an outcome's actual reward value when obtained.

Vroom defines expectancy (*E*) as a momentary belief about the likelihood that a particular act will be followed by a particular outcome. Hence, like other expectancy theorists, Vroom sees an expectancy as a response-outcome association. Expectancies can be described in terms of their strength: maximal strength, designated by the number 1, is subjective certainty that the act will be followed by the outcome; minimal strength, designated by the number 0, is subjective certainty that the act will not be followed by this outcome.

Like other expectancy theorists, Vroom argues that expectancy and valence combine multiplicatively to determine motivation or force. The multiplicative aspect of the theory is important; it means that unless both valence and expectancy are present to some degree, there will be no force. When either or both are 0, the product will be 0 and motivation will be 0. If, for example, a person wants to perform well but does not feel that his effort will result in good performance, he will have no motivation to perform well.

Any action may be interpreted as leading to a number of outcomes; hence, one must consider how the combination of the various outcomes influences behavior. Vroom's theory argues for multiplying the valence of each outcome times the strength of the expectancy that the act will lead to the attainment of the outcome, and then taking the algebraic sum of all the resulting products. Thus, he writes his theory as follows: Force = $\Sigma (E \times V)$, where Σ means that the products for all outcomes are added to determine force. This is a key point in the theory, since it means that tying a valent reward, such as pay, to a desired behavior, such as good performance, will not be enough to motivate the desired behavior. Pay can be highly valued and can be seen as closely related to performance; but if negative consequences, such as feeling tired or being rejected by a work group, are also perceived as related to good performance, there may be no motivation to perform. Finally, according to Vroom, a person will be motivated to perform well in a situation only if performing well has the highest $E \times V$ force in that particular situation. Performing well can have a strong force, but if performing poorly has a stronger force, the person will not be motivated to perform well.

There is one area in which Vroom's theory — and indeed all the expectancy theories — gets into muddy water. This difficulty involves the distinction between acts and outcomes. As Vroom states, "the distinction . . . is not, however, an absolute one. Actions are frequently described in terms of particular outcomes which they affect" (p. 19). Vroom uses the term "action" to refer to behavior that is within the person's repertoire — for example, trying to perform well or seeking a job. Thus, the belief that an act (trying to perform well) will lead to an outcome (performing well) is an expectancy; the relationship between an outcome (performing well) and another outcome (a reward such as pay) is an instrumentality that affects the valence of the original outcome. Many expectancy theorists are even less clear than Vroom is about the distinction between actions and outcomes. Some have tended to ignore the fact that trying to perform an act does not always lead to performing it. In some situations, trying to perform an act is equivalent to performing it; in these situations, it is reasonable to argue that motivation is determined by the kind of outcomes to which performing the act leads, since expectancies are likely to be 1. In many other situations, trying to perform an act does not always lead to performing it. For instance, good job performance does not automatically result from trying to perform well; hence, beliefs — the person's subjective probability — about whether good performance will result must be taken into account to explain behavior.

Expectancy Theory Compared with Drive Theory

Drive theory and expectancy theory are different in a number of ways; however, both theories make similar predictions. Also, they both contain many of the same concepts; both theories include the notion of a reward or favorable outcome that is desired, and both postulate learned connections within the organism. For expectancy theory this connection is a behavior-outcome expectancy, and for drive theory the connection is an S-R habit strength.

Some of the aspects in which the theories differ are not crucial for understanding motivation in organizations (for example, how the theories explain avoidance behavior and the degree to which they assert that effects of anticipated goals can be generalized). However, the theories differ in two respects that are crucial for understanding motivation in organizations. Expectancy theory stresses the importance of forward-looking beliefs about what will occur, while drive theory emphasizes the importance of learned stimulus-response connections.

Extensive research has been done on the relationship between job performance and beliefs about how valued rewards can be obtained in organizations. This research shows that verbal statements of attitudes about (1) the importance of rewards and (2) how rewards are obtained are directly related to performance. The research also shows that a multiplicative combination of these two kinds of attitudes is a predictor of performance. These findings are perfectly predictable from expectancy theory, which emphasizes the importance of knowing a person's response-outcome beliefs and of combining them multiplicatively with the perceived value of the outcomes. Drive theory, on the other hand, stresses the importance of $_sH_R$ and considers how $_sH_R$ combines multiplicatively with drive. It does not stress the importance of the awareness of response-reward connections; thus, it does not lead one to look at these connections in order to predict behavior. Working from drive theory, one would be much more likely to look at *S-R* habit strength than at response-outcome connections in order to predict behavior. Thus, while the research on response-outcome beliefs by no means disproves drive theory, it does provide one reason for preferring expectancy theory.

Expectancy theory gives very loose specifications of how response-outcome connections are built up, thus allowing for the possibility of these connections being formed in a number of ways. Drive theory, on the other hand, postulates that *S-R* habit strengths are built up through repeated associations of stimuli and responses, which seems far too rigid and restrictive. It may be that this process is the only way association can be established among animals, but the necessity of the process where humans are concerned is doubtful. In the case of humans, drive theory's process constitutes one way — but not the only way — that connections can develop. There is evidence that in humans these connections can be formed in a number of ways, including vicariously or by other symbolic means. Ayllon and Azrin (1965) have shown that a simple verbal statement of the existence of a behavior-outcome connection can radically change the beliefs and motivation levels of people toward performing certain behaviors. A number of studies of pay (for example, Atkinson, 1958) have shown that different degrees of motivation occur depending on how the relationship between pay and performance is described. People work harder when they are told pay depends on performance than when they are told pay does not depend on performance. Other studies have shown that people develop behavior-outcome associations from watching other people and from trying something only once. These findings are quite congruent with expectancy theory, since this theory allows for the possibility of expectancies forming in a number of ways.

On the other hand, the sudden changes that do take place in subjective response-outcome probabilities and the consequent changes in motivation are not congruent with drive theory. Drive theory has always emphasized the slow building of associations and the importance of previous experience and temporally close associations. Still, many of the points made by drive theory about how associations come about do appear to be generally valid. Expectancy theory, or for that matter any motivation theory, could profit by specifying some of the more obvious factors that influence response-outcome connections; however, as an over-all theory, the expectancy approach seems to be the most useful one for studying motivation in work organizations.

An Expectancy Model

A number of developments in motivation theory have taken place since Vroom stated his expectancy theory in 1964. The expectancy model presented here draws on these developments to provide the best available model for understanding motivation in organizations. This model is based on four points that the previous overview of the research on human motivation suggests are valid.

1. People have preferences among the various outcomes that are potentially available to them.
2. People have expectancies about the likelihood that an action (effort) on their part will lead to the intended behavior or performance.
3. People have expectancies (instrumentalities) about the likelihood that certain outcomes will follow their behavior.
4. In any situation, the actions a person chooses to take are determined by the expectancies and the preferences that person has at the time.

Figure 3.1 presents an illustration of the expectancy model in diagrammatic form. It shows the major factors that influence the strength of a person's motivation to perform in a given manner. First, motivation is shown to be influenced by the expectancy that effort or action on the part of the person will lead to the intended behavior. Thus, expectancy is simply the person's estimate of the probability that he will accomplish his intended performance, given the situation in which he finds himself. This can be labeled an $E \rightarrow P$ (effort $\rightarrow$ performance) expectancy. For example, a manager may think that he has a 50 percent chance of producing 2000 cars a week in his plant if he tries. If we consider this kind of expectancy as varying from 0 to 1, the manager's $E \rightarrow P$ expectancy could be represented as .5. This kind of expectancy is typically more salient for complex and higher-level tasks than for simple tasks where little ability or skill is required.

Figure 3.1 also shows that expectancies about the consequences of task performance influence motivation. The model shows a number of expectancies, since successful task performance typically leads to a number of outcomes (as does unsuccessful performance). These expectations, which can be labeled $P \rightarrow O$ expectancies (performance $\rightarrow$ outcomes), are subjective probability estimates and can vary from 0 to 1 in the same manner as the $E \rightarrow P$ expectancies. To return to the manufacturing manager example, he may be sure that if his plant does produce 2000 cars a week he will receive a pay increase (his $P \rightarrow O$ expectancy equals 1). At the same time, he may also believe that there is a 50 percent probability that he will receive a promotion if he succeeds in producing 2000 cars. In addition, he may see a number of other outcomes associated with producing 2000 cars, and he may see still other outcomes associated with trying but failing to produce 2000 cars.

In many instances where the $E \rightarrow P$ expectancy is less than 1, it is important to consider what outcomes a person connects with trying to perform in a given way and failing. In other words, where success cannot be assured, it is necessary to consider the person's perceived probability that performance other than the intended one will be the outcome. In the case of the manager, this would involve considering the possibility of trying to produce 2000 cars a week and failing. In some situations, people obtain outcomes simply because they try to perform at a certain level. In these situations, a person will observe many of the same outcomes resulting from successful and unsuccessful performance, and he will realize that he will still receive a number of positive outcomes even though he fails to accomplish the desired

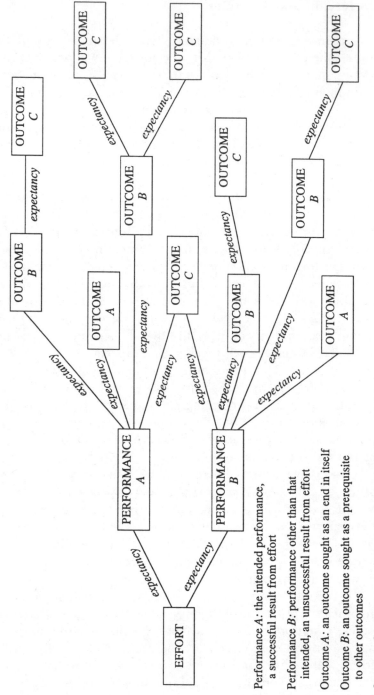

Figure 3.1. Expectancy Motivation Model.

Performance A: the intended performance, a successful result from effort

Performance B: performance other than that intended, an unsuccessful result from effort

Outcome A: an outcome sought as an end in itself

Outcome B: an outcome sought as a prerequisite to other outcomes

Outcome C: an outcome that can be obtained whether or not the effort leads to the intended performance

performance. In some situations, many negative outcomes may be tied to failing to perform at the intended level, which may make trying very unattractive if failure is likely.

The model in Figure 3.1 also shows that only some of the outcomes are seen as leading to other outcomes. This factor is included to stress the point that some outcomes are sought as ends in themselves (for example, personal growth is sought as an end in itself), while others are sought because they lead to other outcomes (for example, money is sought because of what it will buy, not as an end in itself). The attractiveness of any outcome can be thought of as varying from very desirable (+1) to very undesirable (−1). As has been repeatedly stressed, there are two reasons why outcomes that are associated with performance may be valent: (1) they directly satisfy a person's needs, or (2) they lead to an outcome or set of outcomes that satisfy a particular need or set of needs.

→   Overall, then, the model illustrated in Figure 3.1 suggests that a person's motivation to perform in a particular way will be influenced by his expectancies about trying to perform in that way, his expectancies about the outcomes associated with performing at that level ($P \rightarrow O$), and the attractiveness of the outcomes involved. These factors combine to produce a motivational force to perform in the specified manner. For our hypothetical manager, this means that his $E \rightarrow P$ expectancy for producing 2000 cars, his $P \rightarrow O$ expectancies for producing 2000 cars, and the perceived attractiveness of the outcomes combine to determine his motivation to produce 2000 cars.

Figure 3.1 does not show how the various expectancy factors combine to determine motivation. Most expectancy theories have operated on the assumption that the higher the $E \rightarrow P$ expectancy and the more closely performance is seen to be related to positively valent outcomes, the greater will be the motivation. Based on past research, this assumption seems generally valid. Motivation does seem to be greatest when $E \rightarrow P$ is high for successful performance and low for unsuccessful performance and when $P \rightarrow O$ is high for positive outcomes and low for negative outcomes. Some theorists have argued for multiplying the various terms in the expectancy model together in order to obtain a single motivation score. In the case of our model, this approach would involve multiplying all $P{\rightarrow}O$ expectancies by the valence of the outcomes and then adding the products. This sum would then be multiplied by the $E{\rightarrow}P$ expectancy for successful performance. In terms of a formula such as Vroom's, this gives $(E{\rightarrow}P) \times \Sigma[(P{\rightarrow}O)\,(V)]$. This formula can be expanded further to indicate that people often consider both the possibility of attaining their intended level of performance and the possibility of their failing in the following manner: $\Sigma[(E{\rightarrow}P) \times \Sigma[(P{\rightarrow}O)\,(V)]]$.

Some writers have suggested that it is premature to hypothesize multiplicative relationships among these expectancy factors because such relationships go beyond what can be measured (Campbell et al., 1970), and the writers undoubtedly are right. However, it is still important to think of these terms as combining in a basically multiplicative manner for several reasons, probably the most important of which has to do with what happens when either $E{\rightarrow}P$ or $P{\rightarrow}O$ is 0. When $E{\rightarrow}P$ is 0, the prediction is that no motivation will be present; if an additive relationship were hypothesized the prediction would be that some motivation will be present. The no-motivation prediction would seem to fit with the finding that people are not motivated to initiate actions that they have no chance of completing successfully. Similarly, the multiplicative model predicts that if $P{\rightarrow}O$ is 0 for a particular outcome, regardless of what its valence is, that outcome will not influence motivation. The multiplicative model also predicts that if all $P{\rightarrow}O$s are 0, there will be no motivation, even if $E{\rightarrow}P$ is high. This statement is illustrated by the observation that people do not perform many tasks, even though it is obvious that they are able to perform these tasks. The multiplicative combination also allows negative valences to accumulate in such a way that motivation can be negative; negative motivation can be seen in the desires of people to avoid many kinds of activities. Thus, it seems logical to assume that the factors in our expectancy motivation model combine multiplicatively, even though this relationship has not been firmly established.

In organizations, people are often forced to choose among a number of behaviors that are relatively attractive. Simply stated, the expectancy model predicts that people will choose to behave in whatever way has the highest motivational force. That is, people will choose to behave in whatever way has the highest $\Sigma[(E \rightarrow P) \times \Sigma[(P \rightarrow O)(V)]]$ score for them. In the case of productivity, this means people will be motivated to be highly productive if they feel they can be highly productive and if they see a number of positive outcomes associated with being a high producer. However, if for some reason they will receive approximately the same outcomes for being less highly productive, they probably will be low producers.

Managers often ask why their subordinates are not more productive. They seem to feel that people should be productive almost as if it is a question of morality or of instinct. The expectancy approach suggests asking a rather different question: Why should people be productive in a given situation? People are not naturally productive (or nonproductive). Thus, managers who wonder why their people are not more productive should start by comparing the rewards given to good performers with the rewards given to poor performers. Time after time, no real difference is found when this comparison is made. Thus, the workers' perception of the situation is that the good and the poor performers receive the same treatment, and this view is crucial in determining motivation. The example of an automobile assembly-line worker highlights this point. His pay is typically not affected by his performance, and his job is so simple that he receives no satisfaction from doing it well. Being highly productive does nothing more for him than to make him tired. Why should he be productive?

In summary, the expectancy model answers the two questions that were raised at the beginning of this chapter. It argues that both the attractiveness of the outcomes and the person's $E \rightarrow P$ and $P \rightarrow O$ expectancies influence which outcomes a person will try to obtain and how these outcomes will be sought. In order to answer one of these questions, it is necessary to answer the other, since they are so closely related. The choice of a behavior also implies a choice of which outcome will be sought, and the choice of an outcome partially determines what behavior will be attempted.

Chapter 2 discussed the determinants of outcome attractiveness; so far, the determinants of $E \rightarrow P$ and $P \rightarrow O$ expectancies have not been discussed. It is important to understand how these expectancies develop, since they are basic to understanding motivation. Unfortunately, there has been relatively little research on the topic. Still, it is possible to reach some important conclusions about how $E \rightarrow P$ and $P \rightarrow O$ expectancies develop and about what influences them.

Determinants of $E \rightarrow P$ Expectations
(effort · performance)

The single most important determinant of a person's $E \rightarrow P$ expectancies is the objective situation. Sometimes, of course, a person's perception of the situation is not accurate, and as a result the objective situation may not completely determine a person's $E \rightarrow P$ expectancies. However, it seems safe to assume that over time most people's $E \rightarrow P$ perceptions begin to fit reality reasonably well. Several of the other factors that influence $E \rightarrow P$ expectancies tend to encourage this. One of the most influential of these factors is the communication of other people's perceptions of the person's situation. Other people's perceptions are not necessarily accurate, but more often than not they can be a corrective force when a person badly misperceives reality. This communication is most likely to be influential when the person communicating his or her perception is very experienced in the situation and is less emotionally involved in it. For example, the ski instructor can often effectively correct the new skier's misperceptions about the likelihood that the new skier can successfully negotiate a particular turn, since the ski instructor is a more objective and experienced observer. In many situations an older employee can effectively counsel a new employee about the difficulty of doing a job. Often a job looks much more difficult to the new employee than it in fact is, and the result is turnover or low performance.

Learning plays an important role in determining $E \rightarrow P$ expectancies, as well as helping to make these expectancies more accurate. As people gain more experience in a situation, they typically are able to develop more accurate $E \rightarrow P$ expectancies.

After a number of trials at doing something, a person knows from his own experience what his ratio of successful to unsuccessful efforts is. From a straight statistical-sampling perspective, once a large number of trials have occurred, it is possible to estimate the likelihood of a particular event with great accuracy.

There is some evidence that personality factors can cause people's $E \rightarrow P$ probabilities to diverge from reality. Psychologists who have written about personality have emphasized that individuals have a self-image. Sometime during infancy, human beings learn to distinguish themselves from their environment. They learn that they can influence the environment or act on it, and they get feedback about the effectiveness of these actions. Some things that people try to make happen do happen, while others do not happen. From this interaction with their environment, people develop a concept of themselves and of their competence in dealing with the environment. They learn what they can do and what they cannot do. They receive feedback from others about how they are perceived. Out of these experiences, people develop a knowledge of their existence and a self-image — that is, a view of what they are like. A crucial component of people's self-image is the beliefs they have concerning their response capabilities and their value and effectiveness. These beliefs are at the core of what is frequently referred to as self-esteem, and are important for understanding the kinds of $E \rightarrow P$ expectancies people have.

Self-esteem can be influenced either positively or negatively depending on a person's effectiveness in dealing with his environment; but once a person has reached maturity, self-esteem — like a person's needs — appears to become relatively stable. There are large individual differences in self-esteem. Low-self-esteem people are generally poor estimators of their own ability to successfully carry out certain behaviors. They generally tend to underestimate the likelihood that they will be successful, although sometimes they are unrealistically high in their estimates. Not suprisingly, people's self-esteem tends to be related to their $E \rightarrow P$ expectancies; as a result, motivating low-self-esteem people to perform well is difficult, since they are predisposed to believing that they cannot perform well. On the other hand, high-self-esteem people tend to have realistic $E \rightarrow P$ expectancies; thus, they respond more predictably and realistically to their environment. One way an organization can deal with this effect of self-esteem on motivation is by selecting only people who have high self-esteem; another way is by trying to raise the self-esteem of the people already in the organization. The latter solution presumably can be accomplished by providing the right kinds of jobs and leadership; however, the solution does not come easily, given the relative stability of people's self-esteem.

Figure 3.2 summarizes what has been said about the determinants of $E \rightarrow P$ expectancies, which are shown as being directly influenced by four factors: the person's self-esteem, their past experiences, the actual situation, and communications received from others. The figure also shows that the actual situation, in addition to directly influencing the person's $E \rightarrow P$ expectancies, influences what is communicated to the person, making it the crucial determinant of $E \rightarrow P$ expectancies. Because $E \rightarrow P$ expectancies are reality based, by changing the situation in which employees find themselves, organizations can influence employees' $E \rightarrow P$ expectancies — thus influencing motivation. As we shall see, job design has a strong influence on $E \rightarrow P$ expectancies and thus can influence motivation.

Determinants of $P \rightarrow O$ Expectancies
(perform—outcome)

Like $E \rightarrow P$ expectancies, $P \rightarrow O$ expectancies are strongly influenced by the objective situation, by people's past experiences in similar situations, and by what other people say about the situation. For example, one study has shown that people's perceptions of the probability that pay is related to performance are in accord with reality (Lawler, 1967). In this study, pay was clearly related to performance in one group of organizations where managers reported a strong relationship; managers reported a weak relationship in another group of organizations, and evidence supported their perception.

There is a great deal of evidence that verbal reports by

Figure 3.2. Determinants of $P \rightarrow O$ Expectancies.

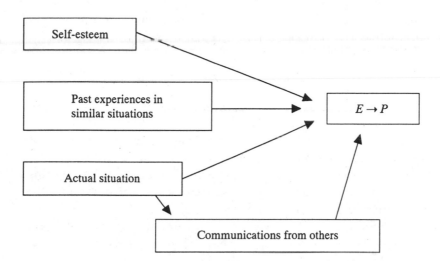

co-workers can strongly influence a worker's $P \rightarrow O$ expectancies. Whyte (1955), in his work on incentive plans, has shown how workers are influenced by other workers' reports on the consequences of performing well. For example, workers can be convinced that if they are highly productive, the pay rate will be reduced, even though they have never seen it happen, and even though the company says it won't happen. Workers believe the event will happen because the event has been predicted by their fellow workers, who represent a high-credibility source. Whyte also shows that workers develop other beliefs about the consequences of high productivity (for example, that high productivity will lead to rejection by other workers) even though they have never experienced such consequences.

Like $E \rightarrow P$ expectancies, $P \rightarrow O$ expectancies tend to be accurate, although there is evidence that under certain conditions $P \rightarrow O$ expectancies may be distorted. Raiffa (1968) has shown that people's subjective probabilities are generally related to actual mathematical probabilities. However, it has also been found that subjective probabilities tend to be larger than actual probabilities at low values, and smaller than the actual probabilities

at higher values. Thus, it seems that people tend to underestimate the possibility of a "sure thing" and to overestimate the
possibility of a "long shot." Some sources have commented that
evidence of the latter is present in the betting and gambling
habits of most Americans.

Some research suggests that $P{\rightarrow}O$ probabilities are influenced by the nature of the outcomes. One group of studies
has shown that, to most people, positive outcomes seem more
likely to occur than negative ones. Other studies have suggested
that people see very positive outcomes as less likely to be obtained than less positive ones. Thus, people exhibit a general
tendency to downgrade the possibility that very positive things
will happen to them; people also downgrade the possibility that
negative things will happen to them.

Some of the research on achievement motivation has sug-
gested that $E{\rightarrow}P$ probabilities can influence certain $P{\rightarrow}O$ probabilities. Specifically, when the $E{\rightarrow}P$ probability is around .5,
the achievement motive is aroused, and $P{\rightarrow}O$ expectancies having to do with achievement-type outcomes are affected. Apparently, when $E{\rightarrow}P$ is very high or very low, people do not see
successful performance on their part as leading to feelings of
achievement or competence, as they do when $E{\rightarrow}P$ is around .5.

Like $E{\rightarrow}P$ probabilities, there is reason to believe that
$P{\rightarrow}O$ probabilities are influenced by people's personalities. Rotter
(1966) has developed a measure of the degree to which people
believe in internal versus external control of rewards. A person
who is high on internal control believes that he can influence
what happens to him and what outcomes he obtains. A person
who is high on external control believes that fate and forces beyond his control influence what happens to him and what outcomes he receives. Rotter suggests that consistent individual
differences appear on this dimension such that some people consistently feel they can influence what happens to themselves,
while others consistently tend to believe that things are beyond
their control.

Research data suggest that internal-control people are
generally better motivated to perform well, presumably since
they see a stronger connection between their behavior and the

goals they seek. In other words, people who are oriented toward internal control are more likely to feel that performance on their part will lead to rewards than are people who believe in external control. Because of this, internal-control people are easier to motivate by the use of rewards that are contingent on their performance.

Rotter's data show fairly large differences between various segments of American society in the degree to which people believe in internal versus external control. Businessmen and college students tend to be high on internal control, while convicts and ghetto youths tend toward external control.

Overall, despite the research on internal versus external control, people's perception of a particular situation is most strongly influenced by the actual situation. One of the reasons that $P \rightarrow O$ beliefs are so important is that they can be greatly influenced by the policies and practices of organizations. Since $P \rightarrow O$ beliefs are based on the actual work situations, and organizations control some important parts of the work situation, organizations can influence $P \rightarrow O$ expectancies by changing the situation. A leader's behavior, the design of jobs, and the pay and promotion systems all influence important $P \rightarrow O$ beliefs and are under the control of organizations. Organizations can also influence $P \rightarrow O$ beliefs by selecting people for membership on the basis of their beliefs in internal versus external control. For example, if the organization wanted (as well it might) to have people with high $P \rightarrow O$ beliefs, it could select people who are high on internal control.

The rest of this book focuses on how certain organizational practices and policies influence $P \rightarrow O$ expectancies. This is the major topic in the chapters on reward systems, job design, and interpersonal influences. The reason for the focus on $P \rightarrow O$ beliefs should be obvious: of the three factors that determine motivation ($E \rightarrow P$ and outcome attractiveness being the other two), $P \rightarrow O$ beliefs can be most easily and directly influenced by organizations. And thus, this is the area in which organizations have the most leverage to influence employee motivation.

Figure 3.3 summarizes what has been said so far about the determinants of $P \rightarrow O$ beliefs. It shows that $P \rightarrow O$ expectancies

Figure 3.3. Determinants of $P \rightarrow O$ Expectancies.

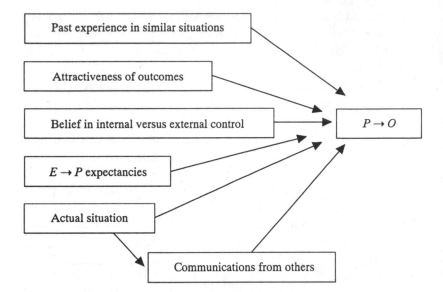

are influenced by past experience, communicated probabilities, $E \rightarrow P$ expectancies, the attractiveness of outcomes, and belief in internal versus external control. It also shows that the actual situation influences what is communicated as well as directly influencing the person's $P \rightarrow O$ expectancies.

Man as a Satisficer with Limited Rationality

Throughout this chapter, support has been given to a rational view of man. However, it is important to distinguish this view from the view of what has been called "economic man." According to the economic man view, there are no limits to the computations man can go through in order to determine which behavior he should attempt. He is always fully aware of all the alternative behaviors that are possible and of all the outcomes that will stem from these behaviors. He also has clear preferences among these outcomes. Thus, any decision he makes is based on full information and is likely to be the optimal decision. Further, his decisions are likely to appear very rational to an observer who is aware of economic man's preferences.

Among other psychologists, Simon (1957) has pointed out that the economic man view is not very realistic. People simply don't behave in this manner. People don't have full knowledge either of all possible behaviors or of all outcomes. They are not capable of highly complex computations, and their behavior does not always appear to be rational to observers. Simon argues that man's behavior is more directed toward satisficing than toward optimizing. By this statement Simon means that man generally looks for a course of behavior that is satisfactory or "good enough," and when he finds it, he acts. He does not continue to search until he has considered all the alternatives so he can then pick the optimal alternative. Man seems to be oriented toward satisficing because of the difficulty and complexity of arriving at an optimal strategy. At times man has to simplify the world so that he can deal with it. It is beyond the cognitive-response capacity of most people to consider adequately all the complexities of the real world in their decision making.

Although Simon does not emphasize the point, much research shows that people do sometimes misperceive situations. For example, their emotions can distort their perceptions to such an extent that they make decisions that look very irrational to an outsider. In one study, Murray (1933) asked five young girls to rate a number of photographs of people, according to how malicious the people appeared to be. The girls played a scary game and then rated the pictures again. The second ratings showed a dramatic increase in the amount of maliciousness assigned to the people in the photographs, presumably because the girls were more frightened. Other evidence shows that the strength of primary needs can influence perception. In studies where people have been asked to identify objects in pictures, the number of food objects that are seen increases as hunger increases. Other studies have shown that subjects avoid perceiving emotionally disturbing stimuli. Still other studies have shown that attitudes and values strongly influence what is seen. Thus, because of their needs, emotions, values, and beliefs, people do misperceive the situations in which they find themselves. These misperceptions can lead them to consider only inappropriate behaviors and not to consider all relevant $P \to O$ expectancies. Thus, the tendency to misperceive situations, like the tendency to satisfice and simplify, often leads to behavior that is far from optimal. A good example of this tendency is the way workers respond to pay-incentive plans when they mistrust management. Instead of responding to the plans with hard work that would earn desired outcomes, they respond by restricting their productivity because they believe that if they are highly productive, management will reduce their pay rates.

Simon (1957) emphasizes that "human behavior in organizations is, if not wholly rational, at least in good part intendedly so." It is precisely because a great deal of behavior is intended to be rational that our model can predict how people will behave in many situations. Although behavior does seem rational to the actor, it may not always be optimal or appear to be rational to an observer for a number of reasons. The observer may not place the same value on outcomes that the actor does. The observer may consider totally different behaviors than the actor does. The observer may have different $P \rightarrow O$ and $E \rightarrow P$ expectancies. Finally, the observer may set a different level at which he is willing to stop his search and act. Thus, the observer may be more easily satisfied, or he may be harder to satisfy. The point remains that the behavior of the actor is intended to be rational and appears to the actor to be rational at the time of the action. The behavior represents the actor's best attempt to deal rationally with the world as he sees it. Because of this, his behavior can be predicted if we know how he perceives the situation and how he values various outcomes.

In using the motivation model as developed thus far, it is important to remember that people don't consider all alternatives and that they satisfice rather than optimize. When people are considering whether to try a behavior such as performing effectively, they don't consider all of the outcomes associated with the behavior. If we try to predict a person's behavior using our model, and if we gather complete data on all his or her perceptions of existing relationships, we still might predict behavior incorrectly because our model would be too complex to allow for valid predictions. If we were to extend the model through all its permutations and combinations, it would undoubtedly end up being much more complicated than the thought process of people. The model, of course, doesn't have to be developed so extensively. In using the present model to predict an individual's behavior, consideration must be limited to only those cognitions that the person is actually using as a basis for decision. We must remember that man does base behavior on perceptions that are simplified and that may not consider all factors. Thus, our model can be viewed as considering a limited number of alternatives, just as people do.

four

Satisfaction and Behavior

Compared to what is known about motivation, relatively little is known about the determinants and consequences of satisfaction. Most of the psychological research on motivation simply has not been concerned with the kinds of affective reactions that people experience in association with or as a result of motivated behavior. No well-developed theories of satisfaction have appeared and little theoretically based research has been done on satisfaction. The influence of behaviorism on the field of psychology had a great deal to do with this lag in research. While psychology was under the influence of behaviorism, psychologists avoided doing research that depended on introspective self-reports. Behaviorists strongly felt that if psychology were to develop as a science, it had to study observable behavior. Since satisfaction is an internal subjective state that is best reported by the people experiencing it, satisfaction was not seen as a proper subject for study. Psychologists thought they should concentrate on those aspects of motivation that are observable (for example, performance, hours of deprivation, strength of response, and so on).

Satisfaction is assigned a role in drive theory and in some of the need theories (for example, the theories of Maslow and

78

Alderfer). According to drive theory, satisfaction and cessation of behavior are due to the satiation of primary drives. Maslow uses the term "satisfaction" quite differently. He does not mean physiological satiation; rather, he means a psychological feeling of contentedness—of having received enough of a desired object. Both Hull and Maslow assume that need satisfaction is important because it influences need strength. However, neither Hull nor Maslow explains what produces satisfaction; their theories lack a clearly defined concept of satisfaction. In essence, all drive theories and some need theories say that the more people obtain of what they want, the more satisfied they will be. In drive theory, satisfaction is treated as a concept that helps explain why something, such as eating, leads to a change in behavior, such as a reduction in food-seeking behavior. Satisfaction is not treated as a variable worth measuring and studying. Studies related to these theories, therefore, have not focused on the causes or consequences of satisfaction; rather, these studies have treated satisfaction as a sometimes useful explanatory concept or intervening variable.

Most of the research on the study of satisfaction has been done by psychologists interested in work organizations. This research dates back to the 1930s. Since that time, the term "job satisfaction" has been used to refer to affective attitudes or orientations on the part of individuals toward jobs. Hoppock published a famous monograph on job satisfaction in 1935, and in 1939 the results of the well-known Western Electric studies were published. The Western Electric studies (Roethlisberger & Dickson, 1939) emphasized the importance of studying the attitudes, feelings, and perceptions employees have about their jobs. Through interviews with over 20,000 workers, these studies graphically made the point that employees have strong affective reactions to what happens to them at work. The Western Electric studies also suggested that affective reactions cause certain kinds of behavior, such as strikes, absenteeism, and turnover. Although the studies failed to show any clear-cut relationship between satisfaction and job performance, the studies did succeed in stimulating a tremendous amount of research on job satisfaction. Usually, these studies have not been theoretically

oriented; instead, researchers have simply looked at the relationship between job satisfaction and factors such as age, education, job level, absenteeism rate, productivity, and so on.
Originally, much of the research seemed to be stimulated by
a desire to show that job satisfaction is important because it influences productivity. Underlying the earlier articles on job satisfaction was a strong conviction that "happy workers are productive
workers." Recently, however, this theme has been disappear-
ing, and many organizational psychologists seem to be studying job satisfaction simply because they are interested in finding
its causes. This approach to studying job satisfaction is congruent
with the increased prominence of humanistic psychology, which
emphasizes human affective experience.

The recent interest in job satisfaction also ties in directly
with the rising concern in many countries about the quality of
life. There is an increasing acceptance of the view that material
possessions and economic growth do not necessarily produce
a high quality of life. Recognition is now being given to the importance of the kinds of affective reactions that people experience and to the fact that these are not always tied to economic
or material accomplishments. Through the Department of Labor
and the Department of Health, Education, and Welfare, the
United States government has recently become active in trying
to improve the affective quality of work life. Job satisfaction is
one measure of the quality of life in organizations and is worth
understanding and increasing even if it doesn't relate to performance. This reason for studying satisfaction is likely to be an
increasingly prominent one as we begin to worry more about
the effects working in organizations has on people and as our
humanitarian concern for the kind of psychological experiences
people have during their lives increases. What happens to people during the workday has profound effects both on the individual employee's life and on the society as a whole, and thus
these events cannot be ignored if the quality of life in a society
is to be high. As John Gardner has said,

> Of all the ways in which society serves the individ-
> ual, few are more meaningful than to provide him

with a decent job. . . . It isn't going to be a decent
society for any of us until it is for all of us. If our
sense of responsibility fails us, our sheer self-interest
should come to the rescue [1968, p. 25].

As it turns out, satisfaction is related to absenteeism and
turnover, both of which are very costly to organizations. Thus,
there is a very "practical" economic reason for organizations to
be concerned with job satisfaction, since it can influence organizational effectiveness. However, before any practical use can
be made of the finding that job dissatisfaction causes absenteeism and turnover, we must understand what factors cause and
influence job satisfaction. Organizations can influence job satisfaction and prevent absenteeism and turnover only if the organizations can pinpoint the factors causing and influencing these
affective responses.

Despite the many studies, critics have legitimately com-
plained that our understanding of the causes of job satisfaction
has not substantially increased during the last 30 years (for example, see Locke, 1968, 1969) for two main reasons. The research on job satisfaction has typically been atheoretical and has
not tested for causal relationships. Since the research has not
been guided by theory, a vast array of unorganized, virtually
uninterpretable facts have been unearthed. For example, a number of studies have found a positive relationship between productivity and job satisfaction, while other studies have found no
evidence of this relationship. Undoubtedly, this disparity can
be explained, but the explanation would have to be based on
a theory of satisfaction, and at present no such theory exists.
One thing the research on job satisfaction has done is to demonstrate the saying that "theory without data is fantasy, but data
without theory is chaos!"

Due to the lack of a theory stating causal relationships,
the research on job satisfaction has consistently looked simply
for relationships among variables. A great deal is known about
what factors are related to satisfaction, but very little is known
about the causal basis for the relationships. This is a serious
problem when one attempts to base change efforts on the research.

This problem also increases the difficulty of developing and testing theories of satisfaction. Perhaps the best example of the
resulting dilemma concerns the relationship between satisfaction and performance. If satisfaction causes performance, then
organizations should try to see that their employees are satisfied;
however, if performance causes satisfaction, then high satisfaction is not necessarily a goal but rather a by-product of an effective organization.

Why has the research on job satisfaction developed so
slowly and in such an atheoretical way? One important reason
seems to be the lack of attention paid to job satisfaction by psychologists interested in learning, development, and other traditional psychological topics. In marked contrast is the area of
motivation where, as we have seen, a number of theories have
been stated. Motivation theories from other areas of psychology have proven very helpful in understanding motivation in
organizations and have formed the basis for our approach to
thinking about motivation in organizations.

Unfortunately, no similar set of theories exists in the area
of satisfaction. What little theory there is comes almost entirely
from the research of industrial psychologists. In some cases this
theory is not explicit but is implied by the way satisfaction is
measured. For example, although Porter (1961) has never presented an actual theory of satisfaction, a particular manner of
defining satisfaction is implicit in his approach to measuring need
satisfaction. His approach indicates that he sees satisfaction as
the difference between what a person thinks he should receive
and what he feels he actually does receive. Before examining in
detail any of the theories of job satisfaction, it is important to
distinguish between the concepts of facet or factor satisfaction
and overall job satisfaction. Facet satisfaction refers to people's
affective reactions to particular aspects of their job. Pay, supervision, and promotion opportunities are frequently studied facets.
Job satisfaction refers to a person's affective reactions to his total
work role.

The kinds of job facets or factors that have been studied
have varied widely among researchers. Some researchers have
chosen to use very concrete, specific factors (for example, wash-

rooms, cafeteria, fringe benefits, and so on) and have ended up with long lists of factors. Other researchers have chosen to use outcome clusters or categories, such as security, status, and autonomy satisfaction; these outcome clusters are similar to the need outcome clusters discussed in Chapter 2.

How many job factors are there? This question, like the question of how many needs there are, has no correct answer. The answer depends on how many outcomes are grouped into a cluster. It is possible to have many groups containing very few outcomes, which will give a large number of factors (for example, instead of grouping all the physical working conditions together, group heat, light, and so on separately). It is also possible to operate on a high level of abstraction and have few groups, each containing a large number of outcomes, thereby producing only a few factors or facets.

A number of studies have tried to determine how many factors there are by looking at the relationships among the different outcomes. When researchers find that the satisfaction ratings given a number of outcomes are correlated, they assume that these outcomes represent a common factor. Thus, factors, or facets, are defined as groups of correlated outcomes. Studies that have taken this approach generally identify five to eight factors. The most common factors are job content, supervision, financial rewards, promotion, working conditions, and co-workers. Note that this list corresponds to the organization of this book, in which separate chapters focus on the impact of job content, interpersonal factors (supervision and co-workers), and extrinsic rewards (promotion and pay) on motivation and satisfaction.

One important reason for distinguishing between facet satisfaction and job satisfaction is that a number of theories argue that job satisfaction is determined by some combination of people's affective reactions to the various facets of their job. However, the theories differ on how these reactions combine to determine satisfaction. This view is somewhat comparable to the idea in motivation theory that the force on a person to behave in a particular way is equal to a combination of the values placed on all the outcomes that are seen to result from behavior.

Theories of Job Satisfaction

Four approaches can be identified in the theoretical work on satisfaction. Fulfillment theory was the first approach to develop. Equity theory and discrepancy theory developed later, partially as reactions against the shortcomings of fulfillment theory. Two-factor theory, the fourth approach, represents an attempt to develop a completely new approach to thinking about satisfaction.

Fulfillment Theory

Schaffer (1953) has argued that "job satisfaction will vary directly with the extent to which those needs of an individual which can be satisfied are actually satisfied" (p. 3). Vroom (1964) also sees job satisfaction in terms of the degree to which a job provides the person with positively valued outcomes. He equates satisfaction with valence and adds "If we describe a person as satisfied with an object, we mean that the object has positive valence for him. However, satisfaction has a much more restricted usage. In common parlance, we refer to a person's satisfaction only with reference to objects which he possesses" (p. 100).* Researchers who have adopted the fulfillment approach measure people's satisfaction by simply asking how much of a given facet or outcome they are receiving. Thus, these researchers view satisfaction as depending on how much of a given outcome or group of outcomes a person receives.

Fulfillment theorists have concluded how facet-satisfaction measures combine to determine overall satisfaction. The crucial issue is whether the facet-satisfaction measures should be weighted by their importance to the person when combined. We know that some job factors are more important than other job factors for each individual; therefore, the important factors need to be weighted more in determining the individual's total satisfaction. However, there is evidence that the individual's facet satisfaction scores reflect this emphasis already and thus do not need to be further weighted (Mobley & Locke, 1970).

*Vroom, V. *Work and Motivation*. Copyright © 1964 by John Wiley & Sons, Inc. This and all other quotes from the same source are reprinted by permission.

A great deal of research shows that people's satisfaction is a function both of how much they receive and of how much they feel they should and/or want to receive (Locke, 1969). A foreman, for example, may be satisfied with a salary of $12,000, while a company president may be dissatisfied with a salary of $100,000, even though the president correctly perceives that he receives more than the foreman. The point is that people's reactions to what they receive are not simply a function of how much they receive; their reactions are strongly influenced by such individual-difference factors as what they want and what they feel they should receive. Individual-difference factors suggest that the fulfillment-theory approach to job satisfaction is not valid, since this approach fails to take into account differences in people's feelings about what outcomes they should receive. Morse (1953) stated this point of view as follows:

> At first we thought that satisfaction would simply be a function of how much a person received from the situation or what we have called the amount of environmental return. It made sense to feel that those who were in more need-fulfilling environments would be more satisfied. But the amount of environmental return did not seem to be the only factor involved. Another factor obviously had to be included in order to predict satisfaction accurately. This variable was the strength of an individual's desires, or his level of aspiration in a particular area. If the environment provided little possibility for need satisfaction, those with the strongest desires, or highest aspirations, were the least happy [pp. 27–28].

Discrepancy theory, which will be discussed next, represents an attempt to take into account the fact that people do differ in their desires.

Discrepancy Theory

Recently, many psychologists have argued for a discrepancy approach to thinking about satisfaction. They maintain that satisfaction is determined by the differences between the actual outcomes a person receives and some other outcome level. The theories differ widely in their definitions of this other outcome level. For some theories it is the outcome level the person feels should be received, and for other theories it is the outcome level the person expects to receive. All of the theoretical approaches argue that what is received should be compared with another outcome level, and when there is a difference — when received outcome is below the other outcome level — dissatisfaction results. Thus, if a person expects or thinks he should receive a salary of $10,000 and he receives one of only $8,000, the prediction is that he will be dissatisfied with his pay. Further, the prediction is that he will be more dissatisfied than the person who receives a salary of $9,000 and expects or thinks he should receive a salary of $10,000.

Katzell (1964) and Locke (1968, 1969) have probably presented the two most completely developed discrepancy-theory approaches to satisfaction. According to Katzell, satisfaction $= 1 - ([X - V] / V)$, where X equals the actual amount of the outcome and V equals the desired amount of the outcome. Like many discrepancy theorists, Katzell sees satisfaction as the difference between an actual amount and some desired amount, but, unlike most discrepancy theorists, he assumes that this difference should be divided by the desired amount of the outcome. If we use Katzell's formula, we are led to believe that the more a person wants of an outcome the less dissatisfied he will be with a given discrepancy. Katzell offers no evidence for this assumption, and it is hard to support logically. A discrepancy from what is desired would seem to be equally dissatisfying regardless of how much is desired. Katzell also speaks of "actual" discrepancies, while most discrepancy theorists talk of "perceived" discrepancies. Note also that by Katzell's formula, getting more than the desired amount should produce less satisfaction than getting the desired amount.

Locke (1969) has stated a discrepancy theory that differs from Katzell's in several ways. First, Locke emphasizes that the perceived discrepancy, not the actual discrepancy, is important. He also argues that satisfaction is determined by the simple difference between what the person wants and what he perceives he receives. The more his wants exceed what he receives, the greater his dissatisfaction. Locke says, "Job satisfaction and dissatisfaction are a function of the perceived relationship between what one wants from one's job and what one perceives it is offering" (p. 316).

Porter (1961), in measuring satisfaction, asks people how much of a given outcome there should be for their job and how much of a given outcome there actually is; he considers the discrepancy between the two answers to be a measure of satisfaction. This particular discrepancy approach has been the most widely used. It differs from Locke's approach since it sees satisfaction as influenced not by how much a person wants but by how much he feels he should receive.

A few researchers have argued that satisfaction is determined by what a person expects to receive rather than by what he wants or feels he should receive. Thus, the literature on job satisfaction contains three different discrepancy approaches; the first looks at what people want, the second at what people feel they should receive, and the third at what people expect to receive. The last of these approaches has seldom been used and can be dismissed. As Locke (1969) points out, the expectation approach is hard to defend logically. Admittedly, getting what is not expected may lead to surprise, but it hardly need lead to dissatisfaction. What if, for example, it exceeds expectations? What if it exceeds expectations but still falls below what others are getting?

It is not obvious on logical grounds that either of the first two approaches can be rejected as meaningless. Both approaches seem to be addressing important but perhaps different affective reactions to a job. There clearly is a difference between asking people how much they want and how much they think they should receive. People do respond differently to those questions (Wanous & Lawler, 1972). In a sense, the two questions help us understand different aspects of a person's feelings toward his present situation. A person's satisfaction with the fairness of what he receives for his present job would seem to be more influenced by what he feels he should receive than by what he ultimately aspires to. The difference between what the person aspires to or wants and what he receives gives us an insight into his satisfaction with his present situation relative to his long-term aspired to, or desired, situation. These two discrepancy measures can and do yield different results. For example, a person can feel that his present pay is appropriate for his present job, and in this sense he can be satisfied; however, he can feel that his present pay is much below what he wants, and in this sense he can be dissatisfied. In most cases, however, these two discrepancies probably are closely related and influence each other. Thus, the difference between the two discrepancies may not be as large or as important as some theorists have argued.

Like the fulfillment theorists, many discrepancy theorists argue that total job satisfaction is influenced by the sum of the discrepancies that are present for each job factor. Thus, a person's overall job satisfaction would be equal to his pay-satisfaction discrepancy plus his supervision-satisfaction discrepancy, and so on. It has been argued that in computing such a sum it is important to weight each of the discrepancies by the importance of that factor to the person, the argument being that important factors influence job satisfaction more strongly than unimportant ones. Locke (1969), however, argues that such a weighting is redundant, since the discrepancy score is a measure of importance in itself because large discrepancies tend to appear only for important items.

Most discrepancy theories allow for the possibility of a person saying he is receiving more outcomes than he should receive, or more outcomes than he wants to receive. However, the theories don't stress this point, which presents some problems for them. It is not clear how to equate dissatisfaction (or whatever this feeling might be called) due to over-reward with dissatisfaction due to under-reward. Are they produced in the same way? Do they have the same results? Do they both contribute to overall job dissatisfaction? These are some of the important questions that discrepancy theories have yet to answer. Equity theory, which will be discussed next, has dealt with some of these questions.

Equity Theory

Equity theory is primarily a motivation theory, but it has some important things to say about the causes of satisfaction/dissatisfaction. Adams (1963, 1965) argues in his version of equity theory that satisfaction is determined by a person's perceived input-outcome balance in the following manner: the perceived equity of a person's rewards is determined by his input-outcome balance; this perceived equity, in turn, determines satisfaction. Satisfaction results when perceived equity exists, and dissatisfaction results when perceived inequity exists. Thus, satisfaction is determined by the perceived ratio of what a person receives from his job relative to what a person puts into his job. According to equity theory, either under-reward or over-reward can lead to dissatisfaction, although the feelings are somewhat different. The theory emphasizes that over-reward leads to feelings of guilt, while under-reward leads to feelings of unfair treatment.

Equity theory emphasizes the importance of other people's input-outcome balance in determining how a person will judge the equity of his own input-outcome balance. Equity theory argues that people evaluate the fairness of their own input-outcome balance by comparing it with their perception of the input-outcome balance of their "comparison-other" (the person they compare with). This emphasis does not enter into either discrepancy theory or fulfillment theory as they are usually stated. Although there is an implied reference to "other" in the discussion of how people develop their feelings about what their outcomes should be, discrepancy theory does not explicitly state that this perception is based on perceptions of what other people contribute and receive. This difference points up a strength of equity theory relative to discrepancy theory. Equity theory rather clearly states how a person assesses his inputs and outcomes in order to develop his perception of the fairness of his input-outcome balance. Discrepancy theory, on the other hand, is vague about how people decide what their outcomes should be.

Two-Factor Theory

Modern two-factor theory was originally developed in a book by Herzberg, Mausner, Peterson, and Capwell (1957), in which the authors stated that job factors could be classified according to whether the factors contribute primarily to satisfaction or to dissatisfaction. Two years later, Herzberg, Mausner, and Snyderman

(1959) published the results of a research study, which they interpreted as supportive of the theory. Since 1959, much research has been directed toward testing two-factor theory. Two aspects of the theory are unique and account for the attention it has received. First, two-factor theory says that satisfaction and dissatisfaction do not exist on a continuum running from satisfaction through neutral to dissatisfaction. Two independent continua exist, one running from satisfied to neutral, and another running from dissatisfied to neutral (see Figure 4.1). Second, the theory stresses that different job facets influence feelings of satisfaction and dissatisfaction. Figure 4.2 presents the results of a study by Herzberg et al., which show that factors such as achievement recognition, the work itself, and responsibility are mentioned in connection with satisfying experiences, while working conditions, interpersonal relations, supervision, and company policy are usually mentioned in connection with dissatisfying experiences. The figure shows the frequency with which each factor is mentioned in connection with high (satisfying) and low (dissatisfying) work experiences. As can be seen, achievement was present in over 40 percent of the satisfying experiences and less than 10 percent of the dissatisfying experiences.

Figure 4.1. Two-Factor Theory: Satisfaction Continua.

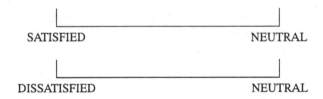

SATISFIED   NEUTRAL

DISSATISFIED   NEUTRAL

Perhaps the most interesting aspect of Herzberg's theory is that at the same time a person can be very satisfied and very dissatisfied. Also, the theory implies that factors such as better working conditions cannot increase or cause satisfaction, they can only affect the amount of dissatisfaction that is experienced. The only way satisfaction can be increased is by effecting changes in those factors that are shown in Figure 4.2 as contributing primarily to satisfaction.

The results of the studies designed to test two-factor theory have not provided clear-cut support for the theory, nor have these studies allowed for total rejection of the theory. In many cases, the studies have only fueled the controversy that surrounds the theory. It is beyond the scope of this book to review the research that has been done on the theory. What we can do, however, is to consider some of the conclusions to which two-factor theory has led. Perhaps the most negative summary of the evidence is the account presented by Dunnette, Campbell, and Hakel (1967). According to them:

> It seems that the evidence is now sufficient to lay the two-factor theory to rest, and we hope that it may be buried peaceably. We believe that it is important that this be done so that researchers will address themselves to studying the full complexities of human motivation, rather than continuing to allow the direction of motivational research or actual administrative decisions to be dictated by the seductive simplicity of two-factor theory [p. 173].

This opinion has been rejected by many researchers as too harsh and negative, and indeed research on the theory has continued since the publication of the Dunnette et al. study. Still, research on the theory has raised serious doubts about its validity. Even proponents of the theory admit that the same factors can cause both satisfaction and dissatisfaction and that a given factor can cause satisfaction in one group of people and dissatisfaction in another group of people. Other researchers have pointed out that results supporting the theory seem to be obtainable only when certain limited research methodologies are used.

The major unanswered question with respect to two-factor theory is whether satisfaction and dissatisfaction really are two separate dimensions. The evidence is not sufficient to establish that satisfaction and dissatisfaction are separate, making this the crucial unproven aspect of the theory. Neither the fact that some factors can contribute to both satisfaction and dissatisfaction nor the fact that, in some populations, factors contribute to satisfaction while, in other populations, these factors contribute

Figure 4.2. Comparison of Satisfiers and Dissatisfiers.

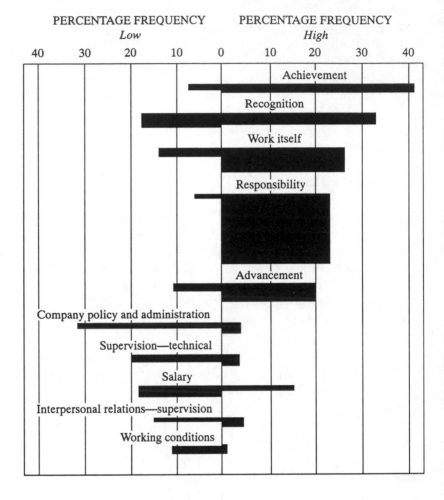

Source: Adapted from Herzberg et al., *The Motivation to Work* (2nd ed.). Copyright © 1959 by John Wiley & Sons, Inc. Reprinted by permission.

to dissatisfaction is sufficient reason to reject the theory. Although these findings raise questions about the theory, they do not destroy its core concept, which is that satisfaction and dissatisfaction are, in fact, on different continua.

Significantly, while considerable research has tried to determine which factors contribute to satisfaction and dissatisfaction, little attention has been directed toward testing the motivation and performance implications of the theory. The study of Herzberg et al. (1959) did ask the subjects (engineers and accountants) to report how various job factors affected their performance. In agreement with the theory, the subjects reported that the presence of satisfiers boosted performance, while the presence of dissatisfiers reduced performance. At best, the results of this study give weak evidence that these job factors influence performance, as suggested by the theory. Only self-reports of performance were used, and in many cases the subjects were reporting on events that had happened some time prior to the date of the interviews. The evidence, although not at all conclusive, at least suggests the kinds of experiences that might lead to a strong motivation to perform effectively. Unfortunately, Herzberg et al. did not develop any theoretical concepts to explain why the job factors should affect performance. Their theory contains little explanation of why outcomes are attractive, and it fails to consider the importance of associative connections in determining which of a number of behaviors a person will choose to perform in order to obtain a desired outcome. Thus, it is not a theory of motivation; rather, it is a theory primarily concerned with explaining the determinants of job satisfaction and dissatisfaction.

Equity Theory and/or Discrepancy Theory

perceived input-output balance

Equity theory and discrepancy theory are the two strongest theoretical explanations of satisfaction. Either theory could be used as a basis for thinking about the determinants of satisfaction. Fortunately it is not necessary to choose between the theories, since it is possible to build a satisfaction model that capitalizes on the strengths of each theory. In this chapter, we will try to build such a model. In many ways, equity theory and discrepancy theory are quite similar. Both theories stress the importance of a person's perceived outcomes, along with the relationship of these outcomes to a second perception. In discrepancy theory, the second perception is what the outcomes should be or what the person wants the outcomes to be; in equity theory, the second perception is what a person's perceived inputs are in relation to other people's inputs and outcomes. Clearly, it could be argued that the two theories are talking about very similar concepts when they talk about perceived inputs and the subject's feeling about what his outcomes should be. A person's perception of what his outcomes should be is partly determined by what he feels his inputs are. Thus, the "should be" phrase from discrepancy theory and the "perceived inputs relative to other people's inputs and outcomes" phrase from equity theory are very similar.

Equity theory and discrepancy theory do differ in that equity theory places explicit emphasis on the importance of social comparison, while discrepancy theory does not. This is a strength of equity theory because it helps to make explicit what influences a person's "should be" judgment. Finally, discrepancy theory talks in terms of a *difference,* while equity theory talks in terms of a *ratio.* For example, equity theory would predict that a person with 16 units of input and 4 units of outcome would feel the same as a person with 8 units of input and 2 units of outcome (same ratio, 1 to 4). Although discrepancy theory does not talk specifically in terms of inputs, if we consider input as one determinant of what outcomes should be, then discrepancy theory would not go along with equity theory. Discrepancy theory would argue that the person with 16 units of input will be more dissatisfied than the person with 8 units of input because the difference between his input and outcomes is greater. The two theories also suggest different types of relationships between dissatisfaction and feelings of what rewards should be. Discrepancy theory would predict a linear relationship such that, rewards being constant, increases in a person's perception of what his outcomes should be would be directly proportionate to increases in dissatisfaction. Equity theory, on the other hand, would predict a nonlinear relationship [satisfaction = (is getting/ should be getting)] such that if a poor ratio exists, a further increase in "should be getting" will have little effect on satisfaction.

In building our "model of satisfaction," we will use the difference approach rather than the ratio approach. This choice is one of the few either/or choices that must be made between the two theories. It is not a particularly crucial choice from the point of view of measurement because methods of measurement in the field of psychology are not precise enough so that discrepancy theory and equity theory would yield very different results. Measurement scales with true zero points and equal distances between all points on the scale (for example, as in measuring weight and height) are required, and such scales are not used when attitudes are measured.

Once it has been decided to think of satisfaction in terms of a difference, the key question becomes what difference or differences should be considered. There is clear agreement that one element in the discrepancy should be what the person perceives that he actually receives. The second element could be one of two other perceptions: (1) what a person thinks he should receive, or (2) what a person wants to receive. As we've already seen, these two perceptions are closely related. However, there is a difference. Overall, it seems preferable to focus more on what a person feels he should receive than on what a person wants to receive.

If satisfaction is conceptualized as the difference between what one receives and what one wants, it is difficult to talk meaningfully about satisfaction with one's present job. Such an approach partially removes satisfaction from the context of the job and the situation. The question "How much do you want?" is an aspiration-level variable, which is not as closely related to the job situation as the question "How much should there be?" An answer to the first question is more a statement of personal goals than a statement of what is appropriate in a particular situation. Research data show that employees consistently give higher answers to the "how much do you want" question than to the "how much should there be" question (Wanous & Lawler, 1972); answers to the "should be" question seem to vary more with such organization factors as job level. Thus, in studying people's feelings about their jobs, it seems logical to focus on what employees feel they should receive from their jobs. This perception would seem to be strongly influenced by organization practices, and it would seem to be a perception that must be studied if we are to understand employees' affective reactions to their jobs and the behavioral responses these reactions produce.

A Model of Facet Satisfaction

Figure 4.3 presents a model of the determinants of facet satisfaction. The model is intended to be applicable to understanding what determines a person's satisfaction with any facet of the job. The model assumes that the same psychological processes operate to determine satisfaction with job factors ranging from pay to supervision and satisfaction with the work itself. The model in Figure 4.3 is a discrepancy model in the sense that it shows satisfaction as the difference between *a,* what a person feels he should receive, and *b,* what he perceives that he actually receives. The model indicates that when the person's perception of what his outcome level is and his perception of what his outcome level should be are in agreement, the person will be satisfied. When a person perceives his outcome level as falling below what he feels it should be, he will be dissatisfied. However, when a person's perceived outcome level exceeds what he feels it should be, he will have feelings of guilt and inequity and perhaps some discomfort (Adams, 1965). Thus, for any job factor, the assumption is that satisfaction with the factor will be determined by the difference between how much of the factor there is and how much of the factor the person feels there should be.

Present outcome level is shown to be the key influence on a person's perception of what rewards he receives, but his perception is also shown to be influenced by his perception of what his "referent others" receive. The higher the outcome levels of his referent others, the lower his outcome level will appear. Thus, a person's psychological view of how much of a factor he receives is said to be influenced by more than just the objective amount of the factor. Because of this psychological influence, the same amount of reward often can be seen quite differently by two people; to one person it can be a large amount, while to another person it can be a small amount.

The model in Figure 4.3 also shows that a person's perception of what his reward level should be is influenced by a

Figure 4.3. Model of the Determinants of Satisfaction.

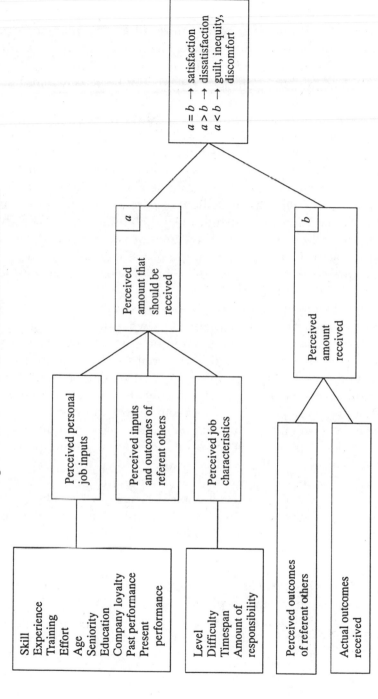

number of factors. Perhaps the most important influence is perceived job inputs. These inputs include all of the skills, abilities, and training a person brings to the job as well as the behavior he exhibits on the job. The greater he perceives his inputs
to be, the higher will be his perception of what his outcomes
should be. Because of this relationship, people with high job
inputs must receive more rewards than people with low job inputs or they will be dissatisfied. The model also shows that a
person's perception of what his outcomes should be is influenced
by his perception of the job demands. The greater the demands
made by the job, the more he will perceive he should receive.
Job demands include such things as job difficulty, responsibilities, and organization level. If outcomes do not rise along with
these factors, the clear prediction of the model is that the people who perceive they have the more difficult, higher-level jobs
will be the most dissatisfied.

The model shows that a person's perception of what his
outcomes should be is influenced by what the person perceives
his comparison-other's inputs and outcomes to be. This aspect
of the model is taken directly from equity theory and is included
to stress the fact that people look at the inputs and outcomes
of others in order to determine what their own outcome level
should be. If a person's comparison-other's inputs are the same
as the person's inputs but the other's outcomes are much higher,
the person will feel that he should be receiving more outcomes
and will be dissatisfied as a result.

The model allows for the possibility that people will feel
that their outcomes exceed what they should be. The feelings
produced by this condition are quite different from those produced by under-reward. Because of this difference, it does not
make sense to refer to a person who feels over-rewarded as being
dissatisfied. There is considerable evidence that very few people feel over-rewarded, and this fact can be explained by the
model. Even when people are highly rewarded, the social-
comparison aspect of satisfaction means that people can avoid
feeling over-rewarded by looking around and finding someone
to compare with who is doing equally well. Also, a person tends

to value his own inputs much more highly than they are valued by others (Lawler, 1967). Because of this discrepancy, a person's perception of what his outcomes should be is often not shared by those administering his rewards, and is often above what he actually receives. Finally, the person can easily increase his perception of his inputs and thereby justify a high reward level.

As a way of summarizing some of the implications of the model, let us briefly make some statements about who should be dissatisfied if the model is correct. Other things being equal:

1. People with high perceived inputs will be more dissatisfied with a given facet than people with low perceived inputs.
2. People who perceive their job to be demanding will be more dissatisfied with a given facet than people who perceive their jobs as undemanding.
3. People who perceive similar others as having a more favorable input-outcome balance will be more dissatisfied with a given facet than people who perceive their own balance as similar to or better than that of others.
4. People who receive a low outcome level will be more dissatisfied than those who receive a high outcome level.
5. The more outcomes a person perceives his comparison-other receives, the more dissatisfied he will be with his own outcomes. This should be particularly true when the comparison-other is seen to hold a job that demands the same or fewer inputs.

Overall Job Satisfaction

Most theories of job satisfaction argue that overall job satisfaction is determined by some combination of all facet-satisfaction feelings. This could be expressed in terms of the facet-satisfaction model in Figure 4.3 as a simple sum of, or average of, all $a - b$ discrepancies. Thus, overall job satisfaction is determined by the difference between all the things a person feels he should receive from his job and all the things he actually does receive.

A strong theoretical argument can be made for weighting the facet-satisfaction scores according to their importance. Some factors do make larger contributions to overall satisfaction than others. Pay satisfaction, satisfaction with the work itself, and satisfaction with supervision seem to have particularly strong influences on overall satisfaction for most people. Also, employees tend to rate these factors as important. Thus, there is a connection between how important employees say job factors are and how much job factors influence overall job satisfaction (Vroom, 1964). Conceptually, therefore, it seems worthwhile to think of the various job-facet-satisfaction scores as influencing total satisfaction in terms of their importance. One way to express this relationship is by defining overall job satisfaction as being equal to Σ(facet satisfaction × facet importance). However, as stressed earlier, actually measuring importance and multiplying it by measured facet satisfaction often isn't necessary because the satisfaction scores themselves seem to take importance into account. (The most important items tend to be scored as either very satisfactory or very dissatisfactory; thus, these items have the most influence on any sum score.) Still, on a conceptual level, it is important to remember that facet-satisfaction scores do differentially contribute to the feeling of overall job satisfaction.

A number of studies have attempted to determine how many workers are actually satisfied with their jobs. Our model does not lead to any predictions in this area. The model simply gives the conditions that lead to people experiencing feelings of satisfaction or dissatisfaction. Not surprisingly, the studies that have been done do not agree on the percentage of dissatisfied workers. Some suggest figures as low as 13 percent, others give figures as high as 80 percent. The range generally reported is from 13 to 25 percent dissatisfied. Herzberg et al. (1957) summarized the findings of research studies conducted from 1946 through 1953. The figures in their report showed a yearly increase in the median percentage of job-satisfied persons (see Table 4.1). Figure 4.4 presents satisfaction-trend data for 1948 through 1971. These data also show an overall increase in the

Table 4.1. Median Percentage of
Job-Dissatisfied Persons Reported from 1946–1953.

Year	Median percentage of job dissatisfied
1953	13
1952	15
1951	18
1950	19
1949	19
1948	19
1946–1947	21

Source: From Herzberg et al., *Job Attitudes: Review of Research and Opinion.* Copyright © 1957 by the Psychological Service of Pittsburgh. Reprinted by permission.

number of satisfied workers, which is interesting because of recent speculation that satisfaction is decreasing. However, due to many measurement problems, it is impossible to conclude that a real decline in the number of dissatisfied workers has taken place.

The difficulty in obtaining meaningful conclusions from the data stems from the fact that different questions yield very different results. For example, instead of directly asking workers "How satisfied are you?" a number of studies have asked "If you had it to do over again, would you pick the same job?" The latter question produces much higher dissatisfaction scores than does the simple "how satisfied are you" question. One literature review showed that 54 percent of the workers tended to say that they were sufficiently dissatisfied with their jobs that they would not choose them again. On the other hand, the straight satisfaction question shows between 13 and 25 percent dissatisfied. However, even this figure is subject to wide variation depending on how the question is asked. When the question is asked in the simple form, "Are you satisfied, yes or no?" the number of satisfied responses is large. When the question is changed so that the employees can respond yes, no, or undecided—or satisfied, dissatisfied, or neutral—the number of satisfied responses drops.

Figure 4.4. Percentage of "Satisfied" Workers, 1948–1971.

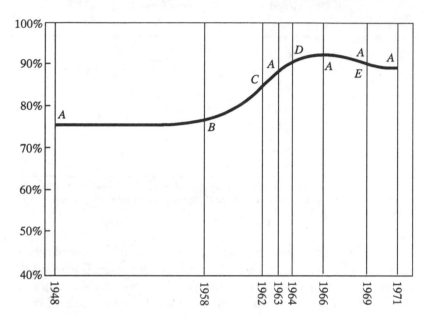

Source: From Quinn, Staines, & McCullough, 1973.

Note: "Don't know" and "uncertain" have been excluded from the base
of the percentages. Sources: A = Gallup, or Gallup as reported by Roper; B =
Survey Research Center (Michigan); C = NORC; D = Survey Research Center
(Berkeley); E = 1969–1970 Survey of Working Conditions.

Because of these methodological complexities, it is difficult
to draw conclusions about the number of workers who are or
are not satisfied with their jobs or with some facet of their jobs.
This drawback does not mean, however, that meaningful research on satisfaction is impossible. On the contrary, interesting and important research has been and can be done on the
determinants of job satisfaction. For example, the relationship
between personal-input factors — such as education level, sex,
and age and seniority — and job or facet satisfaction can be ascer-
tained by simply comparing those people who report they are
satisfied with those people who report they are dissatisfied and
checking the results to see if the two groups differ in any systematic manner. The number of people reporting satisfaction

is not crucial for this purpose. What is important is that we distinguish those people who tend to be more satisfied from those people who tend to be less satisfied. This distinction can be made with many of the better-known satisfaction-measuring instruments, such as the Job Description Index (Smith, Kendall, & Hulin, 1969) and Porter's (1961) need-satisfaction instrument.

A number of studies have tried to determine the amount of employee dissatisfaction that is associated with different job facets. Although these studies have yielded interesting results, some serious methodological problems are involved in this work. As with overall job satisfaction, factors such as type of measurement scale used and manner of wording questions seriously affect the number of people who express dissatisfaction with a given facet. For example, a question about pay satisfaction can be asked in a way that will cause few people to express dissatisfaction, while a question about security satisfaction can be asked in a way that will cause many people to express dissatisfaction. In this situation, comparing the number of people expressing security satisfaction with the number of people expressing pay dissatisfaction might produce very misleading conclusions. This problem is always present no matter how carefully the various items are worded because it is impossible to balance the items so they are comparable for all factors.

Despite methodological problems, the data on relative satisfaction levels with different job factors are interesting. These data show that the factors mentioned earlier as being most important — that is, pay, promotion, security, leadership, and the work itself — appear in these studies as the major sources of dissatisfaction. Porter (1961) designed items using Maslow's needs as a measure of satisfaction. With these items, he collected data from various managers. The results of his study (see Table 4.2) show that more managers express high-order-need dissatisfaction than express lower-order-need dissatisfaction. The results also show that a large number of managers are dissatisfied with their pay and with the communications in their organizations and that middle-level managers tend to be better satisfied in all areas than lower-level managers.

Table 4.2. Differences Between Management Levels in
Percentage of Subjects Indicating Need-Fulfillment Deficiencies.

Questionnaire Items	Percent Bottom management (N = 64)	Percent Middle management (N = 75)	Percent difference
Security needs	42.2	26.7	15.5
Social needs	35.2	32.0	3.2
Esteem needs	55.2	35.6	19.6
Autonomy needs	60.2	47.7	12.5
Self-actualization needs	59.9	53.3	6.6
Pay	79.7	80.0	−0.3
Communications	78.1	61.3	16.8

Source: Adapted from Porter, 1961.

Porter's data also show that managers consider the areas of dissatisfaction to be the most important areas. It is not completely clear whether the dissatisfaction causes the importance or the importance causes the dissatisfaction. The research reviewed earlier suggests that the primary causal direction is from dissatisfaction to importance, although there undoubtedly is a two-way-influence process operating. The important thing to remember is that employees do report varying levels of satisfaction with different job factors, and the factors that have come out high on satisfaction have also been rated high on importance and have the strongest influence on overall job satisfaction.

A study by Grove and Kerr (1951) illustrates how strongly organizational conditions can affect factor satisfaction. Grove and Kerr measured employee satisfaction in two plants where normal work conditions prevailed and found that 88 percent of the workers were satisfied with their job security, which indicated that security was one of the least dissatisfying job factors for employees in these two plants. In another plant where layoffs had occurred, only 17 percent of the workers said they were satisfied with the job security, and job security was one of the most dissatisfying job factors for this plant's employees.

Determinants of Satisfaction

The research on the determinants of satisfaction has looked primarily at two relationships: (1) the relationship between satisfaction and the characteristics of the job, and (2) the relationship between satisfaction and the characteristics of the person. Not surprisingly, the research shows that satisfaction is a function of both the person and the environment. These results are consistent with our approach to thinking about satisfaction, since our model (shown in Figure 4.3) indicates that personal factors influence what people feel they should receive and that job conditions influence both what people perceive they actually receive and what people perceive they should receive. In Chapters 6, 7, and 8 we will discuss the evidence that shows how certain job factors relate to both facet and job satisfaction. These chapters will give detailed information about what determines how satisfied people are with four job factors — promotion, pay, interpersonal relationships, and the work itself — and will show that organizations can significantly influence employee satisfaction in these four areas.

The evidence on the effects of personal-input factors on satisfaction is voluminous and will be only briefly reviewed. The research clearly shows that personal factors do affect job satisfaction, basically because they influence perceptions of what outcomes should be. As predicted by the satisfaction model in Figure 4.3, the higher a person's perceived personal inputs — that is, the greater his education, skill, and performance — the more he feels he should receive. Thus, unless the high-input person receives more outcomes, he will be dissatisfied with his job and the rewards his job offers. Such straightforward relationships between inputs and satisfaction appear to exist for all personal-input factors except age and seniority. Evidence from the study of age and seniority suggests a curvilinear relationship (that is, high satisfaction among young and old workers, low satisfaction among middle-age workers) or even a relationship of increasing satisfaction with old age and tenure. The tendency of satisfaction to be high among older, long-term employees seems to be produced by the effects of selective turnover and the development of realistic expectations about what the job has to offer.

Consequences of Dissatisfaction

Originally, much of the interest in job satisfaction stemmed from the belief that job satisfaction influenced job performance. Specifically, psychologists thought that high job satisfaction led to high job performance. This view has now been discredited, and most psychologists feel that satisfaction influences absenteeism and turnover but not job performance. However, before looking at the relationship among satisfaction, absenteeism, and turnover, let's review the work on satisfaction and performance.

Job Performance

In the 1950s, two major literature reviews showed that in most studies only a slight relationship had been found between satisfaction and performance. A later review by Vroom (1964) also showed that studies had not found a strong relationship between satisfaction and performance; in fact, most studies had found a very low positive relationship between the two. In other words, better performers did seem to be slightly more satisfied than poor performers. A considerable amount of recent work suggests that the slight existing relationship is probably due to better performance indirectly causing satisfaction rather than the reverse. Lawler and Porter (1967) explained this "performance causes satisfaction" viewpoint as follows:

> If we assume that rewards cause satisfaction, and that in some cases performance produces rewards, then it is possible that the relationship found between satisfaction and performance comes about through the action of a third variable — rewards. Briefly stated, good performance may lead to re-

wards, which in turn lead to satisfaction; this formulation then would say that satisfaction rather than causing performance, as was previously assumed, is caused by it.

[Figure 4.5] shows that performance leads to rewards, and it distinguishes between two kinds of rewards and their connection to performance. A wavy line between performance and extrinsic rewards indicates that such rewards are likely to be imperfectly related to performance. By extrinsic rewards is meant such organizationally controlled rewards as pay, promotion, status, and security — rewards that are often referred to as satisfying mainly lower-level needs. The connection is relatively weak because of the difficulty of tying extrinsic rewards directly to performance. Even though an organization may have a policy of rewarding merit, performance is difficult to measure, and in dispensing rewards like pay, many other factors are frequently taken into consideration.

Quite the opposite is likely to be true for intrinsic rewards, however, since they are given to the individual by himself for good performance. Intrinsic or internally mediated rewards are subject to fewer disturbing influences and thus are likely to be more directly related to good performance. This connection is indicated in the model by a semiwavy line. Probably the best example of an intrinsic reward is the feeling of having accomplished something worthwhile. For that matter any of the rewards that satisfy self-actualization needs or higherorder growth needs are good examples of intrinsic rewards [pp. 23–24].*

*Lawler, E. E., and Porter, L. W. The effect of performance on job satisfaction. *Industrial Relations*, 1967, *7*, 20–28. Reprinted by permission of the publisher, Industrial Relations.

Figure 4.5. Model of the Relationship of Performance to Satisfaction.

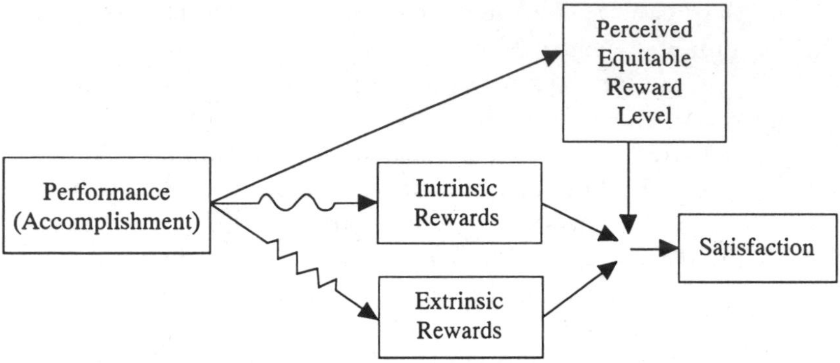

Source: From Lawler, E. E., & Porter, L. W. The effect of performance on job satisfaction. Industrial Relations, 1967, 7, 20–28. Reprinted by permission of the publisher, Industrial Relations.

Figure 4.5 shows that intrinsic and extrinsic rewards are not directly related to job satisfaction, since the relationship is moderated by perceived equitable rewards (what people think they should receive). The model in Figure 4.5 is similar to the model in Figure 4.3, since both models show that satisfaction is a function of the amount of rewards a person receives and the amount of rewards he feels he should receive.

Because of the imperfect relationship between performance and rewards and the important effect of perceived equitable rewards, a low but positive relationship should exist between job satisfaction and job performance in most situations. However, in certain situations, a strong positive relationship may exist; while in other situations, a negative relationship may exist. A negative relationship would be expected where rewards are unrelated to performance or negatively related to performance.

To have the same level of satisfaction for good performers and poor performers, the good performers must receive more rewards than the poor performers. The reason for this, as stressed earlier, is that performance level influences the amount of rewards a person feels he should receive. Thus, when rewards are not based on performance — when poor performers receive equal rewards or a larger amount of rewards than good performers — the best performers will be the least satisfied, and a negative satisfaction-performance relationship will exist. If, on the other hand, the better performers are given significantly more rewards, a positive satisfaction-performance relationship should exist. If it is assumed that most organizations are partially successful in relating rewards to performance, it follows that most studies should find a low but positive relationship between satisfaction and performance. Lawler and Porter's (1967) study was among those that found this relationship; their study also found that, as predicted, intrinsic-need satisfaction was more closely related to performance than was extrinsic-need satisfaction.

In retrospect, it is hard to understand why the belief that high satisfaction causes high performance was so widely accepted. There is nothing in the literature on motivation that suggests this causal relationship. In fact, such a relationship is opposite to the concepts developed by both drive theory and expectancy theory. If anything, these two theories would seem to predict that high satisfaction might reduce motivation because of a consequent reduction in the importance of various rewards that may have provided motivational force. Clearly, a more logical view is that performance is determined by people's efforts to obtain the goals and outcomes they desire, and satisfaction is determined by the outcomes people actually obtain. Yet, for some reason, many people believed — and some people still do believe — that the "satisfaction causes performance" view is best.

Turnover

The relationship between satisfaction and turnover has been studied often. In most studies, researchers have measured the job satisfaction among a number of employees and then waited to see which of the employees studied left during an ensuing time period (typically, a year). The satisfaction scores of the employees who left have then been compared with the remaining employees' scores. Although relationships between satisfaction scores and turnover have not always been very strong, the studies in this area have consistently shown that dissatisfied workers are more likely than satisfied workers to terminate employment; thus, satisfaction scores can predict turnover.

A study by Ross and Zander (1957) is a good example of the kind of research that has been done. Ross and Zander measured the job satisfaction of 2680 female workers in a large company. Four months later, these researchers found that 169 of these employees had resigned; those who left were significantly more dissatisfied with the amount of recognition they received on their jobs, with the amount of achievement they experienced, and with the amount of autonomy they had.

Probably the major reason that turnover and satisfaction are not more strongly related is that turnover is very much influenced by the availability of other positions. Even if a person is very dissatisfied with his job, he is not likely to leave unless more attractive alternatives are available. This observation would suggest that in times of economic prosperity, turnover should be high, and a strong relationship should exist between turnover and satisfaction; but in times of economic hardship, turnover should be low, and little relationship should exist between turnover and satisfaction. There is research evidence to support the argument that voluntary turnover is much lower in periods of economic hardship. However, no study has compared the relationship between satisfaction and turnover under different economic conditions to see if it is stronger under full employment.

Absenteeism

Like turnover, absenteeism has been found to be related to job satisfaction. If anything, the relationship between satisfaction and absenteeism seems to be stronger than the relationship between satisfaction and turnover. However, even in the case of absenteeism, the relationship is far from being isomorphic. Absenteeism is caused by a number of factors other than a person's voluntarily deciding not to come to work; illness, accidents, and so on can prevent someone who wants to come to work from actually coming to work. We would expect satisfaction to affect only voluntary absences; thus, satisfaction can never be strongly related to a measure of overall absence rate. Those studies that have separated voluntary absences from overall absences have, in fact, found that voluntary absence rates are much more closely related to satisfaction than are overall absence rates (Vroom, 1964). Of course, this outcome would be expected if satisfaction does influence people's willingness to come to work.

Organization Effectiveness

The research evidence clearly shows that employees' decisions about whether they will go to work on any given day and whether they will quit are affected by their feelings of job satisfaction. All the literature reviews on the subject have reached this conclusion. The fact that present satisfaction influences future absenteeism and turnover clearly indicates that the causal direction is from satisfaction to behavior. This conclusion is in marked contrast to our conclusion with respect to performance — that is, behavior causes satisfaction. In Chapter 5 we will consider, in terms of our expectancy motivation model (Figure 3.1), why feelings of satisfaction influence turnover and absenteeism.

The research evidence on the determinants of satisfaction suggests that satisfaction is very much influenced by the actual rewards a person receives; of course, the organization has a considerable amount of control over these rewards. The research also shows that, although not all people will react to the same reward level in the same manner, reactions are predictable if something is known about how people perceive their inputs. The implication is that organizations can influence employees' satisfaction levels. Since it is possible to know how employees will react to different outcome levels, organizations can allocate outcomes in ways that will either cause job satisfaction or job dissatisfaction.

Absenteeism and turnover have a very direct influence on organizational effectiveness. Absenteeism is very costly because it interrupts scheduling, creates a need for overstaffing, increases fringe-benefit costs, and so on. Turnover is expensive because of the many costs incurred in recruiting and training replacement employees. For lower-level jobs, the cost of turnover is estimated at $2000 a person; at the managerial level, the cost is at least five to ten times the monthly salary of the job involved. Because satisfaction is manageable and influences absenteeism and turnover, organizations can control absenteeism and turnover. Generally, by keeping satisfaction high and, specifically, by seeing that the best employees are the most satisfied, organizations can retain those employees they need the most. In effect, organizations can manage turnover so that, if it occurs, it will occur among employees the organization can most afford to lose. However, keeping the best performers more satisfied is not easy, since they must be rewarded very well. Chapter 6 points out that, although identifying and rewarding the better performers is not always easy, the effort may have significant payoffs in terms of increased organizational effectiveness.

five

The Decision to Work in an Organization

People don't just happen to join organizations, nor do they automatically show up for work every day. People make motivated, conscious decisions about which occupations and organizations to join and whether to come to work on a given day. These decisions can be called work-participation decisions, since they relate to whether a person will participate in the activities of an organization. All work-participation decisions fit our definition of motivated behavior, since they are voluntary and goal directed. The motivation model illustrated in Figure 3.1 suggests that, like all decisions involving choices among behaviors, work-participation decisions are based on a combination of $E \rightarrow P$ expectancies, $P \rightarrow O$ expectancies, and outcome valences.

It is important to distinguish decisions involving work particiption from those involving work performance. The fact that a person shows up for work tells us little about what he will do once he is there. Often, work-participation decisions are influenced by different outcomes, different $E \rightarrow P$ expectancies, and different $P \rightarrow O$ expectancies from those influencing work-performance decisions. To emphasize this distinction, only work-participation decisions are being treated in this chapter, while the next three chapters will focus on work-performance decisions.

From a theoretical point of view, participation and performance decisions can be treated in the same way, the only difference being the behavior that is focused on in each case. In one case, the behavior is coming to work; in the other case, the behavior is performing in certain ways while at work. A theory or model of motivation can explain both kinds of behavior — as well as many other behaviors — since some general principles of motivation apply to all volitional, goal-oriented behavior.

The behavior of a person actually going to work or not going to work on any given day is often the result of a series of related decisions. First, there is the decision of whether to work, which is influenced by factors such as fear of the stigma associated with not working, attitudes about welfare programs, and knowledge of available employment opportunities. If the person decides to work, he is faced with choosing an occupation, choosing a job within that occupation, and finally deciding whether to go to work on any given day. These choices have been studied separately in the research on the decision to participate. Unfortunately, at this time there is very little research on why people decide not to work. This will undoubtedly change, since this issue is becoming more important. However, until this research is done, the best course is to focus our discussion on the occupation, job-choice, and attendance decisions.

Occupational Preference and Occupational Choice

The range of occuptions open to people is very wide. The *Dictionary of Occupational Titles* lists almost 30,000 different jobs. Of course, no one considers 30,000 different jobs and then decides which one to take. Still, people often consider entering many different occupations during their lives. They develop conceptions of what the occupations are like, and their choices are based on their conceptions. Since misinformation is prevalent about the nature of jobs, people's conceptions can be wrong. Still, millions of people somehow sort themselves into different occupations; at the same time, people are being sorted by representatives of those occupations that limit admission (for example, medicine or law).

In discussing occupational choice, Vroom (1964) distinguishes it from occupational preference. Occupational choice refers to the occupation a person actually tries to enter; occupational preference refers to the occupation that is the most attractive to the person. This distinction is important and ties in directly with our motivation model, which shows that the attractiveness of a behavior (such as joining an occupation) is influenced by the attractiveness of the outcomes that are perceived to be associated with it. Thus, our model suggests that to determine the attractiveness of a given occupation for a person, we must know all the outcomes that the individual perceives to be attainable from that occupation, and we must know the valence he attaches to all the outcomes. We can then apply the formula $\Sigma[(P \rightarrow O)(V)]$ discussed earlier, which indicates that the more positively valued rewards are seen to be attainable by choosing a given occupation, the more desirable membership in that occupation will be.

As stressed in Chapter 3, people do not always try to behave in those ways that lead to the most attractive outcomes, since attractiveness is not the only factor that influences which behavior will be chosen. If attractiveness were the only factor, a few very attractive occupations would be overwhelmed with applicants, which doesn't happen — although some occupations certainly have more applicants than available positions. The major reason more people do not try to enter the most attractive occupations is indicated by the first relationship in the motivation model, $E \rightarrow P$. When $E \rightarrow P$ is 0, there is no motivation, since $E \rightarrow P$ multiplies $\Sigma[(P \rightarrow O)(V)]$ to determine motivation. $E \rightarrow P$ is a reality factor. It indicates that people will not be motivated to enter an occupation, no matter how attractive it is, if they see no probability of being accepted. This accounts for the evidence that many people choose occupations that are not, in their eyes, the most attractive.

For example, Williamson (1939) reported that 37 percent of college men and 46 percent of college women do not list the same occupation as both their preferred and their chosen occupation. Later data collected by Rosenberg (1957) as part of a large-scale study of college students show a lower figure of

22 percent, which is probably due to the fact that Rosenberg collected his data in a time of prosperity when people had a wide range of jobs to choose from, while Williamson collected his data during the Depression. The Rosenberg study also shows that business occupations head the list of occupations that are chosen but not preferred. Of those students choosing business occupations, 40 to 53 percent said they would have preferred another occupation, while only 7 percent of those choosing medicine preferred another occupation. Rosenberg's data further show that students preparing for an occupation they do not prefer are poor class attenders, are relatively uninterested in school work, and have low grades.

Outcome Attractiveness and Occupational Choice

A considerable amount of research evidence indicates that the attractiveness people attach to outcomes is strongly related to their occupational preferences. Other evidence shows that outcome attractiveness predicts occupational choice; but this relationship is weaker than the relationship between outcome attractiveness and occupational preference as would be predicted by the model, since it is influenced by an additional factor: $E \rightarrow P$. For example, many studies have shown that people who place a high value on economic outcomes prefer business occupations (Lawler, 1971). If it is assumed that business occupations are perceived as leading to economic rewards, then the data from these studies make good sense. People who value money highly should prefer careers that they feel will yield the greatest economic return, just as people who value status should prefer those occupations that they feel will provide the greatest status. The results of a study by Stone (1933), shown in Table 5.1, illustrate the kinds of values characteristic of college students preferring certain occupations.

Rosenberg's study (1957) is among those that show a relationship between valuing economic outcomes and choosing business occupations. In this study, students choosing business oc-

**Table 5.1. Characteristic Values of College Students
Indicating Preferences for Different Classes of Occupations.**

Business:	High economic, low theoretical and aesthetic
Banking:	High economic, low religious
Medicine:	High theoretical, low economic and political
Education:	High aesthetic, low economic
Law:	High political, low theoretical
Literature:	High aesthetic and religious, low economic

Source: Based on Stone, 1933, p. 275.

cupations valued extrinsic rewards on a relatively high level and self-expression on a relatively low level; students choosing careers such as social work and teaching valued working with people more than either self-expression or economic rewards. Again, these results make sense on the assumption that business occupations provide economic rewards and careers in social work and teaching provide an opportunity to work with people.

Thus, the evidence suggests that by knowing the attractiveness of outcomes to people we can predict their occupational preferences; to some extent, we can also predict their occupational choices, since people choose those occupations that provide the rewards they value. A crucial factor in these predictions is a fairly well developed, society wide knowledge of the rewards provided by different occupations. If there was no general agreement on what rewards different occupations offer, then occupational choices and preferences could not be predicted by knowing only the attractiveness of outcomes; both a person's $P \rightarrow O$ expectancies and outcome preferences would have to be known. As stressed in Figure 3.3, $P \rightarrow O$ expectancies are based on reality, and there are clear differences in the kinds of rewards offered by different occupations. Thus, if we know a person values money, we can predict that he will prefer a business career, since it can be a high-paying career and he will probably perceive it as such. We can be less sure, however, that he will actually choose a business career, since his choice will be based on a combination of his $E \rightarrow P$ expectancies, his outcome preferences, and his $P \rightarrow O$ expectancies.

Outcome Attractiveness, P→O Expectancies, and Occupational Preference

According to our motivation model, the best predictions of occupational preferences should come from a combination of outcome preferences and $P \rightarrow O$ expectancies. Several studies have shown that occupational preferences can be predicted by combining outcome-attractiveness measures with $P \rightarrow O$ expectancies about various occupations. Vroom (1964) asked college students to rank five occupations according to ability to provide 15 outcomes. He also asked the students to indicate the attractiveness of the outcomes and to specify their occupational preferences. Vroom's data showed that the most preferred occupations were seen as providing outcomes that were most attractive to the person. Wanous (1972b) partially replicated Vroom's study. Wanous' results also showed that occupational preferences could be predicted by a combination of $P \rightarrow O$ expectancies and outcome-attractiveness ratings; the most attractive occupation to an individual was the occupation that he saw as providing those outcomes he valued. Thus, research data offer reasonably good support for the view that occupational preferences can be predicted from a combination of a person's $P \rightarrow O$ expectancies and the attractiveness he assigns to various outcomes. However, these data do not prove that this combination is a better predictor than either the attractiveness ratings or the $P \rightarrow O$ expectancies alone.

Outcome Attractiveness, P→O Expectancies, E→P Expectancies, and Occupational Choice

According to our motivation model, the best prediction of occupational choice — unlike occupational preference — can't be obtained from simply knowing a person's outcome preferences and $P \rightarrow O$ expectancies. A person's $E \rightarrow P$ expectancies must also be considered in predicting his occupational choice. Unfortunately, no study has directly tested whether a person's occupational choice is best predicted by a combination of his $E \rightarrow P$ and $P \rightarrow O$ expectancies and the attractiveness he assigns to various outcomes. Thus, it is impossible to determine directly whether considering $E \rightarrow P$ expectancies will allow for better prediction of occupational choices that might be obtained if only $P \rightarrow O$ expectancies and outcome attractiveness are considered. However, some relevant evidence can be considered.

A study by Korman (1966b) supports the argument that the $E \rightarrow P$ factor is important and that people don't always choose the occupation that is most attractive to them because they believe it is beyond their abilities. Self-esteem is one of the variables influencing a person's expectancy that his effort will lead to successful performance. In an occupational choice situation, the higher a person's self-esteem, the more likely he should be to choose the occupation that is most attractive to him — even though entry into the occupation may be highly competitive. In other words, the person who has high self-esteem sees a good chance of success in whatever he does; therefore, his $E \rightarrow P$ expectancy will not be the deciding factor in his choice of an occupation. People who are high in self-esteem will base their occupational choices simply on the degree to which certain occupations are seen to fulfill their needs. For the person who is low in self-esteem, the opposite condition should exist; his $E \rightarrow P$ expectancy may be very significant in discouraging him from trying to join many occupations that he finds attractive. Thus, for high-self-esteem people, there should be a correspondence between preferred occupation and chosen occupation, whereas preferred occupation should not correspond with chosen occupation for low-self-esteem people.

Korman's (1966b) data support the view that self-esteem is an important determinant of whether an individual will choose the occupation that is, in fact, most attractive to him. His data show that persons with high self-esteem are more likely than others to choose occupations that they feel will satisfy their important needs. Thus, for people with high self-esteem, occupational attractiveness is predictive of choice, while it is not for persons with low self-esteem.

Personal Factors and Occupational Choice

A great deal of evidence shows that personal factors — such as sex, religion, and family background — are related to occupational-choice decisions. For example, several studies have shown that children tend to pick their parents' occupation. Other studies have shown that children from wealthy families tend to choose high-paying occupations with greater frequency than children from low-income families do. Significant differences exist among the kinds of occupations chosen by members of different ethnic and religious groups. Protestants are more likely to attain high-status occupations than are Roman Catholics; Jews are more likely to attain high-status occupations than are Italians; whites are more likely to attain high-status occupations than are blacks (Vroom, 1964). Finally, there is abundant evidence that women choose different occupations than men do. Rosenberg (1957) noted that half of the men he studied planned to enter law, engineering, farming, or business, whereas only one-twentieth of the women he studied planned to enter these occupations.

Unfortunately, few of the research studies that have shown a relationship between personal-background factors and occupational choices have collected data to explain the differences. However, our motivation model can explain many of these differences if we assume that people from different backgrounds have different $E \rightarrow P$ and $P \rightarrow O$ beliefs and that they rate the attractiveness of outcomes differently. For example, the effect of sex on choices can be partially explained by a group of research studies showing that women value money less than men, and social contact more than men. Combined with the possible effects of sex discrimination on women's $E \rightarrow P$ beliefs for certain occupations, this could account for their tendency not to choose business occupations. Similarly, the tendency of children to choose the same occupations as their parents can be explained by evidence that children's values and interests do correspond to those of their parents.

Conclusions

Overall, the evidence supports the view that individuals tend to prefer those occupations that they perceive as offering outcomes that are attractive to them. Somewhat less support is available for the proposition that occupational choices are influenced by both preferences and perceptions of the likelihood of actually joining the occupation. Clearly, more research is needed on the role of $E \rightarrow P$ perceptions in career-choice decisions. Despite some gaps in the research on occupational choice and preference, a seemingly safe conclusion is that our motivation model is a valid approach to thinking about these topics.

Organizations and Job Choice

Once the decision to enter an occupation has been made, a job seeker must choose an organization. Every person makes this decision at the beginning of his work career, and the decision is constantly being made by every employee who considers changing jobs. People are constantly choosing among jobs; in some cases they choose among jobs they do not have, while in other cases they choose between the job they hold and a job being offered to them.

The job-choice decision — like the occupational-choice decision — is a voluntary, goal-oriented decision and should be explainable by our motivation model. There is, in fact, every reason to believe that job-choice and occupational-choice decisions are based on the same type of decision-making process. The decisions are similar, since they involve choosing among mutually exclusive behaviors. In both decisions, the possibility is present that the most desirable behavior cannot be accomplished. Desirable jobs — like desirable occupations — are often difficult to enter.

The major difference between the two decisions is that occupational-choice decisions are often made first and seem to be more permanent. The occupational choice decision is a higher-order, first-screening decision that limits the number and range of job openings an individual considers. In the occupational-choice decision, the behavior is that of choosing a career, whereas in job choice, the behavior is that of choosing among organizations in which to work and among specific jobs in the chosen organization.

The two decisions may also differ in the amount and kinds of information available to the individual as a basis for his decision. In his job-choice decision, the individual often has more information than he does in his occupation-choice decision. The following account shows how a job-choice decision is made by a business school student:

> He begins to search for possibilities and eventually discovers a series of alternatives. He then concentrates on evaluating these alternatives in terms of the degree to which they will permit attainment of each of his goals. Through visits to the organization, brochures prepared by its personnel or public relations staff, and conversations with friends, teachers, or parents he forms *judgments* of the likelihood that he will be able to attain particular goals through a given organizational membership [Vroom, 1966, p. 214].

Presumably, the student then joins the organization that he feels will offer the best opportunity to attain his goals. This description fits very well with the events we would predict based on our motivation model, except Vroom doesn't mention the importance of $E{\rightarrow}P$ expectancies. Just as in occupational choice, a reality factor comes into play in job-choice decisions because a person will not try to obtain a very attractive job if he feels he cannot. Vroom's description of the job-choice decision may be misleading in that it shows the person conducting an organized, rational search for alternatives. Although this activity may typify some people's job-choice behavior, as was pointed out in Chapter 3, many decisions are made on the basis of inaccurate, incomplete information and limited consideration of alternatives (Simon, 1957).

Vroom's (1966) data partially support our view of what influences job-choice decisions. He asked graduating business-administration students to rate the jobs they were considering in terms of likelihood of providing 15 goals. The students were also asked to rank the goals in order of importance. The data showed that the students preferred jobs in those organizations that were seen as instrumental for the satisfaction of their most important needs, and they joined these organizations after graduation.

Unfortunately, very few other studies provide results that test the theories presented here about how people make job choices. Much of the research has looked at the effect of economic variables (for instance, on turnover and labor supply) but has not directly examined the psychological processes that underlie job-choice decisions. Still, the research is interesting, and several findings seem to fit well with our approach to explaining job choices (see Organization for Economic Cooperation and Development, 1965; Yoder, 1956; and March & Simon, 1958). These data show that:

1. Organizations that pay higher-than-average wages seem best able to attract and retain high-quality labor.
2. Turnover is high in organizations where wages are low in relation to other organizations in the area.
3. The stimulus to leave an organization is greatest when employees in other organizations seem to be making more money.
4. Turnover is low in time of recession or depression.

The first three findings indicate that people tend to gravitate toward higher-paying jobs, particularly if the jobs are local and highly visible. These three findings suggest that people often choose jobs that they perceive to have the highest instrumentality for one goal — pay. If we assume that the perceived differences between working as an A in company X and working as an A in company Y are very small, then differences in wages should have a great influence on the decision of where to work. This could be true even for people who do not value money very highly, if the one clearly visible difference between the two companies is the salary. The person who is in the job market for the first time is particularly likely to take the highest-paying job. This person is usually not too good at assessing the degree to which jobs provide noneconomic rewards, so he is more likely to feel that starting salary is the only clear difference among jobs. This speculation leads to the prediction that most new graduates will accept the highest-paying job they are offered in their chosen occupation.

People's tendency to take jobs affording the most opportunity to attain their goals leads to the expectation that people who value money highly will almost gravitate toward high-paying companies. This relationship should hold whether the people are choosing a job for the first time or choosing between their present job and one in another company. The relationship would not be expected to hold if the low-paying company were seen to offer other desirable rewards that the high-paying company did not offer. The fourth finding mentioned above probably comes about because alternative jobs are fewer during a recession, and as a result a person is less likely to find a job that is more attractive than his present job.

Although the unemployed person who is choosing a job is similar in many ways to the person who is deciding whether to leave his present job, he is also different in one very important respect. The person who doesn't have a job is likely to take whatever job offers more rewards, even if the difference is very small. On the other hand, the experienced worker would be relatively unlikely to change jobs for a small difference in extrinsic rewards. For one thing, he may envision a number of costs associated with leaving his present job—such as giving up long-term friendships and adopting new behavior patterns. Thus, he may feel that a small increment in extrinsic outcomes is not worth the initial cost. The new job seeker has no such costs, and he can give more weight to differences in whatever outcomes are attractive to him.

In addition to differences among pay scales, job applicants look at many other factors. A study of students looking for accounting jobs found that students have rather well-developed images of the large national CPA firms (Rhode, Sorensen, & Lawler, 1975). The students saw clear differences among the social climates of the firms, along with differences in the prestige and integrity of the firms and differences in the opportunities the firm provided for them to grow and develop their skills. These differences influenced the students' choices of where to apply for jobs. Organizations realize this, and the next section will examine how organizations try to influence the applicant's perceptions of factors such as an organization's climate and prestige.

Individuals and Organizations
Attracting and Selecting Each Other

In most job-choice situations, people have to make choice decisions about jobs they have never personally experienced. If they are thinking of changing jobs, they may have a great deal of experience with their present job but very little with the other jobs they are considering. Or they may have personal experiences with none of the jobs, which is true of new graduates. This raises the question of how people develop their $P \rightarrow O$ expectancies when they have never personally experienced a job.

There is relatively little research on just how individuals gather information about jobs and organizations. However, some inferences are possible based on research done in other areas and using our motivation model. First, it seems likely that people do not gather all the information they can. In most cases, there are many sources of information about a particular job or organization, including company advertising, company recruiters, and former and present employees. If a person were to gather all the available information, he would not only find it very time consuming, he would undoubtedly suffer from information overload and be unable to process all the information.

Further, it is not always strategically wise for the person to collect all the information he needs. Often, in the selection process, the individual is trying to accomplish two things: (1) he is trying to attract the organization so he will get a job, and (2) he is trying to gather information about the organization. At times, these two desires can come into conflict. For example, a student may want to know whether an organization would view his long hair as being widely deviant from its standards, but, in his desire to obtain the job, he may get a haircut. In short, it seems reasonable to assume that in this search process, as in many others, people end up satisficing rather than optimizing. They don't consider all the alternatives, and they don't have

complete information about the consequences of choosing each
of the alternatives.

Individuals attach varying degrees of credibility to information that reaches them through different channels. Social psychologists often have pointed out a strong source-credibility
effect; that is, information from some sources is much more
readily believed than information from other sources. What are
the sources of information about jobs that generally are given the
highest credibility? Although there has been little research in
this area, it seems likely that advertisements have low credibility, as do statements made by recruiters and employment agen-
cies, which leaves us with statements made by present and past
employees. These statements probably have the highest credibility, especially when the present or past employee is a friend
of the person considering the job.

Word-of-mouth advertising in the form of comments by
employees can be a double-edged sword in the sense of both
attracting and driving away potential employees. Therefore, one
advantage of having a satisfied work force would be to attract
job applicants, thus improving the number and perhaps quality of the applicants. On the other hand, the existence of a large
number of dissatisfied and bitter employees could present real
problems for an organization trying to attract new employees.
Dissatisfied employees are likely to say unkind things about the
organization that are likely to be believed. Thus, the future quality of the organization's work force could be seriously impaired.

Basic to a good selection program from the organization's
point of view is a large supply of applicants. Without a favorable selection ratio (a large number of applicants per position
to be filled), no selection program is of value. However, a good
selection program must not only attract many applicants, it must
also attract qualified applicants. Ideally, an organization should
encourage intelligent self-selection among prospective applicants,
so that only people who can do the job and who will work for
a significant period of time will actually apply. Attracting qualified people who do not stay on the job is dysfunctional from
the organization's point of view because this turnover uses
money, time, and resources. Attracting unqualified people is

costly because the applications have to be processed and ultimately rejected, frequently giving unqualified applicants a bad
impression of the organization.

There has been very little research on how organizations
attract members and on the effectiveness of various approaches.
Especially lacking is research on what kinds of job-applicant expectations result from various attraction efforts. Organizations
try in numerous ways to attract job applicants; for example,
they advertise on the radio, in newspapers, and in magazines.
They make movies for high school seniors. One movie used by
the telephone company to attract applicants for the operator's
job shows beautiful girls talking to men all over the world who
compliment them on their sexy voices; background music is
provided by the New York Rock and Roll Ensemble. Organizations sometimes offer bonuses to current employees who find
an applicant the company hires. Most of this advertising is
directed toward impressing people with specific rewards associated with holding a particular job. In other words, this advertising is directed toward influencing $P \rightarrow O$ expectancies. Organizations also invest in general image-building advertising,
which pictures the organization as exciting, dynamic, presti-
gious, and progressive. Presumably, this advertising attracts job
applicants because it creates the perception in applicants that
certain rewards will be associated with joining the organization.

In their advertising to attract people, it is interesting to
note that organizations seldom mention the negative aspects of
working for them in general or of any particular job. For many
years, advertisements in college newspapers to attract seniors
stressed the security, pay, and promotion opportunities that
different companies had to offer. Now these advertisements stress
challenge and opportunity. They have, in short, switched to
stressing different rewards, but they still talk only about the positive aspects of the job. Thus, organizations seem to follow a
strategy of attracting every prospective applicant rather than
allowing intelligent self-selection to take place.

Most organizations describe their jobs as positively as possible without being completely dishonest. This strategy, in effect,
gives up the potential advantages of intelligent self-selection in

return for the advantage of having a large number of applicants from which to select. A study by Weitz (1956) illustrates the problem with this approach. He was asked to deal with the high turnover of insurance salesmen, and he diagnosed the problem as being due to the unrealistic expectations that had been built up in the men during the attraction and selection process. He dealt with this problem by giving the applicants a realistic picture of the job, thus allowing self-selection to take place. When this was done, people seemed to develop more realistic $P \rightarrow O$ expectancies, which made the job seem less attractive to some people but prevented those people whose needs could not be met by the job from taking it. Those who took the job after such a description tended to be more satisfied and to stay longer. The approach of giving realistic information would seem to have wide applicability. It has already been used in hiring telephone operators and automobile assembly-line workers. In the latter case, the applicants were shown a movie that depicted the bad parts of the job and that included workers quitting and complaining about the boring work (Wanous, 1972a).

The kinds of selection programs used by the organization may also influence the perceived attractiveness of working for the organization. A study by Alderfer and McCord (1970) points out that the manner of conducting the selection interview directly influences the probability that a person will take a job with a company. These researchers found that students were more attracted to working for companies when interviewers were perceived as taking a personal interest in them and when potential careers were discussed with them.

Because the selection process does influence the attractiveness of jobs, organizations are faced with a difficult dilemma when considering different selection procedures. The ideal selection system would both attract the best applicants and provide all the information the organization needs in order to choose intelligently among these applicants. The problem is that many of the selection devices producing good selection information also appear to affect the applicants negatively. Certain tests, such as personality tests that ask questions about religion and sex, are good examples; although the tests are sometimes valid, they often make the organization that gives them seem less attractive to the applicant. Other examples are stress interviews and simulations that focus on the toughest parts of the job (for example, see OSS Staff, 1948). There also seems to be a limit to the amount of information an organization can collect without driving the applicant away. Many individuals simply will not sit still for all the testing, interviewing, and so on that could be done by organizations to gather enough information on which to base their selection decision.

Unfortunately, how people react to different selection procedures has not been sufficiently researched; thus, it is difficult to predict how much of each type of selection procedure a person will accept. There probably are large individual differences in how much a person will accept and in how people will react to different selection procedures. The organization is always faced with balancing its desire to attract the best people with its desire to gather valid selection data. The typical interview is a microcosm of these competing desires. Part of the time the interviewer is in the role of attracting the person, and part of the time he is in the role of trying to evaluate the person. This conflict can produce obvious stress and strain in the interviewer. The situation faced by the interviewer is similar to that faced by the job applicant who tries to both attract the organization and gather information about it. In a sense, deciding how to behave in the selection situation is a game played by both the organization and the job applicant, and how each one plays it depends on where he perceives he stands with respect to the other at that moment. How each one plays it also has a very strong influence on the likelihood that the selection process will result in a decision that is good for both the applicant and the organization.

Satisfaction and Turnover

Chapter 4 showed that job dissatisfaction can cause people to quit their jobs, which is highly congruent with the view in this chapter of how people choose jobs. When our motivation model was presented in Chapter 3, it was stressed that people base their $P \rightarrow O$ expectancies on their past experiences. A person's feelings of job satisfaction represent a summary statement of his experience in a certain situation. The person who is dissatisfied is saying that his job has not provided the outcomes he feels it should, whereas the person who is satisfied is saying that his job has provided the outcomes he feels it should. Looking into the future, the satisfied person tends to believe that he will receive the outcomes he desires, whereas the dissatisfied person does not feel the job is likely to provide the rewards he desires (Wanous, 1972a).

Feelings of satisfaction are related to turnover because they influence people's $P{\to}O$ expectancies. In short, the dissatisfied employee tends to have low $P{\to}O$ expectancies about his present job; as a result, he is more likely to find another job that will provide the kind of outcomes he desires. Hence, he is much more likely to think about quitting (Wanous, 1972a) and to actually quit when faced with an alternative job that is reasonably attractive.

The dissatisfied employee is also much more likely to be searching for other job possibilities. Since he has desires that are not being met by his present job, he tends to actively search for a situation where he can get what he wants. All the research on motivation shows that organisms with unsatisfied needs tend to search their environment more actively than organisms whose needs are satisfied. Thus, dissatisfaction seems to cause turnover for two reasons: (1) it causes people to search their environment for more attractive alternatives, and (2) it influences the degree to which people feel their jobs will provide in the future the rewards they desire.

Career Strategies

Although people's approaches to developing their careers have not been thoroughly researched, some evidence is worth considering. It shows how people try to plan their moves from one job to another and from one occupation to another so they will develop careers that give them the outcomes they desire. It also shows that people differ widely in what they want from their work careers.

Several studies have considered the kinds of career strategies used by managers who aspire to upward mobility. Table 5.2

presents the strategies a number of British managers reported using. Improving qualifications was the most frequently mentioned strategy. The second most frequently mentioned strategy was choosing jobs that were stepping-stones. A study of American executives also points to the importance of the stepping-stone job strategy in executive's career strategies (Glickman, Hahn, Fleishman, & Baxter, 1968). This study mentions other strategies used by managers to advance their careers. The "hitch your wagon to a star" principle was frequently mentioned, and the authors suggest that an analysis of the promotions people got indicated its effectiveness. It is not uncommon to find the top management of organizations dominated by people who all worked together in a certain department early in their careers (in one company, the group is known as the "marketing mafia"). Taking on risky assignments, solving major crises ("crises create heroes"), and acquiring a special competence that is unveiled at an appropriate time were other frequently used approaches.

Martin and Strauss (1956) have described the importance of sponsor/protégé relationships. According to them, the protégé may complement his superior by being strong in an area of the superior's weakness; the protégé may serve as a detail

Table 5.2. Distribution by Mentions of Perceived Career Strategies.

	Autoline (N − 40)	Novoplast (N = 41)	Both (N = 81)
Wait	6	9	15
Do job well	14	8	22
Make it easy to leave	4	1	5
Improve one's knowledge of the firm	4	1	5
Improve one's qualifications	19	16	35
Improve interpersonal relations	13	12	25
Change content of job	3	2	5
Get out of dead-end job	7	10	17
Choose jobs that are stepping-stones	10	17	27
Ask for move or explanation	9	9	18
Leave for another company	5	9	14
Other	2	4	6

Note: Each manager interviewed gave multiple responses.

Source: From Sofer, C. *Men in Mid-Career: A Study of British Managers and Technical Specialists.* Copyright © 1970 by Cambridge University Press. Reprinted by permission.

man, advisor, hatchet man, or information gatherer. An especially powerful sponsor may have a cluster of protégés surrounding him, and a skillful, upwardly mobile protégé may have several
sponsors. The success of the whole system depends on the sponsor being promoted and on his ability to carry his protégés along
with him. Apparently, this system works often, since Martin and
Strauss conclude that the "top management echelons of many
companies are made up of interlocking chains . . . [comprised
of] certain powerful sponsors and their adherents" (p. 109).

A group of English sociologists did an interesting study
of 229 blue-collar workers who tended to see their jobs and their
careers quite differently from upwardly mobile managers (Goldthorpe, Lockwood, Bechhofer & Platt, 1968). These workers,
most of whom were unskilled, saw their relationship with their
employers as a strictly financial one in which they did the work
so they could do other things off the job. Few workers were attracted by the idea of promotion; in fact, most workers desired
to continue to be paid well for doing the same job. Only 8 percent liked the idea of promotion and had done anything to increase their chances of being promoted. Most of these workers
simply did not see promotion as something that would provide
them with greater need satisfaction. They wanted more leisure
time and less stress in their lives, and becoming a manager was
not seen as likely to provide these. Interestingly, the workers
who saw their jobs in purely financial terms were those who were
socially mobile in a downward direction; that is, they tended
to occupy a lower social class than their parents. Dubin (1956)
has collected data from which he concludes that, in the United
States, "for almost three out of every four industrial workers
studied, work and the workplace *are not* central life interests"
(p. 131). Still, Morse and Weiss (1955) report that 80 percent
of a sample of workers say they would continue working even
if it were not financially necessary. People in professional occupations were particularly likely to say that they would continue
working.

Several studies have shown that work is a central life interest for managers. For example, Sofer (1970) found that work
played a very large or dominant role in the lives of 57 percent

of the managers he studied. One study has shown that, although managers may strongly identify with work, they do not necessarily have upward mobility aspirations (Tausky & Dubin, 1965). In this study only 10 percent of the managers were classified as strivers — that is, managers who are working hard to be upwardly mobile. According to Tausky and Dubin, "one of the great analytical myths carried over from the popular culture is the belief that business bureaucracy is peopled by strivers" (p. 729). In general, people vary widely in their career perspectives on at least two dimensions: (1) the degree to which they are involved in and identify with their work, and (2) their mobility aspirations. Although these two dimensions are related, they are not perfectly correlated, as shown by the number of people who identify with their work but are not upwardly mobile. The data also suggest that managers are more involved in their work and are more upwardly career oriented than are workers.

How do people develop such different career orientations? One approach to answering this question is to go back to childhood experiences and look at how self-concept is developed, how outcome preferences are established, and how perceptions of rewards available in different occupations are formed. Working in England, Carter (1966) has provided a great deal of data on how childhood experience influences individual careers. His research illustrates the strong impact of social class on the self-images individuals develop and on the perceptions of different careers. He talks of four classes: (1) traditional respectable families, (2) newly affluent families, (3) solid working-class families, and (4) the roughs. The first two classes raise their children to aspire to higher-level jobs, and communicate to them that blue-collar jobs are beneath them. The working-class parents "do not think in terms of moving up the social scale significantly." They are mostly semiskilled or unskilled workers, and they teach their children that their jobs are respectable and that the children should take these same jobs. The "roughs" have no aspirations for their children and, in fact, teach their children that work is distasteful. "These children are ready-made for the 'dead-end' jobs."

On the surface it may not be obvious that the employee

who chooses a job requiring a minimum amount of work is motivated by the same process as the employee who chooses a risky job in hope of being promoted. However, at a deeper level of analysis, they are both trying to do the same thing; that is, they are both choosing jobs on the basis of their career goals. Their goals are probably different — thus, the difference in their behavior. The fact is that both employees have career goals reflecting their needs, self-image, and perceptions of rewards that are available in different jobs, and the behavior of both employees is geared toward the attainment of these career goals. One employee plays it safe to achieve his desired career goals (that is, to keep a good-paying but not too demanding job), whereas the other employee takes chances to achieve his desired career goals (that is, to become a top executive).

Controlling Turnover

More and more organizations are reporting high turnover figures for all types of employees. Studies of college graduates indicate that five years after graduation at least 50 percent have changed organizations, many deciding to take up a new occupation. Studies of nonmanagement employees show that turnover runs more than 40 percent a year in many jobs. In some assembly line jobs, turnover runs as high as 275 percent a year. Increasingly, people seem to be planning on and actually having careers that involve multiple organizations and even multiple occupations. Thus, some of the turnover is difficult to avoid since it represents people who took jobs knowing that they would stay only a short time. For example, as part of his career, an accountant may plan to take a job with one of the large public accounting firms merely for the training and experience it offers. His first job might be nothing more than a stepping-stone to the kind of job he ultimately seeks (he may wish to be a vice president or comptroller of a large firm). Thus, accounting firms often lose more than 90 percent of their people after ten years.

Some turnover is also due to changes that take place in people and is therefore hard to control. People change the kinds of goals they set for themselves, and they change their concepts of how capable they are of functioning well in a certain environment. Because of these changes, a job that was satisfying to a person can come to be seen as inappropriate and dissatisfying. Under these conditions, an organization must try to find a new job for the person, or he will almost surely quit. Often, in this situation, there is nothing the organization can do to influence the person's decision to leave.

Admittedly, some turnover is not under the control of the organization; however, much of it is controllable. Turnover often stems from people being dissatisfied with their jobs and with their careers for reasons that the organization can change. For some reason, their job isn't providing them with the rewards or outcomes that they feel it should, and they decide to try a somewhat similar job in another organization because they perceive it as more likely to satisfy their needs. Organizations can reduce this turnover by providing people with the rewards they want and giving people a better idea before they take the job of what is in store for them.

Given the high cost of turnover and the fact that it is controllable, a strong case can be made for organizations adopting a policy of trying to control their turnover. Since organizations never seem to have enough interesting jobs, pay, promotions, and so on to keep everyone happy, the issue becomes whom to reward. One strategy is to reward everyone equally, which has the unfortunate effect of causing the better performers to be the most dissatisfied and the most likely to leave. If the better performers are to be satisfied, they must receive more rewards than the poor performers because, as the satisfaction model represented in Chapter 4 points out, they feel they should receive more. This argues for a strategy of giving more rewards to those people whom the organization wants to retain. In terms of our satisfaction model, this means offering them the kinds of outcomes they value. To implement this strategy, organizations must know whom they want to retain, what outcomes are valued by the people they want to retain, and what outcome level is needed to retain those they want to retain; and they must be able and willing to give the outcomes. All too often, organizations don't control their turnover because they simply aren't prepared to gather the kind of information they need. They don't know whom they want to keep, they don't know what outcomes the employees value, they don't know what reward levels to give, and they aren't able to reward people differentially. The result is that turnover occurs among the better performers. This turnover could be prevented by an investment of time and effort on the part of the organization.

Job-Attendance Decision

Employees make daily decisions about whether to participate in the activities of their organizations. They decide whether to go to work each day. Judging from the absenteeism figures reported by many organizations (often as high as 10 percent), many people decide not to go. Of course, some of the people who are absent from work on a given day are not voluntarily absent; medical or other reasons keep them away. However, other people can go to work but make a conscious decision not to. People have to be motivated to go to work each day. As our motivation model indicates, they decide whether to go to work by comparing the perceived consequences of the other behaviors they are considering with the outcomes associated with going to work. They are motivated to go to work only when they feel that this behavior will lead to more positively valued outcomes than any alternate behaviors.

Job satisfaction is related to absenteeism. We would expect this from our motivation and satisfaction models for the same reason that satisfaction is related to turnover. When a person says that he is dissatisfied with his job, he is saying that it does not provide him with the rewards he feels it should. Since past experience influences $P \rightarrow O$ expectancies, people who are dissatisfied tend to feel that going to work is not likely to provide the outcomes they value; hence, they are less likely to go. Three kinds of outcomes have been shown to have a strong influence on job-attendance decisions: social factors, job design, and pay.

Whyte (1948) has shown that being a member of a closely knit social group seems to motivate people to go to work regularly. People who belong to such groups presumably associate more rewards with going to work (for example, the satisfaction of social needs) than do people who are not group members. They enjoy the companionship they obtain at work, and they look forward to finding out what the people at work have been doing. To miss work means to miss out on one day's events in the life of the group. Often, the social part of work can become more important than the performance aspects, so that people come not so much to work as to see their friends. Group members also see some negative consequences associated with not going to work that do not operate for nongroup members. When asked, they often say that other people will have to work too hard if they do not go to work, and they say they feel uneasy about this (Whyte, 1948). In short, it is not surprising that people who belong to a cohesive social group are more likely to go to work, since job attendance is more attractive to them than staying away.

At first glance it may seem that organizations have little control over whether cohesive social groups develop, but this is not true. Many organization policies and practices influence whether groups will form. For example, the physical layout of the work area is controlled by management and has a strong influence on group formation. The simple act of dividing a large room into small rooms with six people in each encourages group development. Similarly, if work is laid out so people can talk, it encourages group development. One organization found that it could reduce turnover in some production jobs by placing the machinery in a way that allowed the employees to walk together and talk, whereas previously they were always walking in different directions. Organizations also influence group formation by their personnel-placement practices. If the organization rotates people frequently, it is more difficult for groups to form. However, organizations can encourage group formation by allowing people to choose whom they will work with. Although the formation of cohesive groups usually leads to reduced turnover, it doesn't always lead to increased performance. In fact, as will be discussed in Chapter 8, it may have a negative effect on performance.

A number of studies have shown how the work itself can influence job attendance. When jobs are meaningful, challenging, and involve responsibility, employees are more likely to be motivated to come to work. The reason seems to be that jobs with these characteristics provide outcomes that satisfy people's higher-order needs. They provide people with the opportunity to experience achievement, competence, and self-realization. When people experience these feelings at work, their jobs tend to be more attractive (Ross & Zander, 1957).

Routine, repetitive jobs simply do not allow people to satisfy these kinds of needs. Thus, it is not surprising that people who work on repetitive, simple jobs tend to be absent more often than people who work on interesting jobs. They see fewer positive outcomes associated with coming to work. The highest absence rates in any organization are usually found on the assembly line jobs, which is partly due to the lack of possible social contact and greatly due to the lack of satisfaction from doing the work itself. Other studies have shown that absence rates decrease dramatically as the interest and complexity of jobs increase.

It is important to note that more interesting work does not motivate everyone to come to work. Clearly, only those people who want the rewards it has to offer will be motivated to come. In fact, some people will be driven away from work because they don't want the responsibility and stress that go with more complex work. For example, the workers mentioned earlier in the study by Goldthorpe et al. (1968) did not want challenging work.

There is surprisingly little research on the effect of different pay systems on absenteeism. However, it is clear that pay can affect job-attendance decisions. A recent study by Lawler and Hackman (1969) provides strong support for this point. In working with a company that had been experiencing high absenteeism among part-time janitorial employees, a plan was developed that offered a cash bonus to workers who showed up regularly. The plan was designed to affect directly the perceived consequences of going to work and not going to work. The plan was developed by members of three work groups within the organization. Figure 5.1 shows the results for these workers; the bonus plan did lead to higher job attendance. This, of course, suggests the importance of tying pay to the kind of behavior that is to be motivated. The data clearly show that relating pay closely to attendance had the effect of increasing attendance.

Figure 5.1. Impact of Pay Plan on Attendance.

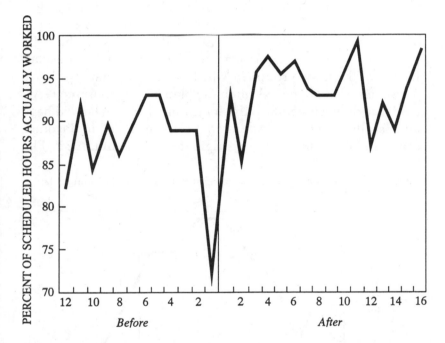

Source: From Lawler, E. E., & Hackman, J. R. The impact of employee participation in the development of pay incentive plans: A field experiment. *Journal of Applied Psychology,* 1969, *53,* 467–471. Copyright © 1969 by the American Psychological Association, and reproduced by permission.

The pay plan developed by the groups involved in the study was imposed on two similar work groups elsewhere in the organization. The data show that the plan was not as effective when it was imposed. Whereas the workers who developed the plan felt a commitment to seeing that it was successful, other workers saw the plan more as a management tool imposed on them to get them to come to work—which it was. These data emphasize that the mechanics of a plan do not determine its success. Success is also very much influenced by how the plan is introduced, how it is accepted, the workers' initial experience with it, and the superior/subordinate trust levels. These points will be discussed in more detail in Chapter 6, where pay plans will be considered.

In a follow-up study of the bonus plans, Scheflen, Lawler, and Hackman (1971) collected data on the impact of the plans after one year. Attendance had risen in the groups in which the plan had been imposed. Management had discontinued the plan in two of the three groups in which it had originated. Figure 5.2 shows what happened when the plan was discontinued. Attendance dropped significantly, indicating that the plan did have an effect on attendance. Attendance remained high in the other group in which the plan was originated and maintained. The

Figure 5.2. The Effect on Attendance of Eliminating the Bonus Plan.

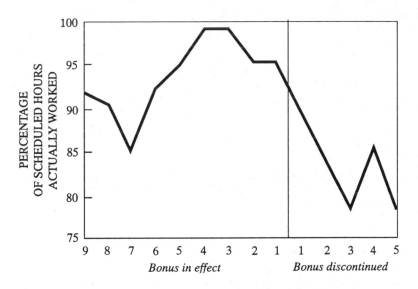

Source: From Scheflen, K. D., Lawler, E. E., & Hackman, J. R. Long-term impact of employee participation in the development of pay incentive plans: A field experiment revisited. *Journal of Applied Psychology,* 1971, *55,* 182–186. Copyright © 1971 by the American Psychological Association, and reproduced by permission.

researchers attributed the dropping of the plan to their own failure to gain management commitment to the plan.

Haire (1956) has pointed out that many organizations pay people for attendance rather than for performance. But are organizations really paying for attendance? Given the amount of leave a person can have without losing any pay, many organizations seem to pay not so much for attendance as for membership; that is, they make pay contingent on remaining on the organization's membership rolls and meeting the organization's minimal attendance requirements. The effect is to allow a person to decide a number of times during a year not to show up for work without suffering any financial loss. In terms of our motivation model, then, this policy has the effect of reducing the perceived positive consequences of going to work on certain days and therefore leads to lower attendance.

In summary, organizations can influence the job-attendance decisions employees make. Absenteeism doesn't just happen; it is a form of motivated behavior that can be influenced by what organizations do. Like turnover, absenteeism is determined by the kinds of outcomes people feel are associated with coming to work. The practices and policies of organizations directly influence the rewards people see associated with coming to work. By fitting jobs to the needs of their employees, by tying pay to attendance, and by encouraging the development of cohesive social groups, organizations can tie positive outcomes to job attendance and go a long way toward reducing and controlling absenteeism.

The Decision to Work in the Future

The evidence reviewed in this chapter clearly shows that organizations can influence the decisions people make about work. By the jobs they design and the work environment they create, organizations influence absenteeism and turnover. As a general rule, organizations have less control over the occupational choices people make. These choices are influenced more by events in society as a whole over which organizations have relatively little control (for example, the status of different occupations and the values of society). Until recently, organizations haven't had to be too concerned with people deciding not to work. Almost everyone wanted to work, and as a result organizations simply worried about competing with other organizations. The emphasis is changing as more and more people decide not to enter work organizations (for example, see Reich, 1970; Roszak, 1969). If this trend continues, work organizations may have to change their practices and policies in order to attract people into the labor market.

What can organizations do to make work more attractive? Making jobs more interesting, paying higher wages, and encouraging the formation of cohesive groups have already been mentioned. Beyond these, organizations can be much more flexible in the kinds of work arrangements they establish for their employees. The typical pattern of every employee coming to work at the same time and working for the same period just doesn't fit everyone. One way to attract people to work would be to allow them to design their own hours and even to allow them to work only part of the year. For example, husbands and wives could split the same job, with one working for six months and the other working for six months, or each working half the day. Also, some employees could work four 10-hour days a week while others could work five 8-hour days a week. Flexible work arrangements are just one example of how organizations can design work to suit individuals and thus make work in organizations more attractive. If present trends continue, more and more of this kind of individualization of the employer/employee relationship may be necessary for organizations to attract people.

six

Extrinsic Rewards and Job Performance

One of the most salient attributes of work organizations is the power to give tangible outcomes. Among the most obvious rewards are pay, promotion, interesting work, status symbols, and fringe benefits. The giving and withholding of these rewards can have a tremendous influence on motivation and satisfaction, as shown by a number of studies in this area. The amount of influence a particular extrinsic reward can have is, of course, determined by just how important it is to the person. This chapter will focus on how important the various extrinsic rewards are and how these rewards affect performance. Satisfaction with extrinsic rewards will also be considered. The major emphasis will be on rewards of pay and promotion, since they are given in all work organizations and since they have been subjected to the most research. With few exceptions, statements about their effects on motivation and satisfaction hold true for other extrinsic rewards.

The Importance of Extrinsic Rewards

Herzberg et al. (1957) reviewed a number of studies that had attempted to determine the importance of job factors by simply

143

asking people to rate these factors in terms of importance. As presented in Chapter 2, Figure 2.5, the results of this review show that an extrinsic reward (promotion), intrinsic factors (discussed in Chapter 7), and an interpersonal factor (discussed in Chapter 8) are rated as relatively high in importance. Surprisingly, pay was ranked only seventh. A later review found that, on the average, pay is ranked closer to third on a scale of importance (Lawler, 1971). This review also points out that substantial variances exist among studies and among persons in rating factors such as pay and other extrinsic rewards, which is consistent with the previous chapters' approach to the concept of outcome importance or attractiveness.

We would expect the importance of outcomes such as pay and promotion to vary as a function of the strength of a person's need at any given time and as a function of the kind of needs these outcomes can satisfy for the person. Pay might be first in importance for one individual because it satisfies his strong need for security; for another individual, pay might be first because it satisfies his need for esteem; for still another individual, pay might be last in importance because it cannot satisfy his strong social needs. To understand the impact of a pay plan on these individuals, we have to look at how important rewards such as pay are to them and why these rewards are important. Looking at the average importance of rewards such as pay or promotion can give us at best only an idea of whether they are important to enough people to use as motivators.

Some interesting research points out various factors that distinguish people for whom pay is very important from those for whom it is less important. For example, a study of piece-rate pay plans by Dalton (1948) distinguishes between rate-busters (employees who are very productive and to whom pay is very important) and restricters (employees who restrict their productivity and to whom pay is less important). Dalton sees the two groups as quite different in terms of family background. The restricters were typically sons of unskilled industrial workers; they grew up in large cities where they were active in boys' gangs. They tended to be Democrats, and they referred to the rate-busters as "Republican Hogs." Their religious preference was usually Catholic, and they belonged to many social groups (for example, clubs such as the Elks). In general, the rate-busters had grown up on farms or in small towns where they lived under the close supervision of parental authority. They tended to be "lone wolves" and typically did not join in group activities. Most were Republicans and owned their own homes. For the rate-buster, money seemed to be a "mark of virtue," because it was a sign that he worked hard. Dalton summarized the two types as "the country born (or middle-class born), lone-wolf, Republican, money-saving and investing worker without outside interests versus the city-born, gregarious, New Deal Democratic, spending worker" (in Whyte, 1955, p. 46).

The career-orientation research reviewed in Chapter 5 highlighted some of the differences between workers who value promotion and those who don't. Other studies have shown that factors such as pay satisfaction, job level within the organization, and how pay is determined influence the importance of pay and promotion. Altogether, the studies show that significant and comprehensible individual differences exist in the importance people assign to extrinsic rewards. The studies suggest that organizations have relatively little control over the degree to which their members will value various extrinsic rewards. Outcome importance is influenced at least as much by a person's background as by what happens to the person after joining the organization. This is not to say that organizations have no control; they clearly do (for example, changes in pay rates will change the importance of pay). However, other factors over which the organization has little control also have an important influence. The one action an organization can take if it wants to have members who value or don't value certain extrinsic rewards is to try to select its members on this basis. For example, if organizations want to use pay as an incentive, they could select workers who value money. Dalton's research suggests that this could be accomplished by looking at certain background factors. There are psychological tests that measure the value orientations and needs of individuals. However, it is not easy to identify those people in a selection situation for whom pay is important, since people answer test questions in a way that

is designed to enable them to get the job, and all selection instruments are of limited validity.

Approaches Relating Pay to Performance

The motivation model presented in Chapter 3 indicates that outcomes will motivate job performance only if they are important and appear to be tied to performance. Research shows that
to most people in most situations rewards such as pay and promotion are important. Thus, when such rewards are tied to performance so that their attainment appears to be dependent on
good performance, they should motivate good job performance.
In fact, many studies have shown that tying pay to performance
does increase motivation (Lawler, 1971).

There are innumerable approaches to tying pay closely
to job performance, most of which have been tried at one time
or another. Many approaches are very similar and can be grouped
for discussion purposes. It is important, however, to discuss
separately those pay plans that relate individual performance
to individual pay and those that relate group performance to
different levels of group reward. In the group plans, everyone
in a given group gets the same pay regardless of individual contribution, since pay is tied to performance of the total group.
Evidence suggests that the difference between group and individual plans is significant both in terms of how they are seen
by employees and in terms of their effects. It is also worthwhile
to distinguish between two types of group plans: one type is based
on work-group performance, or "subunit performance" (Porter
& Lawler, 1965); another type—for example, the Scanlon Plan—
is based on the performance of a total organization, usually a
whole company or major division or plant.

Individual Pay Plans

The best-known individual-incentive plan is the piece-rate approach, in which payment is tied to the number of units produced
by the workers. Literally thousands of piece-rate plans have been
devised and put into practice. All piece-rate incentive plans are

based on some type of measurement of what constitutes normal or standard production in a given job. Such a measurement is needed for determining how much will be paid for each piece in simple piece-rate plans and for determining the time savings that result from above-average performance in standard time plans. The difficulty of measuring performance and arriving at time standards and equitable piece rates has been a continuing source of concern and focus of research among behavioral scientists (for example, see Viteles, 1953). Every study has shown that time standards and piece rates are not based solely on objective, accurate, reliable, and verifiable data and therefore can be a source of unending controversy. Perhaps the one unanswered question with respect to such measures concerns the degree of their susceptibility to error. Industrial engineers often claim an accuracy of plus or minus 5 percent, while the research of behavioral scientists suggests that the errors are usually much larger (Whyte, 1955).

The piece-rate plan is not the only form of individual-incentive plan. In fact, it is only the second most commonly used plan. Merit raises based on individual job performance constitute the most frequently used incentive plan. Under such a system, an employee's salary is adjusted regularly, based on his performance during a preceding time period — usually six to twelve months. Performance is measured by a superior's evaluation.

Many studies have pointed out that both piece-rate pay systems and merit-raise pay systems are often ineffective in their attempts to tie pay to performance. Neither can tie individual pay perfectly to performance. Still, compared with straight hourly pay and systems in which raises are not merit based, they do achieve some success in relating pay to performance. Thus, it is possible to compare situations where employees are working under piece-rate or merit-raise conditions with situations where employees are paid on fixed-rate systems and find out something about the effect on performance of relating pay to performance.

Taylor's (1911) early work provides one of the first examples of how employee motivation can be changed by tying pay more closely to performance. Taylor took a "thrifty Dutch-man" who was shoveling pig iron, redesigned his job, and put him on a piece-rate plan that offered more money if he shoveled more pig iron. Taylor's subject responded with a several hundred percent increase in productivity. Part of this increase seemed due to the pay-incentive system, thus providing dramatic evidence that tying pay to performance can affect motivation.

A 1945 government survey of 514 wage-incentive plans in the United States showed that the change to these plans had resulted in average production increases of 39 percent and average unit labor cost reductions of 11.6 percent. Viteles (1953) cites the Murray Corporation as an example of what can happen when a company switches from a fixed-wage payment system to an individual-incentive plan; the change led quickly to average plantwide production gains of 16 percent. Furthermore, accident rates fell, and cooperation with supervisors increased.

Many such cases have been reported, but all of them suffer from the same methodological flaw that is present in Taylor's (1911) original experiment. In addition to changing the Dutch-man's pay, Taylor changed a number of other factors (for example, how he did the work and the shape of his shovel). In the Murray Corporation, the introduction of wage incentives was accompanied by the formation of new standards (which meant new work procedures), by changes in shifts and length of work week, and by a change in union/management relations. Thus, it is impossible to attribute the changes in productivity solely to the changes in the wage plan. The same criticism can be made of most of the studies of companies that have changed from fixed-wage systems to incentive-pay systems. As Viteles states, "The installation of a wage incentive plan is generally accompanied by other changes in working conditions, personnel policies, and practices which are frequently major in character" (1953, p. 29).

Fortunately, a few studies represent a methodological improvement over the type discussed above. These studies made an effort to see that only the pay system was changed during the period studied. Some even included a control group in which nothing was changed.

In the Western Electric studies (Roethlisberger & Dickson, 1939), one of the first of many experimental manipulations applied to workers in the relay-assembly test room was the installation of a piece-rate incentive plan. It was actually a group plan, but because of the small size of the group individual pay was closely related to individual performance. Following the installation of this plan, production went up about 16 percent.

After the researchers found that in the relay-assembly test room they had obtained an increase in productivity that could not be attributed to any one of the changes they had instituted, they decided to conduct some additional studies to isolate the cause of the increased productivity. To do this, they set up a mica-splitting test room and a second relay-assembly test room. The second relay-assembly test room was designed to test the hypothesis that the results obtained in the first relay-assembly test room were due to economic causes. In this room only the method of payment was changed; the workers were put on a piece-rate payment plan. This resulted in a 12.2 percent increase in production. Although this increase was not as large as that in the original room, it suggests that a considerable amount of the increased productivity found in the original room was due to the change in the pay system. More important, it provides evidence that tying pay more closely to performance can result in increased productivity.

Wyatt (1934) reported a study in which he switched employees from a fixed weekly pay system to a competitive bonus system designed to relate pay to individual productivity. The immediate effect of introducing the bonus system was a production increase of 46 percent, a rate that was maintained throughout a 15-week period. A piece-rate system was then introduced, which resulted in a further increase in output of 30 percent. This new level of production was maintained throughout the remaining 12 weeks of the study.

In another well-controlled study, Burnett (1925) had four subjects work on a cross-stitching task for eight weeks, during which they were paid an hourly rate. Later, the subjects worked for five weeks on a piece rate that was based on their hourly output. Nothing was changed between the work periods except the method of payment. The immediate effect of adopting the piece rate was an average increase in output of 7.2 percent. This rose to 18 percent for the third week and 20.2 percent for the fourth week. During the last two weeks, production fell off slightly, but the results clearly suggested that tying pay more closely to performance did bring about the substantial increase in productivity during the five-week experimental period.

In a more recent series of studies among psychotics in a mental hospital, Ayllon and Azrin (1965) tested the effects of tying token rewards to certain kinds of behavior (for example, serving meals or doing clerical work). The patients could use the tokens to buy certain privileges around the hospital and commodities at the hospital commissary. This well-designed series of studies presents strong evidence that, by relating the giving of tokens to certain kinds of work behavior, the frequency with which patients will volunteer to do work in a mental hospital can be dramatically increased. Figure 6.1 shows how effective the token rewards were in influencing work behavior. During days 1 to 20, when the receipt of tokens was contingent on performance, the 44 patients worked a collective total of 45 hours a day. The first day that the token/performance contingency was removed, the amount of work fell to about 35 hours. On the third day, it went down to about 20 hours; by day 36 of the experiment, amount of work had dropped to 1 hour per day. When the token rewards were again made contingent on performance (day 41), the time spent productively immediately increased to 45 hours a day and stayed there during the next 20 days.

Atkinson and Reitman (1956) did an experiment with two conditions. In the first condition, subjects were given achievement-arousing instructions for performing a task but were offered no financial reward. In the second condition, subjects were given the same achievement-arousing instructions and were told that a $5 prize would be awarded for the best performance. The results showed that the offer of a financial reward led to increased performance in general, especially among people who had low achievement motivation. People who had high achievement motivation worked hard without the offer of a financial reward.

Figure 6.1. The Total Number of Hours of the
Onward Performance by a Group of 44 Patients.

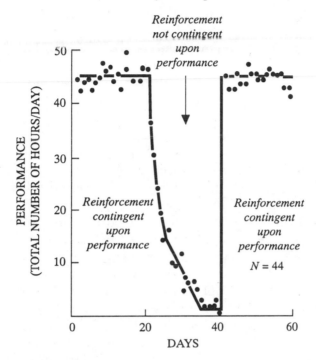

*Reinforcement
not contingent
upon
performance*

*Reinforcement
contingent
upon
performance*

*Reinforcement
contingent
upon
performance*

N = 44

PERFORMANCE
(TOTAL NUMBER OF HOURS/DAY)

DAYS

Source: From Ayllon, T., & Azrin, N. H. The measurement and reinforcement of behavior of psychotics. *Journal of Experimental Analysis of Behavior,*
1965, *8,* 357–383. Copyright © 1965 by the Society for the Experimental Analysis of Behavior, Inc. Reprinted by permission. Additional information and related
research can be found in *The Token Economy: A Motivational System for Therapy and
Rehabilitation* by T. Ayllon and N. H. Azrin, Appleton-Century-Crofts, 1968.

To summarize, a substantial amount of evidence supports
the prediction of our motivation model that tying individual performance to financial rewards results in increased performance.
This evidence comes from many different kinds of studies. Unfortunately, much of it comes from studies of poor quality; but
some of it comes from rather carefully controlled laboratory experiments. Even the most conservative results from these studies
seem to suggest that individual-incentive plans can increase
productivity by 10 to 20 percent.

Group and Organization Subunit Incentive Plans

Two studies have compared the effectiveness of individual-incentive plans and group-incentive plans. Marriott (1949) studied the relationship between the size of the work group and the output of male production workers on group-incentive plans in two British factories. In both factories, he found a general tendency for production to decrease as the size of the group increased. He also reported that workers who were paid on an individual-incentive basis were higher producers on the average than workers in even the smallest work group. Babchuk and Goode (1951) studied a sales group that developed its own group-incentive system, which encouraged cooperation and improved the interpersonal relationships in the group.

These two studies illustrate the positive and negative features of group-incentive plans. As the Marriott study points out, these plans often do not lead to as high productivity as individual plans, although they generally are better at motivating productivity than pay plans that do not relate pay to productivity. Campbell (1952) has suggested one explanation for this. Like Marriott, he found lower productivity in larger groups, but he also found that in larger groups employees saw less relationship between their pay and their performance. In large groups, pay is clearly not as closely tied to individual performance as in small groups or individual plans. Thus, group plans would be expected to have less motivation value than individual plans, since they lead to lower performance→pay subjective probabilities. On the other hand, group plans can encourage cooperation and eliminate some of the problems—such as restrictive norms and dysfunctional competition—that are associated with incentive plans. Because of these strengths, group plans are preferred in situations in which cooperation among employees is important and should be rewarded and in which individual performance is very difficult to measure.

Companywide Incentive Plans

A substantial number of companywide incentive plans have been tried. Typically, they offer everyone in the company some form of extra payment based on a measure of organizational effectiveness. The key characteristic of these plans is that all employees holding similar jobs get the same bonus regardless of individual contribution. The measure of company effectiveness may be profitability, sales, or some other measure that reflects corporate success. In the best-known plan, the Scanlon Plan, a measure of labor cost relative to productivity is often used.

The Scanlon Plan is undoubtedly the best researched of the companywide incentive plans. Puckett (1958) studied the impact of the plan in nine firms and reported increases in productivity that are extremely impressive. In the first year under the plan, productivity increased an average of 22.5 percent. In the second year, productivity increased an average of 23.7 percent over the base period. Puckett discredits the common criticism that the plan is successful only in firms experiencing severe economic problems. He points out that several of the companies he studied were already quite profitable, and the plan made them still more successful. He is less convincing in answering the criticism that the plan works only in small companies. He found no relationship between company size and the success of the plan for the firms he studied, but his sample covered a very limited size range. The largest organization had under 1200 employees, which is hardly large enough to prove that the Scanlon Plan can work as well in large organizations as in small ones. In fact, the overall record of the Scanlon Plan shows that it has seldom been tried in large firms. The largest firms that have tried the plan employ approximately 7200 people; most of the firms employ fewer than 1000 people (Schultz, 1958).

The Lincoln Electric Plan (Lincoln, 1951) represents an interesting attempt to combine the advantages of an individual plan with those of a companywide plan. The total amount of money given as bonus is determined by the profitability of the company, but the amount each individual receives is based on a rating of his performance. Thus, someone could receive no bonus, even though the company had a good ear, and someone could receive a large bonus in a mediocre year. The plan tries to relate individual performance more closely to individual pay while encouraging employees to work together in a cooperative spirit to increase the total amount of bonus money. As with most companywide incentive plans, it is difficult to establish how successful this one has been. Lincoln (1951) presents considerable evidence that the plan has been very successful. His data show that, in 1949, Lincoln Electric Company had sales of over $25,000 per employee, while the industry average was less than $15,000. The data also show that sales per employee have steadily risen since the plan was installed. Based on this and other evidence, Lincoln argues that the plan has greatly increased productivity.

Since measures of organization success vary in the degree to which they are under the control of the members of the organization, the choice of measure is important. For example, the Scanlon Plan uses a labor-cost figure rather than profits, since cost is more under the control of the employees; hence, there is a much closer relationship between employee behavior and employee pay. Organization size can also be an important determinant of the effect of companywide plans. The larger the company, the greater the separation between individual performance and company performance. In one sense, companywide plans exaggerate the advantages and disadvantages inherent in group-based plans; that is, they facilitate cooperation among organization members more than group plans, but they break down even further the connection between performance and pay. For several reasons it is difficult to make any strong statements about how effective various companywide incentive systems have been. First, in addition to changing the payment system, most of the plans involve a number of other changes. Thus, we cannot tell what role, if any, changes in the payment system have played in changes in organizational effectiveness. When a company adopts the Scanlon Plan or the Lincoln Electric Plan, it is adopting not a method of wage payment but a philosophy of management, one part of which is concerned with wages. Second, where companies have changed to companywide plans, it has been impossible to establish adequate control groups; thus, it is impossible to prove that increased effectiveness is due to any of the changes that have been made. However, this criticism is not too damaging to those studies that have found large and consistent increases in organizational effectiveness, since these increases are not likely to be mere chance phenomena.

Unintended Consequences
of Tying Rewards to Performance

Several case studies have documented the negative side effects of tying promotion to performance, which include lack of cooperation among peers competing for the same promotion, trying to make the competition look bad, and individuals trying to make their own performance look better than it actually is. The latter of these can be accomplished by individuals either presenting invalid data to the system designed to measure their performance or performing well in only those aspects of their performance that are measured. This can be very dysfunctional if it means neglecting good performance in an area that is difficult to measure but that is important for the effectiveness of the organization. Promotion on the basis of performance is especially likely to lead to dysfunctional side effects when it involves two or more individuals competing for a single job. Severe problems are caused when the individuals who are competing have interdependent jobs (jobs that require cooperation).

Pay is less often a reward that one person gets at the expense of another, since many people can and often do get pay increases in organizations. Still, much evidence shows that certain kinds of pay-incentive plans cause a number of side effects. Like promotion systems, pay plans can lead to (1) neglecting certain aspects of performance, (2) reporting invalid data, and (3) perceiving a relationship between good performance and negative outcomes.

Neglecting Aspects of Performance

Reward systems motivate employees to perform well in those aspects of their jobs that are measured by the performance-evaluation system. The problem is that the evaluation system doesn't always measure all the behaviors that need to be performed. The results are that those behaviors that aren't measured tend to be ignored or performed poorly. Berliner (1961) has described the situation faced by plant managers in the Soviet Union who are placed on a production-based pay-incentive plan and given unreasonably high production goals on the assumption that this is best for the overall economy.

> . . . the incentives that motivate managers to strive
> for the fulfillment of their production targets are
> the same incentives that motivate them to evade
> the regulations of the planning system. Because of
> the tightness of the supply system . . . managers are
> compelled to defend their enterprise's position by
> overordering supplies, by hoarding materials and
> equipment, and by employing expediters whose
> function is to keep the enterprise supplied with
> materials at all costs, legal or otherwise [p. 369].

Cohen (1966), in discussing the Soviet situation, points out that the dysfunctional consequences that occur because of the managers' rigid obsession with meeting their production goals should not be taken as evidence that the American system is necessarily better. The American system stimulates its own form of societally dysfunctional behavior. According to Cohen, "the American system is admirably contrived to encourage deviance on an enormous scale in the area of merchandising" (p. 83). The reason is simply that the American control and reward systems are based not on productivity but on profits.

Babchuk and Goode (1951) have provided an interesting case study that highlights how pay systems can cause employees to behave dysfunctionally. They studied a selling unit in a department store where a pay-incentive plan was introduced on the basis of employee sales volume. Total sales initially increased but in a way that was not functional as far as the long-term goals of the organization were concerned. Considerable "sales grabbing" and "tying up the trade" occurred as well as a general neglect of such unrewarded and unmeasured functions as stock work and arranging merchandise for displays.

Pay-incentive systems frequently fail to motivate cooperative behavior, even when it contributes to organizational effectiveness. Pay plans often are based on measures of individual productivity or performance that do not reflect how much cooperative behavior has taken place. For example, pay plans typically fail to reward the employee who loans his co-worker a needed tool because it is crucial that the other worker get his job done. In fact, if this action causes the employee's production to suffer, he may even lose money. Pay plans often fail to reward the manager who shuts down his production line for maintenance at the time when it is optimal from the point of view of the rest of the organization.

Invalid Data

Reward systems often encourage the production of two kinds of invalid data: invalid data about what can be done, and invalid data about what has been done. The research on budgets and on piece-rate payment systems provides a number of good examples of situations in which organizations are given invalid data about what can be done. To understand how and why invalid data occurs, it is worth reviewing a few of the case studies that have illustrated this phenomenon.

Whyte (1955) has provided some graphic case examples of how individuals distort the data fed into production-measuring systems. Most of Whyte's examples are cases in which individuals under pay-incentive systems distort data about the kind of production that is possible on a given job. The following quote illustrates one worker's attitude toward the measurement system and the men who run it.

> ". . . you got to outwit that son-of-a-bitch! You got to use your noodle while you're working, and think your work out ahead as you go along! You got to add in movements you know you ain't going to make when you're running the job! Remember, if you don't screw them, they're going to screw you! . . . Every movement counts! . . .
>
> "Remember those bastards are paid to screw you," said Starkey. "And that's all they got to think about. They'll stay up half the night figuring out how to beat you out of a dime. They figure you're

going to try to fool them, so they make allowances for that. They set the prices low enough to allow for what you do."

"Well, then, what the hell chance have I got?" asked Tennessee.

"It's up to you to figure out how to fool them more than they allow for," said Starkey.

". . . When the time-study man came around, I set the speed at 180. I knew damn well he would ask me to push it up, so I started low enough. He finally pushed me up to 445, and I ran the job later at 610. If I'd started out at 445, they'd have timed it at 610. Then I got him on the reaming, too. I ran the reamer for him at 130 speed and .025 feed. He asked me if I couldn't run the reamer any faster than that, and I told him I had to run the reamer slow to keep the hole size. I showed him two pieces with over-size holes that the day man ran. I picked them out for the occasion! But later on I ran the reamer at 610 speed and .018 feed, same as the drill. So I didn't have to change gears. And then there was a burring operation on the job too. For the time-study man I burred each piece after I drilled and reamed, and I ran the burring tool by automatic feed. But afterwards, I let the burring go till I drilled 25 pieces or so; and I just touched them up a little by holding them under the burring tool" [pp. 15–16].*

Gardner (1945) has also pointed out that employees often give invalid data in industry and provides an example of how it can occur.

In one case, a group who worked together in as-sembling a complicated and large-sized steel frame-

work worked out a system to be used only when
the rate setter was present. They found that by
tightening certain bolts first, the frame would be
slightly sprung and all the other bolts would bind
and be very difficult to tighten. When the rate setter
was not present, they followed a different sequence
and the work went much faster [pp. 164–165].

Argyris (1951, 1964), Hofstede (1967), and others have
pointed out that employees often provide misleading data when
they are asked to give budgetary estimates. Not surprisingly,
they usually tend to ask for much larger amounts than they need.
On the other hand, when only a low budget estimate will get
a project approved, a low estimate is submitted (for example,
under some program, planning, and budgeting systems; see
Lyden & Miller, 1968). Managers submit high budget requests
because they realize their requests will be cut. The bargaining
process they go through is similar to the one that goes on between the time-study man and the worker who is on a piece-
rate plan. The time-study man and the manager's superior both
try to get valid data about what is possible in the future, and
the employees who are subject to the control system often give
invalid data and try to get as favorable a standard, or budget,
as they can.

There are also many cases in which employees have fed
control systems invalid information about the work that has been
done. Roethlisberger and Dickson (1939), in their classic study
of the bank wiring room, point out how employees can control
the kinds of production reports given by their work group. In
this case, the employees were on a pay-incentive plan and wanted
to show a consistent daily production figure. They did this by
not reporting what they produced on days when production was
high and by overstating their production on days when production was low.

Research on giving blood provides a dramatic example
of individuals' falsifying data to obtain money (Titmus, 1971).
In the United States, many commercial blood banks pay donors
for the blood they give. In large cities, there is a high incidence
of patients contracting hepatitis after receiving transfusions. The

research shows that the incidence of hepatitis is much higher among patients receiving commercial blood than among those receiving free blood. Apparently, the blood of paid donors is more likely to be infected than the blood of voluntary donors. Blood banks have to rely on their donors to give accurate medical histories to prevent the collection of infected blood. As Titmus points out:

> . . . it has been repeatedly shown that paid donors — and especially poor donors badly in need of money — are, on the average and compared with voluntary donors, relatives, and friends, more reluctant and less likely to reveal a full medical history and to provide information about recent contacts with infectious disease, recent innoculations, and about their diets, drinking, and drug habits that would disqualify them as donors [p. 151].

Perceiving Good Performance Related to Negative Outcomes

Perhaps the best example of how pay systems can affect the relationship between performance and other outcomes is provided by the research on piece-rate pay plans. There is considerable evidence that restriction of output often results when workers are placed on piece-rate plans because the incentive plans cause a number of negative outcomes to be associated with good performance. In the Western Electric studies (Roethlisberger & Dickson, 1939), a rigidly enforced policy of output restriction was discovered. Workers who exceeded the quota could expect to receive a "bing" (punch on the arm) and to be rejected and degraded by the other members of the group. More recent studies (Collins, Dalton, & Roy, 1946; Dalton, 1948; Dyson, 1956; Roy, 1952; Whyte, 1955) have provided additional evidence to support the point that restriction is widespread and that it comes about because negative consequences such as social rejection and interpersonal abuse are tied to high performance.

Several studies have tried to determine why norms against high productivity develop and why negative social outcomes are tied to performing well (Hickson, 1961; Viteles, 1953). Data from these studies suggest that workers may feel that more productivity will lead to negative economic consequences. In one study, 30 percent of the workers felt that high production would lead to higher production quotas, 11 percent felt that it would result in lower piece rates, and a smaller percentage thought that higher productivity would result in no change in wages. Many workers (23 percent) felt that high productivity would be unpopular with other workers. A later study by the Opinion Research Corporation (1949) showed that workers also feared they might work themselves out of a job if they responded to wage-incentive plans by producing a great deal. Overall, 50 percent of one group of workers felt that increased output would be bad for them.

Sociologist Donald Roy's description of his experiences while working on a piece-rate job reflects how group pressure operates, and suggests that fear of rate changes is an important basis for production restriction:

> From my first to my last day at the plant I was subject to warnings and predictions concerning price cuts. Pressure was heaviest from Joe Mucha, day man on my machine, who shared my job repertoire and kept a close eye on my production. On November 14, the day after my first attained quota, Joe Mucha advised:
> "Don't let it go over $1.25 an hour, or the time-study man will be right down here! And they don't waste time either! They watch the records like a hawk! I got ahead, so I took it easy for a couple of hours."
> Joe told me that I had made $10.01 yesterday and warned me not to go over $1.25 an hour. He told me to figure the setups and the time on each operation very carefully so that I would not total over $10.25 in any one day.
> Jack Starkey spoke to me after Joe left. "What's the matter? Are you trying to upset the applecart?"

Jack explained in a friendly manner that
$10.50 was too much to turn in, even on an old
job. "The turret-lathe man can turn in $1.35 . . .
but their rate is 90 cents, and ours 85 cents."

Jack warned me that the Methods Department could lower their prices on any job, old or
new, by changing the fixture slightly or changing
the size of the drill. According to Jack, a couple
of operators (first and second shift on the same drill)
got to competing with each other to see how much
they could turn in. They got up to $1.65 an hour
and the price was cut in half. And from then on
they had to run that job themselves, as none of the
other operators would accept the job [in Whyte,
1955, p. 23].

One explanation of why production restriction and gold-
bricking develop is presented in Figure 6.2. It suggests that when
a piece-rate incentive plan is installed in a situation where mistrust exists between management and employees, the employees
will begin to believe that high productivity will lead to negative
economic consequences. This, in turn, will (1) lead to the creation of informal pressure groups in which employees seek to protect their economic interests by using social means to control
other employees' production and (2) destroy any perception that
high production leads to high pay. The net result is that the
individual worker will see more negative than positive outcomes
associated with high productivity and consequently will restrict
his production (Lawler, 1971).

This argument suggests that group pressures develop because of the economic structure. This does not mean that social sanctions are not real and important causes of the restriction in themselves. It merely suggests that they have an economic
basis and that they are likely to appear only when certain economic realities and beliefs exist.

Many of the side effects associated with tying rewards to
performance do not appear when rewards are distributed on the
basis of group or companywide performance. In these cases, the

Figure 6.2. Model of the Determinants of Production Restriction.

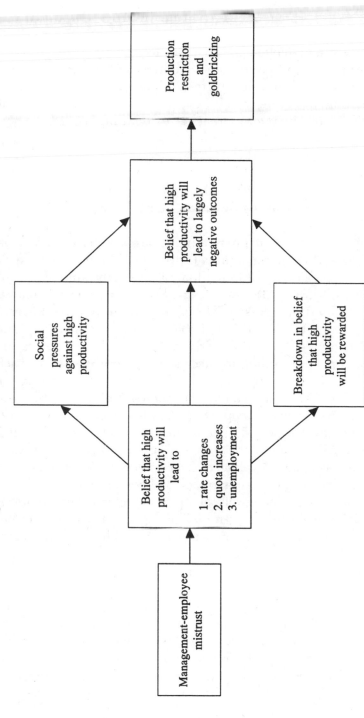

Source: From *Pay and Organizational Effectiveness: A Psychological View* by E. E. Lawler. Copyright © 1971 by McGraw-Hill Book Company. Used by permission of the publisher.

opposite situation often prevails. Norms develop that favor good performance, and positive social outcomes become associated with good performance. Further, cooperation is encouraged rather than discouraged. However, as we shall see next in our discussion of different approaches to relating rewards to performance, no approach is without its disadvantages, including group and companywide plans.

Evaluating the Different Approaches to Relating Rewards to Performance

The various approaches to relating rewards to performance can be classified according to three factors: (1) whether the rewards are given on a group or individual basis, (2) the kind of reward that is given, and (3) how performance is measured. One researcher used this classification system in evaluating different pay systems (Lawler, 1971). Table 6.1 lists the major types of pay-incentive plans and provides a general effectiveness rating for each plan according to three separate criteria. First, each plan is evaluated in terms of how effective it is in creating the perception that pay is tied to performance. This rating indicates the degree to which the approach actually ties pay closely to performance over a period of time and the degree to which employees believe that higher pay will follow good performance. Second, each plan is evaluated in terms of how well it minimizes the perceived negative consequences of good performance. This criterion refers to how well the approach eliminates situations in which social ostracism and other negative consequences become associated with good performance. Third, each plan is evaluated in terms of whether it contributes to the perception that important rewards other than pay (for example, recognition and acceptance) stem from good performance. The ratings potentially range from +3 to −3, with +3 indicating that the plan has generally worked very well in terms of the criterion, and −3 indicating that the plan has not worked well. A rating of 0 indicates that the plan has generally been neutral or average.

A number of trends appear in the ratings presented in Table 6.1. Looking at the criterion of tying pay to performance,

Table 6.1. Ratings of Various Pay-Incentive Plans.

Type of plan		Performance measure	Tie pay to performance	Minimize negative side effects	Tie other rewards to performance
Salary reward	Individual plan	Productivity	+2	0	0
		Cost-effectiveness	+1	0	0
		Superiors' rating	+1	0	+1
	Group	Productivity	+1	0	+1
		Cost-effectiveness	+1	0	+1
		Superiors' rating	+1	0	+1
	Organizationwide	Productivity	+1	0	+1
		Cost-effectiveness	+1	0	+1
		Profits	0	0	+1
Bonus	Individual plan	Productivity	+3	−2	0
		Cost-effectiveness	+2	−1	0
		Superiors' rating	+2	−1	+1
	Group	Productivity	+3	0	+1
		Cost-effectiveness	+2	0	+1
		Superiors' rating	+2	0	+1
	Organizationwide	Productivity	+3	0	+1
		Cost-effectiveness	+2	0	+1
		Profits	+1	0	+1

Source: From *Pay and Organizational Effectiveness: A Psychological View* by E. E. Lawler. Copyright © 1971 by McGraw-Hill Book Company. Used by permission of the publisher.

we see that individual plans are rated highest, group plans are next highest, and organizationwide plans are lowest. This reflects the fact that in group plans to some extent and in organizationwide plans to a great extent an individual's pay is not directly a function of his own performance. In these situations, an individual's pay is influenced very strongly by the behavior of others with whom he works and, if the payment is based on profits, by external market conditions.

Bonus plans are generally rated higher on the first criterion than are salary increase plans. Under bonus plans, a person's pay may vary sharply from year to year in accordance with his most recent performance, which does not usually happen with salary increase programs. Organizations seldom cut anyone's salary; as a result, pay under a salary increase plan reflects not just recent performance but performance over a number of years. Consequently, pay is not seen to be closely related to present behavior. On the other hand, bonuses typically depend on recent behavior; if someone performs poorly, it will show up immediately in his pay. Thus, a person under a bonus plan cannot coast for a year and still be highly paid, as he can be under the typical salary increase plan.

Finally, approaches that use objective measures of performance are rated higher on the first criterion than are those that use subjective measures. In general, objective measures enjoy higher credibility; that is, employees will often grant the validity of an objective measure, such as sales volume or units produced, when they will not accept a superior's rating. Thus, when pay or any reward is tied to objective measures, it is usually clear to employees that pay is determined by their performance. Also, objective measures are often public criteria; when pay is tied to these measures, the relationship is much more visible than when it is tied to a subjective, nonverifiable measure, such as a superior's rating. Overall, then, individually based bonus plans that rely on objective measures produce the strongest perceived connection between pay and performance.

Ratings on the ability of pay programs to minimize the perceived negative consequences of good performance show that most plans are neutral on this criterion. That is, they neither contribute to the appearance of negative consequences nor help to eliminate any that might be present. Individual bonus plans do receive a minus rating on this criterion, which reflects the fact that piece-rate plans often lead to situations in which social rejection, firing, and running out of work are perceived by individuals to result from good performance. The perceived negative consequences of good performance may cancel out the positive motivational force that piece-rate plans typically generate by tying pay closely to performance.

The final criterion for pay plans, tying rewards other than

pay to performance, generally has higher ratings for group and organizationwide plans than for individual plans. Under group and organizationwide plans, it is generally to the advantage of everyone for an individual to work effectively. Thus, the good performer is much more likely to be encouraged by his fellow workers to perform well than he would be in situations where good performance might harm others.

It should be clear from this short review that no one pay plan represents a panacea for an organization's motivation problems, since no one type of pay program is strong in all areas. The same is true for any reward system that ties rewards to performance; each one has its strengths and weaknesses. Table 6.1 could just as well have evaluated promotion systems or systems that distribute status symbols on the basis of performance. The same strengths and weaknesses would appear. If the rewards are given on a group basis, the connection between individual behavior and performance is weakened; similarly, if the performance measure is not objective, the connection is weakened. Giving extrinsic rewards on an individual basis typically produces negative side effects, whereas giving them on a group basis can generate social support and cooperation. It really doesn't matter what extrinsic reward is involved as long as it is valued by its potential recipients.

Which Rewards Should Be Tied to Performance?

If an organization decides to motivate good performance by the use of extrinsic rewards, it faces the problem of which reward or rewards to use. Which rewards are likely to be most effective in motivating performance? A partial answer to this question was given in the discussion of outcome importance in Chapter 2, where it was stated that the more important the outcome, the more effective it can be in motivating performance. As we have seen, research on reward importance suggests that promotion and pay are the two most important extrinsic rewards that most organizations have to offer. However, the research also suggests that there are large individual differences in the degree to which these rewards are valued. For some people money is not very important, and for some people promotion is something to be avoided. Thus, in deciding which rewards to use, an organization has to consider individual differences or it may end up trying to motivate people with rewards they do not value. Organizations may have to take a diagnostic stance with respect to their members; that is, they may have to try to determine which rewards are important to which members and then structure the rewards accordingly. Since organizations have relatively little control over how important extrinsic rewards are to people, they must fit the system of motivation to their employees.

Both pay and promotion have certain advantages and disadvantages as rewards. Using pay as a reward can be very expensive, since large amounts of money are often needed to motivate people. However, pay also has some advantages as a reward: it can be given on a group basis or an individual basis, and it can be given in widely different amounts. Unfortunately, promotion is not such a flexible reward. It is difficult to give promotions on anything but an individual basis. Also, promotion can be given only when an opening occurs in an existing position or a new position is created, although promotion can be held out as an incentive at all times. Thus, an organization that relies on promotion as its major reward can get into difficulty because of its poor flexibility.

It is often difficult to tie promotion closely to performance because of the many situational factors that interfere with a direct performance-promotion system. For example, organizations often need to promote people on the basis of potential rather than on the basis of past performance. There are situations in which performance in lower-level jobs may not be a good indication of performance in a higher-level job. In this case it may be foolish for the organization to promote the best performers, since others may do the job better. This situation often occurs in research and development labs where the positions involved are research scientist and manager; the best scientists often don't make the best managers.

Pay and promotion are not the only rewards that can be used to motivate performance. Certain status symbols and prizes (such as vacations and even trading stamps) can be tied to good performance, as can special privileges (such as leaving early). In addition, superiors can give recognition and greater job security to those who perform well. The effectiveness of any of these rewards, of course, depends on how important they are and whether they can be tied to performance. The problem with many of these rewards is that they are not important to many people and they are difficult to relate to performance.

Performance can also be motivated by punishment. Significant negative outcomes can be attached to poor performance, making it less attractive than good performance. If dismissal is believed to result from poor performance, it may be a significant motivator. However, the threat of dismissal produces dysfunctional effects. For example, many managers develop "just-in-case files" and "cover-your-ass files" to protect them against the charge that they have performed poorly. The threat of dismissal can produce other self-protective and defensive behaviors that are not necessarily functional (for example, risk-avoidance). Employees have been known to say "you can't be fired for what you don't do but you sure can for what you do." In addition, punishment tells the person only what not to do, it doesn't indicate what should be done.

Punishments such as reprimands and criticism from superiors can also be tied to poor performance in the hope of making it unattractive. Again, this is only effective if the employee assigns a negative valence to reprimands and criticisms, which is often not the case. Situations can develop in which these punishments have a positive valence. For example, in certain work groups, being criticized by the boss can lead to increased status in the work group if the group has an antimanagement value system.

Perhaps the only safe conclusion about which rewards and punishments should be used is that it depends on the situation. It makes sense to use only those rewards and punishments that are important to the people in the organization and that can be tied to performance. The use of any other rewards and punishments will simply be a waste of time and effort. It may not even be advisable to use all of those that are important, since they may lead to negative side effects or they may be too expensive. The point remains, however, that if an organization wants to motivate performance it must find those rewards and/or punishments that are important and that can be clearly tied to performance.

How Should Performance Be Evaluated?

The importance of the performance-evaluation process to the success of any extrinsic-reward system cannot be stressed strongly enough. An organization must have an effective performance-appraisal system if it is to use extrinsic rewards to motivate performance. For any reward to be a motivator, it must be tied to performance. For this to happen, the measures of performance must meet a number of criteria: (1) they must respond to the behavior of the individual; (2) they must include all the behavior that needs to be performed; (3) they must be perceived by the people in the organization as valid measures of their behavior; and (4) they must involve goals that people feel are obtainable.

A number of different measures are used to evaluate performance. Many organizations appraise their employees by rating them on various personality traits (for example, responsibility, attitude, cooperativeness). Needless to say, this is a very subjective process and is likely to lead to defensive reactions on the part of the person being appraised. When a person is told that he has been rated low in responsibility, his natural reaction is to think of all the times he behaved in a responsible manner and to present these to the evaluator. This reaction is not likely to produce behavior change or to increase motivation. The problem with trait rating is that traits are not sufficiently tied to concrete behavior. Telling a person that if he is responsible he will receive a pay raise does not tell him how he needs to behave. Further, any feedback the person receives based on that rating tends not to have a positive effect. Much research shows that evaluative, nonbehaviorally related feedback tends to produce defensive behavior and does not motivate good performance.

Trait ratings are also difficult to make and tend to produce invalid data. Superiors tend to dislike rating their subordinates on traits such as responsibility, and they tend to do it poorly

(Campbell, Dunnette, Lawler & Weick, 1970). They have trouble defining and discriminating among the various traits; as a result, the ratings produced are often invalid and difficult to explain.

Many organizations simply ask superiors to give a single rating of overall job performance for each subordinate. Such ratings can be done validly by many superiors. Evidence shows that separate raters agree when they assess the performance level of a given employee. Such ratings have additional advantages: (1) an employee is compared with his peers, and thus relative standing is apparent; (2) a global rating is derived from a number of behaviors and thus is rather inclusive; and (3) superiors are willing to make such ratings. Because of these advantages, global ratings are often used in organizations as a basis for making raise and promotion decisions. However, they are poor from a motivational point of view because they fail to specify what behavior constitutes good performance. They are also a poor source of feedback because they don't tell the individual in behavioral terms what he has done right or wrong.

Many management theorists have recommended evaluating employees in terms of specific objectives (for example, see Meyer, Kay, & French, 1965; Drucker, 1954; Odiorne, 1965). In this process (sometimes called "management by objectives" or M.B.O.), the superior and subordinate jointly decide on a set of goals and on how performance against these goals will be measured. When the time for the appraisal comes, both the superior and the subordinate are in a good position to evaluate the subordinate's performance. Meyer et al. (1965) found that only under an objectives-oriented system does performance appraisal lead to increased motivation and improved performance. Superiors are better able to rate whether subordinates did or didn't perform a particular behavior, such as reaching a sales goal or handling returned merchandise well, than how responsible a person is. Thus, these performance ratings are based on more explicit and objective criteria and are more valid and reliable than the performance ratings based on personality traits. Since it is possible to talk about specific behaviors, subordinates tend to be less defensive and are better able to hear any criticisms of their performance. Finally, discussing specific behaviors and objectives can contribute to a better understanding between the superior and the subordinate about the nature of the subordinate's job.

Difficulty of Goals

When the performance-evaluation process involves setting goals or standards, the perceived difficulty of the goals is very important and has a strong impact on employee motivation. Achievement motivation is highest on tasks that participants see as moderately difficult (Atkinson, 1964). Apparently, when people see themselves as having approximately a 50-50 chance of performing a task successfully, good performance on the task becomes very attractive to them because it becomes associated with feelings of achievement and competence. This finding indicates that standards and goals seen as moderately difficult to achieve will produce the most intrinsic motivation. Thus, if achievement motivation is to be maximized, budgets, production standards, and other performance goals should be set so that employees have about a 50-50 chance of reaching them. According to our motivation model from Chapter 3, goals set much higher will appear to be too difficult to achieve, and people will abandon any hope of achieving them. If goals are set too low, they will not be seen as challenging, and intrinsic motivation will not come into play.

Subordinate Participation

Traditionally, the performance-appraisal process has been a superior-active, subordinate-passive situation (White & Barnes, 1971). The superior was supposed to evaluate the subordinate's performance and report his findings to the subordinate; the subordinate, on the other hand, was a passive but attentive listener who was supposed to find out about his performance from his supervisor. Since the classic article by McGregor (1957), this view of how the process should take place has been more frequently questioned. McGregor initiated the change by suggesting that the subordinate should have a more active role in the process. Recently, White and Barnes (1971) have suggested that appraisal become a two-way process, involving collaboration between the superior and the subordinate.

Why should the subordinate participate in the performance-appraisal process? A major part of the answer to this question can be found in the fact that most writers who have argued for participation have also argued for basing appraisals on specific objectives instead of personality traits. Participation is a necessity if meaningful motivating goals and objectives are to be set; it is not necessary for trait ratings. The subordinate-passive view is highly congruent with the trait-rating approach, since under this approach the subordinate can contribute little to his own appraisal. Thus, the argument for participation is tied to the argument that appraisals should be based on meaningful, mutually set goals. Much evidence shows that when subordinates are given the opportunity to participate in decisions, they are much more committed to those decisions. They feel responsible for the decisions, and they are motivated to see that the decisions work. Apparently, their self-esteem and feelings of competence become involved, and they feel bad if a decision they made turns out poorly. The same thing occurs when subordinates participate in setting their own goals. They feel a sense of ownership of the goals, and their feelings of self-esteem and competence are tied to achievement of the goals; as a result, they are motivated to achieve these goals.

Participation can also help establish meaningful, moderately difficult goals. Subordinates frequently have important information about the level at which the goals should be set. As pointed out previously, goal difficulty is a very important influence on motivation. There is always the danger that unilaterally set goals may be unrealistic because the superior simply lacks information about where they should be set.

Relationship of Appraisal to the Reward System

Based on their study of the performance-appraisal process, Meyer et al. (1965) argue that salary actions should be separated from the appraisal process because salary actions dominate all else in a discussion. These researchers found that it was impossible in the same meeting to talk meaningfully about salary and other factors such as development needs, past performance, and future goals. Their study highlights the major problem organizations face when using pay, or for that matter any important extrinsic reward, to motivate good performance. To be a significant motivator of performance, pay must be closely tied to performance, which can be done well only if a performance-appraisal program exists that measures performance validly and makes explicit the pay-performance connection. However, when pay decisions are tied to the performance-appraisal process, a number of negative consequences result. The subordinate's whole stance toward the process changes. Suddenly, the process is a contest in which he has to do his best to get a raise, be promoted, or whatever. He tries to make himself look good on those measures that will determine his pay, which often leads him to give invalid data about the performance he is capable of so that his objectives will be set low (Whyte, 1955). It may also lead him to produce invalid data about how he has performed so that he will look good. Clearly, the issue of how much to separate or combine the various appraisal functions is a crucial one.

Alternatives for combining or separating appraisal functions range from having all the functions built into one appraisal system and discussed at the same session, to having separate appraisal systems for each function. Either of these extremes seems unsatisfactory. When everything is combined in one session, many important issues are never discussed (for example, personal development and training). Having separate appraisal systems also seems impractical because the natural spillover from one to another is ignored. It might be possible, however, to have relatively separate discussion sessions for the different functions if the more salient functions were dealt with in the first session. That is, if a development session were held after the reward decisions had been made, it should be possible to talk about development needs without salary lurking too strongly in the background. This approach essentially recognizes the spillover and tries to minimize it. Even with this approach, there will be some spillover, producing side effects that can be eliminated only if no effort is made to relate rewards to performance as measured by the appraisal system.

When Should Extrinsic Rewards Be Used to Motivate Performance?

Obviously, under some conditions, extrinsic rewards probably shouldn't be used to motivate performance because the dysfunctional consequences of using them will outweigh the functional ones. Style of management is one important determinant of whether extrinsic rewards should be used to motivate performance. For many reasons, it is difficult to tie rewards and performance together in autocratic organizations. For example, one way of making the connection between pay and performance clear is to have open salary information. In an organization that generally adopts a democratic or participative approach to management, this practice should develop naturally. As employees begin to participate more in evaluating themselves and others, they will gradually come to know other employees' salaries as well as the general pay scale of the organization. However, given the structure of an autocratic organization, it is difficult to imagine a policy of openness in effect. Salary openness demands trust, open discussion of performance, and justification of salaries, none of which are likely to occur in an autocratically run organization. They are, however, an integral part of a democratic approach to management.

Participative performance appraisal is often a necessary practice if rewards are to be clearly tied to performance. It is also likely to fit well with a democratic but not with an autocratic style of management. Similarly, a high level of superior/subordinate trust is needed if effective performance appraisals are to be done. This trust can easily develop where a history of participative decision making exists. It is much more difficult to develop when autocratic management is practiced.

What kind of extrinsic-reward system will work in an organization run along autocratic lines? The evidence suggests that the more objectively based the plan is, the more likely it is to be successful. Plans that tie rewards to "hard" criteria (such as quantity of output, profits, or sales) and thus require a minimum level of trust stand a much better chance of succeeding in the autocratic organization than approaches that depend on joint goal setting and "soft" criteria (such as trait ratings). However, in most organizations there are a number of jobs that lack any hard criteria for measuring performance — jobs in which trust and participation are needed if extrinsic rewards are to act as an incentive. In these job situations, the more participative organization is in a better position to use extrinsic rewards to motivate performance than the autocratic organization. However, even in participative organizations, it isn't always possible to develop measures of performance that are inclusive and that are seen as valid by the individual and his manager. When this is true, it is impossible to relate rewards clearly to overall performance, and thus the giving of rewards differentially to employees will only cause bitterness, mistrust, and dysfunctional behavior.

Motivating people with extrinsic rewards can be very expensive, particularly if the extrinsic reward is money. An organization must be willing and able to give certain employees very large raises and/or bonuses if pay is to motivate performance. If a company cannot afford to do this or is not willing to, it should forget about using pay to motivate performance. Sometimes the nonfinancial costs of a pay-incentive plan can be great. For example, great stress can be placed on the interpersonal relationships in the organization because the superior has to evaluate his subordinates and differentially reward them. This can be dysfunctional if the superiors are not prepared to handle it well. Even if organizations are willing to absorb the financial and nonfinancial costs of relating pay to performance, pay may not be important to the employees and therefore will not be a possible source of motivation. For example, in one factory that employed large numbers of unmarried women, time off the job was more important than money; when the women were told they could go home after a certain amount of work was done, productivity increased dramatically. Several earlier attempts to use pay to motivate higher productivity had failed.

In summary, organizations should try to use extrinsic rewards as a motivator if the following practices can be put into effect: (1) important rewards can be given and tied to performance; (2) information can be made public about how the rewards are given; (3) superiors are willing to explain and support the reward system in discussions with their subordinates; (4) rewards can vary widely, depending on the individual's current performance; (5) performance can be objectively and inclusively measured; (6) meaningful performance-appraisal sessions can take place; and (7) high levels of trust exist or can be developed between superiors and subordinates. On the other hand, if many of these practices do not exist and cannot be initiated, it may be better not to use extrinsic rewards as motivators. Merely adopting some of the practices that are necessary if rewards are to be effective motivators (for example, openly stating reward levels), or putting all of the practices into an organization in which conditions are not right (for example, where good superior/subordinate relations do not exist) may only make the organization less effective and the employees more unhappy.

Satisfaction with Extrinsic Rewards

Many studies have considered both the determinants and consequences of satisfaction with extrinsic rewards. The research shows that because dissatisfaction with extrinsic rewards leads to many negative consequences, extrinsic-reward satisfaction is an important issue in any organization. Before we look at the consequences of dissatisfaction, let us consider the research on the determinants of satisfaction.

Determinants of Satisfaction

A model of the determinants of facet satisfaction was presented in Chapter 4 (Figure 4.3). It led to a number of predictions about who will be satisfied with their level of extrinsic rewards. The model showed that dissatisfaction is likely to occur among people who perceive themselves to have higher inputs than other people who receive the same level of reward. It also showed that, other things being equal, satisfaction will be directly related to the level of reward an individual receives. Of course, in practice other things tend not to be equal, and as a result extrinsic-reward satisfaction is not perfectly related to the amount of reward received. Some people have lower inputs and therefore are satisfied with lower levels of reward. Still, much research shows that extrinsic-reward satisfaction is strongly and directly related to the amount of reward received, especially when people with similar jobs and similar backgrounds are compared.

A recent study shows why pay satisfaction is strongly related to the amount of pay received (Lawler & Porter, 1963). The data from this study show that people's perceptions of what their pay actually is rise with an increase in pay, but their perceptions of what it should be do not necessarily rise. Figures 6.3 and 6.4 show perceptions of pay going up along with raises in income and perceptions of what pay should be remaining relatively stable. The decreasing distance between the lines in both figures shows that higher pay does bring higher satisfaction. A comparison of the two figures shows that highly paid, lower-level managers are more satisfied with their pay than are lowly paid, higher-level managers, even though the higher-level managers receive more pay.

Figure 6.3. Responses of Vice-Presidents to Questions Asking How Much They Are Paid and How Much They Should Be Paid as a Function of Actual Pay.

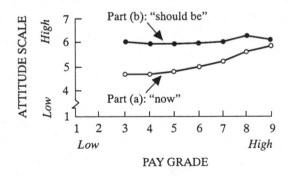

Source: From Lawler, E. E., & Porter, L. W. Perceptions regarding management compensation. Industrial Relations, 1963, 3, 46–47. Reprinted by permission of the publisher, Industrial Relations.

Figure 6.4. Responses of Lower-Level Managers to Questions
Asking How Much They Are Paid and How Much
They Should Be Paid as a Function of Actual Pay.

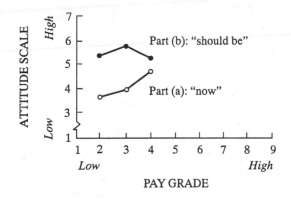

Source: From Lawler, E. E., & Porter, L. W. Perceptions regarding management compensation. *Industrial Relations,* 1963, *3,* 46–47. Reprinted by permission of the publisher, Industrial Relations.

Much research shows that unless they are rewarded more highly, people who have high inputs tend to be the most dissatisfied. For example, one study has shown that better performers feel they should receive more pay than poorer performers (Porter & Lawler, 1968). Figure 6.5 shows that managers who rate themselves as good performers feel that they should receive more pay than managers who rate themselves as poor performers. It also shows that both groups report they receive about the same pay, thus creating the situation in which the higher performers are more dissatisfied.

Other personal-input factors and certain job-demand factors have also been shown to be related to extrinsic-reward satisfaction. For example, a group of research studies shows that pay dissatisfaction will increase as job level increases unless pay increases greatly. Other studies have shown that pay dissatisfaction increases as education level increases (Klein & Maher, 1966). Overall, the research evidence on extrinsic-reward satisfaction is consistent with the model of facet satisfaction presented in Chapter 4. Satisfaction does seem to vary directly as a func-

Figure 6.5. Need-Fulfillment ("Is Now") and
Perceived-Equitable-Reward ("Should Be") Attitudes
for High and Low Performing Managers as Rated by Self.

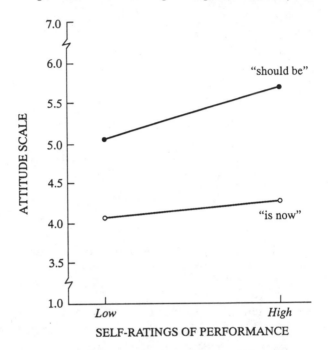

Source: From Porter, L. W., & Lawler, E. E. *Managerial Attitudes and Performance.* Copyright © 1968 by Richard D. Irwin, Inc. Reprinted by permission of the publisher, Irwin-Dorsey Press.

tion of a person's perceived inputs and outcomes; higher inputs lead to higher dissatisfaction unless accompanied by higher outcomes.

Consequences of Extrinsic-Reward Dissatisfaction

Chapter 4 discussed a number of consequences of job dissatisfaction. Many of the same points are applicable to extrinsic-reward satisfaction. It is clear from many research studies that extrinsic-reward dissatisfaction leads to the same negative effects as total job dissatisfaction. Figure 6.6 summarizes the negative effects of extrinsic-reward dissatisfaction.

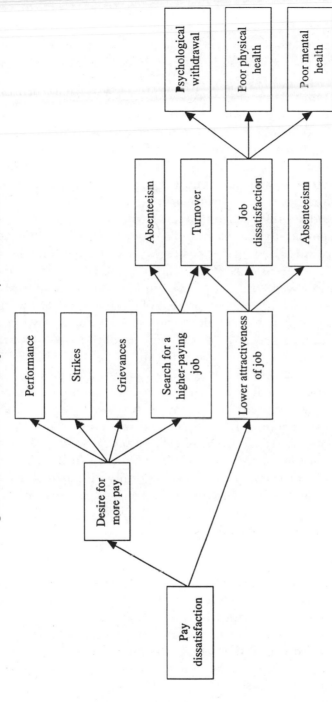

Figure 6.6. Model of the Consequences of Pay Dissatisfaction.

Source: From *Pay and Organizational Effectiveness: A Psychological View* by E. E. Lawler. Copyright © 1971 by McGraw-Hill Book Company. Used by permission of the publisher.

Much evidence shows that total job satisfaction will be low if extrinsic-reward satisfaction is low. This is to be expected, since overall job satisfaction is influenced by extrinsic-reward satisfaction. It is precisely because extrinsic-reward satisfaction exerts such a strong influence on total job satisfaction that it is related to factors such as absenteeism and turnover. As was pointed out in Chapter 4, job satisfaction tends to be consistently related to these membership decisions. Typical of the studies showing a relationship between extrinsic-reward satisfaction and attendance behavior is one by Weitz and Nuckols (1953) and another by Metzner and Mann (1953). The former study reported that 83 percent of a group of employees who said their pay was adequate were still with a company at the end of a year, whereas only 67 percent of those who said their pay was too low were still with the company. Metzner and Mann (1953) reported that only 45 percent of those white-collar workers who were absent four or more times in six months were satisfied with their pay, whereas 60 percent of those who were absent once or not at all were satisfied.

The relationship between extrinsic-reward satisfaction and factors such as strikes and grievances also seems understandable in terms of the impact of extrinsic-reward satisfaction on total job satisfaction. In Chapter 4, it was pointed out that job dissatisfaction seems to cause strikes and grievances, both of which represent actions that employees take to increase their overall satisfaction and their satisfaction with particular facets of their jobs, such as amount of extrinsic rewards received.

Who Should Be Satisfied?

In Chapter 4, the point was made that it is very important who in an organization has high and low job satisfaction. Since satisfaction is related to turnover, those people who are most highly dissatisfied are also most likely to leave. This doesn't present a problem if the poorer performers are dissatisfied, but it does present a problem if the good performers are dissatisfied. This point is applicable whether the discussion centers on total job satisfaction or extrinsic-reward satisfaction; it matters very much who is dissatisfied.

Organizations have only a limited amount of extrinsic rewards to give out. For example, in the case of money, they must decide how much money they are going to invest in each of their employees. Since they do not have an unlimited amount of money, what is given to one person is taken away from another. It is possible to increase satisfaction by increasing pay. Thus, in deciding how much money to spend on pay, organizations are deciding how satisfied they want their employees to be; in allocating rewards such as pay among individuals, they are essentially making decisions about who they want to be satisfied and whom they want to retain.

To be satisfied, the good performer must receive substantially more than the poor performer because he sees himself as having higher inputs. He is also most likely to receive attractive offers from other organizations. This reasoning suggests that in an organization that pays everyone roughly the same the poorer performers will be the most satisfied and will tend to stay, whereas the good performers will leave. It also suggests that many organizations could cut their turnover costs without increasing their salary costs simply by distributing pay so that the good performers receive more.

Pay Secrecy

It is impossible to maintain secrecy about who receives most of the extrinsic rewards that are given. For example, promotions cannot be kept secret, but information about one reward, pay, can be kept secret. In fact, in many organizations, information about the pay received by managers is kept secret on the assumption that secrecy will reduce pay dissatisfaction.

The model presented in Chapter 4 of the determinants of facet satisfaction emphasizes that pay comparisons do influence satisfaction. However, there is no evidence to indicate that secrecy eliminates pay comparisons. There is evidence that when pay secrecy exists, people base their comparisons on inaccurate information, innuendo, and hearsay. If pay secrecy leads employees to estimate the pay of others correctly, then pay satisfaction should be roughly the same with or without secrecy. On the other hand, if secrecy leads people to underestimate the pay of relevant others, satisfaction should be lower with secrecy. Whether secrecy leads to over-, under-, or accurate estimates of other people's pay is a researchable topic and has been studied extensively. The research shows that secrecy tends to lead people to overestimate the pay of others at the same management level and that the greater the overestimation, the greater the dissatisfaction. This finding suggests that pay secrecy may do more to cause pay dissatisfaction than to reduce it.

On the basis of available data, it seems quite possible that, other things being equal, an organization might be able to raise the satisfaction level of its employees by making pay rates public. Unfortunately, no research has directly measured the effect on employee satisfaction of an organizational change from a secret system to a public system. The consequences would probably depend on how well pay had been administered prior to the change. If it had been poorly administered and a number of unjustifiable pay differences existed, then the change would cause problems—temporarily, at least. In the long run, however, it would probably be beneficial if it forced the organization to take a critical look at its pay procedures and to straighten out any irregularities that existed. All too often, managers make bad pay decisions because they think that people will not know what they have done. If pay has been well administered, the typical company would seem to have much to gain by making pay public. Accurate pay information can clearly show employees that pay is related to performance, and it can eliminate any pay dissatisfaction that might result from overestimating other people's pay.

Data collected by Beer and Gery (1968) suggest what can happen when people gain more information about pay rates. Employees who had accurate information about the pay rates in a company were more favorable to the idea of merit pay than were those who had little information. This finding is hardly surprising, since it seems logical that employees will be more willing to accept the risk of a merit system if they have clear evidence that the company can be trusted to distribute pay fairly. With pay secrecy, it is difficult to build this trust.

Tying Extrinsic Rewards to Performance

This chapter has emphasized that the relationship between extrinsic-reward level and performance has a crucial influence on organizational effectiveness. When extrinsic rewards are related to performance, the result is higher motivation and a tendency for turnover to be centered among the poorer performers. Despite the obvious advantages of organizations tying rewards to performance, rewards often are not tied to performance in many organizations. There are some situations in which tying rewards to performance is dysfunctional; however, organizations often do not relate rewards to performance even when doing so would be highly functional.

Research has shown that pay is not consistently related to performance. This is true even in organizations that claim to have merit pay programs. For example, Svetlik, Prien, and Barrett (1964) show that a negative relationship exists between amount of salary and performance as evaluated by superiors. Another study has shown that managers' pay is relatively unrelated to superiors' performance evaluations (Lawler, 1967). Two other studies also indicate that at the managerial level pay is not always related to performance (Haire, Ghiselli & Gordon, 1967; Brenner & Lockwood, 1965). The evidence in both studies consists of salary-history data, which indicate some interesting tendencies. For example, the raises managers get from one year to another often show no correlation to each other. If the companies were tying pay to performance, the lack of correlation would mean that a manager's performance in one year was quite unrelated to his performance in another year. This assumption simply does not fit with what is known about performance; that is, a manager who is a good performer one year is very likely to be a good performer the next year. Thus, we must conclude that the companies studied were not tying pay to performance. Apparently, either pay raises were distributed on a random basis or the criteria for awarding raises were frequently changed. As a result, recent raises were often not related to past raises or to performance. One study has shown that pay is related to job level, seniority, and other nonperformance factors (Lawler & Porter, 1966).

Overall, the evidence suggests that organizations do not consistently pay for performance and that pay is influenced by many nonperformance factors. The same is probably even more true of the way other rewards are administered. Promotions certainly are not always given to the best performers, sometimes for good reasons. It is important to promote the person who will do well in the higher-level job, and this may or may not be the person who has performed best in the lower-level job. Thus, like pay systems, promotion systems often turn into compromises in the sense that promotions are made on the basis of a number of criteria.

One reason why rewards are not closely related to performance in organizations is that some employees object to this manner of administering rewards, and employees obviously influence how rewards are administered. Studies done among blue-collar workers to determine their preferences with respect to pay plans show that they object to many kinds of merit-based reward systems. They particularly objected to piece-rate pay plans. Salary-increase plans are the preferred payment plan. Interestingly, opposition to piece-rate pay plans is lower among employees who have worked under them and higher among union members. In a study done on the management level, it was found that, although managers believed that performance should be the most important determinant of their pay, they also wanted to be paid on the basis of the nonperformance factors in which they excelled (Lawler, 1966). For example, the managers who had been with the organization a long time thought that seniority should be an important determinant of reward level, those who were well educated thought that education level should be, and so on. Thus, it seems likely that in any organization there will be pressures from various groups to base reward on factors other than performance. Even though a minority of the people in an organization might feel education or seniority should be very important in determining rewards, they can often influence the reward system, particularly if they are managers and are in the position of giving the rewards.

The best way to summarize the discussion of extrinsic rewards is to stress again the importance of who receives the extrinsic rewards given out by an organization. Each organization has a limited quantity of rewards to give; how they are given determines who will continue to work for the organization, how hard people will work, and the attitudes of the employees toward the organization. The giving of extrinsic rewards represents an investment in people, and a crucial issue in any organization concerns how this investment is made. One effective way to understand an organization is to look at how the extrinsic rewards it has to offer are actually distributed among its members and how the employees perceive the distribution. The study of the relationship between extrinsic-reward satisfaction and performance in an organization can also provide some important insights into the eventual impact of an organization's reward-distribution system (Porter & Lawler, 1968). A strong positive relationship between satisfaction and performance indicates a reward system that is functioning well and that is rewarding good performance. On the other hand, a zero or negative relationship between satisfaction and performance indicates a poorly functioning reward system and should be taken as a signal of potential problems. Specifically, such relationships mean that motivation is likely to be low because rewards are not clearly tied to performance. They also mean that turnover in the organization is likely to be centered among the better performers.

In Chapter 7, we will focus on how job design influences motivation and satisfaction. Like pay and promotion, job design has a strong influence on motivation, but in a different manner. Instead of influencing motivation through an impact on the giving and receiving of extrinsic rewards, job design's influence comes from its impact on certain intrinsic rewards.

seven

Job Design
and Job Performance

The psychological literature on employee motivation contains considerable evidence that job design can influence satisfaction, motivation, and job performance. It influences them primarily because it affects $P \rightarrow O$ beliefs concerning intrinsic rewards such as feelings of self-esteem, achievement, and competence. It also affects the valence of certain outcomes and $E \rightarrow P$ beliefs about good performance. Before discussing the evidence supporting this view, we need to consider two alternative job design strategies; specifically, we will compare the scientific management approach with the job enrichment approach.

The Scientific Management Approach

The scientific management approach to designing jobs became popular in the early 1900s; it is now considered the traditional approach. It assumes that jobs (particularly lower-level jobs) should be simplified, standardized, and specialized. Consistent with this approach has been a pervasive tendency in organizations to break work down into very small segments and to standardize the procedures for performing these work segments. As Frederick W. Taylor (1911) suggested more than 60 years ago:

> The work of every workman is fully planned out
> by the management at least one day in advance,
> and each man receives in most cases complete writ-
> ten instructions, describing in detail the task which
> he is to accomplish. . . . This task specifies not only
> what is to be done but how it is to be done and the
> exact time allowed for doing it [p. 39].

The mechanized assembly line represents the ultimate development of the scientific management approach. It contains many
simplified, standardized jobs that are machine paced.

Before considering the actual consequences of putting people to work on jobs designed according to the principles of scientific management, some of the expected advantages of designing jobs according to this approach should be enumerated. Jobs
have been and continue to be designed based on this approach
because economic and engineering advantages are expected to
be derived. Three of the expected economic advantages have
to do with the kind of training and skills workers need to successfully perform the jobs. First, jobs of this nature require little training, which is very important from a cost standpoint,
since training is expensive. Training programs demand that a
training staff be hired and that workers be supported during
their training periods. A second expected economic advantage
stems from the fact that the jobs can be filled with low-skill people. Presumably, low-skill people are a cheap commodity that
is usually readily available. Third, because low-skill people are
required and little training is needed, workers become relatively
interchangeable. If a worker is absent, production can go on
as usual because he can be easily replaced.

Another advantage of assembly line jobs is that the high
degree of mechanization usually means that the worker has to
put forth less physical effort, and thus he is not likely to get phys-
ically tired in the same way as a worker who is digging ditches.
When combined with mechanical pacing, standardization creates conditions under which quality is carefully controlled and
production should be predictable; everyone is doing a simple
task for which one standardized way has been prescribed, so

mistakes should be unlikely. Each part of the manufacturing process is being done by someone who is trained to do only that part and to do it in the best way. This is assumed to lead to higher quality than having one individual do many different steps in the manufacturing process, since this individual can never become as expert in doing any one operation as the individual who has only one to do. Production should be predictable because it is determined by the speed at which the assembly line is run, and thus it can be controlled by management.

In short, designing jobs to be machine paced, standardized, specialized, and simplified appears to give managers more control over workers. With one quick look at a worker, a supervisor can usually tell if he is performing correctly. All the supervisor has to see is whether the employee is at his machine and doing the simple action he has been trained to do. Also, the supervisor can know the job almost as well as the worker, making it easy for him to determine whether the work is being done properly. With a more complicated job, the worker might know the job better than his supervisor; as a result, the supervisor would be in a poor position to determine whether the worker is doing things correctly. Finally, because the company has invested little in training assembly line workers, the foreman can easily replace them if they don't perform correctly. Thus, for these workers, being fired is a meaningful threat.

The problem with jobs designed according to the principles of scientific management is that they typically do not produce the results claimed by the advocates of this approach. For obvious reasons, the employees simply do not behave as they are supposed to; thus, many of the expected economic savings never materialize. Specifically, expected savings from reduced training costs often are never realized because of the higher turnover on routine jobs. Some companies report turnover in excess of 100 percent per year for their assembly line jobs. If too many workers leave, even minimal training costs begin to become significant, thereby countering some of the expected economic advantages of simplified jobs. Further, as turnover increases, other costs go up — expenses of recruitment, selection, payroll, accounting, having inexperienced workers on the job, and supervision. When these costs are totaled, turnover can be a significant expense. Recent research indicates that it costs organizations at least five times an employee's monthly salary to replace him. This means it costs at least $2000 to replace even a lower-level employee and much more to replace higher-level employees.

Absenteeism also tends to be high on standardized, specialized, and simplified jobs; it, too, is expensive. Employees are likely to use all their paid sick leave and vacation time, and a large "float" of extra workers must be maintained to fill in for absentees. As a result, the organizations get fewer hours of work per employee per dollar spent.

Another expected advantage of the scientific management approach is its use of cheap labor. However, as experience in the automobile industry so clearly demonstrates, the work is so dissatisfying that companies have to pay high wages to get workers even to accept assembly line jobs. The typical worker on the automobile assembly line is making at least a dollar an hour more than he has made on any of his previous jobs — more than he could make on most other jobs, given his skills.

An interesting, unexpected cost of using the assembly line approach appeared in a recent study of a research and development laboratory (Hall & Lawler, 1969). When asked what the hardest part of his product-design job was, an engineer reported "making the product assembly-line proof," which meant designing the product in such a manner that it could be assembled in only one way regardless of how hard the worker tried to assemble it another way. Why was this important? Because of the boredom and monotony of working on the line, it seems that workers simply do not notice what they are doing and frequently put things together wrong — even though (or perhaps because) they are performing a single, simple, repetitive action. Part of the problem also seems to be caused by workers consciously trying to put things together in different ways to add some variety to their jobs. There are many classic stories of automobile workers ingeniously varying the names on the hoods and trunks of cars as a way of relieving the boredom that comes from spending all day every day putting the same few letters on cars. Cars have also been known to come off assembly lines with soda bottles in the doors and various parts missing.

Another type of design problem is also present when organizations use assembly lines and work simplification. It is very difficult to set up a "balanced" line — that is, a line on which every job takes the same length of time. Every time demand for the product fluctuates and the number of people on the line changes, the line has to be balanced again. Industrial engineers must be hired for this time-consuming job, which means added expense for the organization. Even where lines are well balanced, all workers do not have equal tasks; as a result, some workers spend time waiting for preceding workers to finish their tasks. In some instances, the result is that more labor time is required for the assembly line production of products than for individualized production. For example, in an automobile company, the industrial engineers were surprised to find that it would take less time for a single worker to assemble a control mechanism than it was taking the assembly line. Why was an assembly line being used? Individual assembly had never been considered.

Having to design products so they are assembly-line proof suggests that the assembly-production method does not always create conditions under which high quality is assured. Perhaps it eliminates some of the quality problems that might normally develop due to someone not knowing how to make something, but it does not motivate employees to do high-quality work; to the contrary, it seems to motivate them to do low-quality work. The traditional answer to this problem has been to hire more quality-control inspectors and to use more sophisticated control procedures. This may result in some improvement, but all too often it leads to the "too much control — too little quality" phenomenon. Also, these methods are very expensive; by the time the controls are installed, many of the cost savings resulting from the assembly line approach are lost.

When considering the financial advantages of installing an assembly line, it is extremely important to consider the tremendous investment in required machinery. Further, this method of production is relatively inflexible; that is, both the people and the machinery are keyed to produce one product, and both find it very difficult to produce something else. Assembly lines are inflexible in terms of rate of productivity. Each time their speed is changed, they must be balanced, which often means extensive shifting of people. Inflexibility of this type can be a serious problem for companies in fields where demand is variable and somewhat unpredictable, resulting in constant readjustment of the product mix. Obviously, this is not easy where heavily mechanized assembly lines exist, since both human and mechanical inflexibility are present.

The Job-Enrichment Approach

Since the early 1950s, many social scientists concerned with job design and motivation have argued strongly against the scientific management approach. They have suggested replacing it with the job-enrichment approach, which is based on the assumption that jobs should be complex, challenging, and interesting. A distinction is often made between vertical and horizontal job expansion. Horizontal expansion consists of increasing the number of tasks a person does and is often referred to as job enlargement, whereas vertical expansion consists of increasing the autonomy and responsibility of the employee for what he does and how he does it and is often referred to as job enrichment. Most writers have argued that jobs must be expanded both vertically and horizontally if they are to be motivating, satisfying, and truly enriched.

The expected advantages of enriched jobs are many. Basically, the arguments in favor of this approach contend that enriched jobs produce greater motivation and satisfaction than simplified jobs. The increased motivation means that the employees will be more productive and will produce higher-quality work. The increased satisfaction is economically desirable because of its association with turnover and absenteeism.

Of course, some obvious costs are associated with the enrichment approach. Initial training usually takes longer. Workers are clearly less replaceable because they often are doing complex jobs. The mechanical assistance offered by the assembly line is lost in many instances, which means that the employee may have to put forth more effort. Further, skilled workers are needed to do the jobs, which can mean higher wages. Proponents of this approach argue that the disadvantages are more than offset by the expected gains due to increased motivation and satisfaction (for example, see Ford, 1969).

Many studies have attempted to measure the effects of job-enrichment programs. Almost without exception, these studies show that some positive gains are derived when jobs are enriched. In most cases, productivity is higher after enrichment. One literature review (Lawler, 1969) found that in six of ten studies productivity increased as a result of enrichment; in all ten studies, job enrichment led to higher work quality. One study (Marks, 1954) was carried out in a company that made hospital appliances. Before the change, the products were made on an assembly line. Several new job designs were tried, all of which combined jobs so as to increase their complexity. For example, in one of the new designs the workers assembled the whole product, controlled the sequence and pace of the assembly, and inspected the finished product. These new job designs led to slightly lower productivity but increased quality. Defects were cut almost in half as a result of the job design changes.

In another study (Kuriloff, 1966), an electronics firm that manufactured measuring instruments on an assembly line was experiencing work quality, turnover, absenteeism, and production-flexibility problems. To solve these problems, the firm enriched the jobs of the assembly line workers. Instead of assembling only one part of the instrument, each worker had to assemble a whole instrument. In many cases, this represented a week's work for one employee. When the employee finished the instrument, he tested it, signed it, and sent it to the customer. If any problems developed with the instrument, the worker was personally responsible for correcting it. Immediately after the change to enriched jobs, productivity and quality dropped because the employees did not know how to assemble the instruments. However, six months after the change, productivity had returned to its previous level and quality was higher. As a result of the change, satisfaction increased while turnover and absenteeism decreased.

In another study, Ford (1969) reports that job enrichment resulted in a 27 percent decrease in turnover, which saved his company $245,000. Many studies have reported similar results; thus, substantial evidence shows that job enrichment affects satisfaction, absenteeism, and turnover, as well as work quality. However, studies by Blood and Hulin (1967) and by Turner and Lawrence (1965) do suggest an important qualification. They found significant individual differences in how people respond to enriched jobs. Basically, they found that "town workers" (people from small town and rural backgrounds) responded to enrichment as predicted by the proponents of the approach. However, workers from big city backgrounds did not show high productivity, high-quality work, and satisfaction when they worked on enriched jobs; nor did they show lower absenteeism and turnover. Thus, any theory that attempts to explain the effects of job design on motivation must be prepared to account for significant individual differences in workers' responses to enriched jobs.

Why Does Job Design Affect Motivation?

It is clear from the research evidence that job design does affect employee attitudes and behavior. Whether jobs are enriched makes a difference. Admittedly, individual responses to enriched jobs may vary, but most employees do respond differently to enriched jobs than to jobs designed according to the principles of scientific management. The question that remains concerns why job design has an important influence on motivation. At the beginning of this chapter, it was suggested that job design might influence motivation by affecting three of the components of the motivation model presented in Chapter 3. Let's consider how this might occur.

Effects on P→O Beliefs

Depending on how the work is arranged, jobs can provide various kinds of opportunities for employees to satisfy important needs and to achieve important goals. For example, some jobs may provide opportunities for workers to satisfy social needs; other jobs may provide personal-growth-need satisfaction, or material-need satisfaction. The design of the job is often crucial in determining what kinds of rewards it will provide. Most assembly line jobs simply do not provide employees the opportunity to experience achievement and accomplishment.

Job design also influences what the employee must do to obtain many rewards. On some jobs, the employee simply has to show up for work. For example, as stated in Chapter 5, some jobs are designed so that satisfaction of social needs is readily available to any employee who shows up for work. Other jobs offer need satisfaction only if the employee works effectively. A baseball player is likely to satisfy his needs for competence and growth only if he performs moderately well. On still other jobs, performance does not affect the kinds of rewards a person receives. The assembly line worker, for example, typically receives no more rewards when he performs well than when he performs poorly.

Job design can affect performance motivation because it can affect the degree to which the achievement of many intrinsic rewards and outcomes is dependent on work behavior. Thus, following the motivation model in Chapter 3, jobs increase motivation when they can positively affect a person's $P \rightarrow O$ beliefs with respect to good performance.

The following hypothetical case illustrates the effect of job design on $P \rightarrow O$ beliefs. Consider, for example, a hypothetical female employee who is primarily motivated to obtain social satisfactions. Assume that this woman loves to participate in interesting conversations and that she usually feels best about herself when she finds that she has been helpful or stimulating to another person through social interaction. Imagine that this woman works on a manufacturing job making small electrical fixtures at a circular table with five other female employees. Further, assume that the work is fairly simple, demanding only minimal skill and attention and thereby providing considerable opportunity for conversation while at work. It would be predicted that this employee and others similar to her would (1) have good attendance on the job, (2) tend to have relatively long tenure on the job, and (3) have adequate but certainly not especially high levels of performance. Since the job is structured so that the employee can satisfy her strong social needs while at work, she probably would find work an attractive place to be — thus, the prediction of low absenteeism and long tenure. Moreover, since the task is not demanding, she would be able to maintain an adequate level of performance without losing the chance to engage in social activities. There is no incentive in the way the work is designed for this employee to try to perform at especially high levels.

Now consider the situation if the same woman held a job as a customer-service representative for a public utility company, in which her duties consisted mainly of answering telephone calls from customers and dealing with the problems they presented. The employee should show very high levels of performance and, at the same time high job satisfaction, good attendance, and long tenure with the organization. Such a job would be nearly optimal for our hypothetical employee; she could, while on the job, satisfy her personal needs best by working hard and striving toward the goals of the organization — that is, by being as helpful as possible to the customers who call in for assistance. Moreover, the harder and more effectively she worked on the job, the more she would be able to satisfy her own needs and achieve her personal goals. If the same employee worked on a noisy assembly line job which provided few interaction opportunities, different behavior would be expected. Since working effectively would not satisfy her social needs and in fact might hinder their satisfaction, we would expect low performance. Further, since work attendance would not satisfy her social needs, we would expect poor attendance and turnover.

The point of this example is that the way the work is designed strongly affects both the kinds of satisfactions that are potentially available in the work setting and the kinds of behaviors that must be engaged in to achieve these satisfactions. In other words, job design strongly influences people's $P \rightarrow O$ beliefs and therefore their behavior. The example also shows that what happens on the job is a joint function of the actual $P \rightarrow O$ associations that are created by the job design and the kinds of needs or goals that are of major importance to the employee. Other evidence, which will be reviewed later, shows that enriched jobs create different $P \rightarrow O$ beliefs than simplified jobs. People who work on enriched jobs see a relationship between performing well and feelings of growth, self-respect, and competence. This is why enriched jobs seem to produce higher motivation.

Effects on Outcome Attractiveness

Compelling research data establish that tasks and jobs can affect the attractiveness of outcomes to individuals on both short- and long-term bases. Performing various kinds of tasks and experiencing the consequences of that performance can affect substantially the individual's subsequent needs and goals.

One of the major theorists whose work is relevant to this discussion is David C. McClelland of Harvard University. According to McClelland (1951), if an individual has found that he experiences a good deal of pleasure (or pain) while working on some particular kind of task, that affective state will become associated with the cues that are present at the time of the experience. In subsequent situations in which those cues are present (such as performing the same task again or performing a similar task), the prior affective state would be reactivated. This reactivated affective state can increase the attractiveness (or unattractiveness) of the outcomes associated with performing the task.

Many experiments conducted by McClelland and his associates have shown that the cues emitted by tasks (and other aspects of work situations) do in fact arouse various needs to above-normal levels. These experiments have focused on the achievement motive and have shown that achievement motivation can be aroused by certain kinds of tasks. When this motivation is aroused, achievement-type outcomes are valued more highly by employees.

Suppose the hypothetical woman with strong social needs is placed suddenly on a challenging enriched job that involves social isolation. One effect might be to make her dissatisfied and to cause her to quit because she can't satisfy her social needs.

However, the challenging nature of the job could arouse her achievement motivation, which might result in her trying to obtain outcomes associated with accomplishment and growth and becoming less concerned with satisfying her social needs. Since in the new job she could obtain achievement-related outcomes through good performance, she might become very motivated to perform well. Thus, rather than causing her to quit, the job change might cause her to become a more effective employee. The key determinant of her reaction would be whether the new job aroused her achievement motivation, which in turn would be determined by her previous learning and by the characteristics of the task.

Some research evidence shows that experience on a task or job may affect the long-term needs or goals of employees. In one study, Breer and Locke (1965) varied the degree to which collective, interdependent task behavior was required of subjects. One effect of working on tasks requiring interdependent behavior was an increase in the value the subjects placed on collective endeavors. Presumably, in subsequent tasks, these subjects would respond more readily to opportunities to engage in performance activities with other people. Since the Breer and Locke data were collected in the laboratory during a short time period, the degree to which the changes observed were long-lasting is open to question. Even if the attitudinal effects of participating in a Breer and Locke experiment did not persist, the results suggest that a more prolonged and intense task experience could alter the personal orientations of the participants on an enduring basis.

A case illustrating this point is provided by Kornhauser's (1965) study of automobile workers in Detroit. Kornhauser compared the reactions of employees who worked on low-level, routine, repetitive jobs with demographically similar employees whose jobs were more complex and more under the control of the workers themselves. The findings showed that individuals who worked on the lowest-level jobs tended to show less initiative regarding work activities and had a less active orientation toward life and toward their careers. In addition, they showed less personal ambition and less desire for personal growth. For example, when asked whether he would "push hard" to change things in his life, one worker responded, "'I quit pushing, I guess. There's a time when I did but the last 8 or 10 years I sorta slowed down' (he was 42 at the time); 'I guess I just got tired of trying to get somewhere and you don't'" (p. 241).

Kornhauser took pains to demonstrate that his findings regarding such reactions were due to the job experience of the workers rather than to some pattern of a priori personal characteristics, and his case is a convincing one. He concludes: "Factory employment, especially in routine production tasks, does give evidence of extinguishing workers' ambition, initiative, and purposive direction toward life goals" (p. 252). It seems likely that work on challenging jobs might increase people's desires for growth, self-esteem, and autonomy, although Kornhauser doesn't make this point.

One important function that well-designed tasks can serve, then, is to arouse needs in the work situation. Thus, for example, if an individual has learned that he experiences positive feelings about himself when he succeeds in accomplishing a moderately difficult task, a need to achieve will be aroused every time that individual finds strong cues of moderate difficulty in subsequent tasks. Because of the need arousal, the attractiveness of various outcomes changes.

Effects on E→P Beliefs

Job design can easily affect beliefs about the likelihood that effort will lead to successful performance. The assembly line job is designed so that most people can perform the job successfully. However, many jobs are designed so that people are not sure whether high effort on their part will lead to good performance. Many managerial jobs are sufficiently complex and difficult so that high effort alone does not guarantee good performance. The corporation president, like the baseball batter, can "strike out" even though he puts forth the effort. Some corporation presidents feel that they are doing well if they make the right decision 50 percent of the time. If $E{\rightarrow}P$ beliefs did not influence the strength of $P{\rightarrow}O$ beliefs and outcome valences, motivation would be highest when $E \rightarrow P$ is high. In other words, motivation should be highest when people are certain that effort will lead to performance. The motivation model presented in Chapter 3 indicated that motivation is determined by the formula $(E \rightarrow P) \times \Sigma[(P \rightarrow O)(V)]$. Since the other factors in this formula are multiplied by $E \rightarrow P$, the resulting figure would be highest when $E \rightarrow P$ is highest. This would seem to argue for designing jobs so that they can be easily done according to scientific management. However, this argument is fallacious because $E \rightarrow P$ beliefs do influence $P \rightarrow O$ beliefs.

Research has shown that $P \rightarrow O$ beliefs concerned with achievement motivation are influenced by $E \rightarrow P$ probabilities. The strongest $P \rightarrow O$ beliefs for achievement motivation result when effort is seen to have approximately a 50-50 chance of leading to good performance. Apparently, when $E \rightarrow P$ is very high (or very low), people do not see successful performance as leading to feelings of achievement or competence; and the $\Sigma[(P \rightarrow O)(V)]$ term in the model is lower. Because increases in the $E \rightarrow P$ term can decrease the $\Sigma[(P \rightarrow O)(V)]$ term, they often do not increase motivation.

There is also evidence that the $E \rightarrow P$ probability can influence outcome attractiveness; most outcomes are valued more when they are obtained as a result of high effort or accomplishing a difficult task. For example, honors and prizes are valued more when they are difficult to obtain. Thus, in many instances, motivation may be highest when the $E \rightarrow P$ probability is not perfect because of the potential influence of this factor on the attractiveness of the outcomes associated with good performance. In summary, once $E \rightarrow P$ exceeds .5, further increase in it only serves to decrease the value of $\Sigma[(P \rightarrow O)(V)]$, thus potentially negating any increase in it. Because of this effect, the highest motivation may well come when the $E \rightarrow P$ probability term is around .5.

Job Characteristics and Their Effect on Motivation

At this point, more detailed statements must be made about how specific job characteristics affect motivation, so that we can under-

stand why people react as they do to enriched jobs and to assembly line jobs. This is also necessary so that we can specify
how jobs need to be designed to maximize individual satisfaction and motivation.

We know from the research on achievement motivation
that task difficulty is one task characteristic that influences motivation and satisfaction. But what are the others? The work of
Kurt Lewin (for example, see Lewin, Dembo, Festinger & Sears,
1944) and Chris Argyris (1964) suggests some of them. They
argue that individuals experience higher-order-need satisfaction
when they learn that they have accomplished something they
believe is personally worthwhile or meaningful. In more concrete terms, such satisfaction should be obtained when an employee works effectively on a job that (1) allows him to feel
personally responsible for a meaningful portion of the work,
(2) provides outcomes that are intrinsically meaningful or are
otherwise experienced as worthwhile, and (3) provides feedback
about what is accomplished. The harder and better an individual
works on a job with these characteristics, the more likely he will
be to obtain higher-order-need satisfaction. Further, as he gains
experience on the job, he will be even more motivated to perform effectively because he will learn that good performance does
in fact lead to higher-order-need satisfaction. The three general
job characteristics mentioned above are central in influencing
motivation and satisfaction and will be described in more detail so they can serve as a useful basis for analyzing jobs (see
also Hackman & Lawler, 1971).

1. *The job must allow a worker to feel personally responsible for
a meaningful portion of his work.* What is accomplished must be
through the individual's own efforts. He must realize that the
work he does is his own, and he must believe that he personally
is responsible for whatever successes and failures occur as a result
of his work. Only if what is accomplished is seen as one's own
can an individual experience a feeling of personal success and
a gain in self-esteem.

The autonomy dimension, as specified by Turner and
Lawrence (1965), represents one effort to measure the degree
to which workers feel personally responsible for their work. In

jobs high on measured autonomy, employees have responsibility for scheduling their work and for determining work methods; in jobs low on autonomy, employees have little say about scheduling or about which procedures are used in doing the job.

2. *The job must involve doing something that is intrinsically meaningful or otherwise experienced as worthwhile to the individual.* If a worker feels that the results of his efforts are not very important, it is unlikely that he will feel especially good if he works effectively. There are at least two characteristics that a job must have in order to be experienced as meaningful by employees with relatively high desires for higher-order-need satisfaction. First, the job must include a sufficiently whole piece of work to allow the worker to perceive that he has produced or accomplished something of consequence. This would be expected when a job is high on task identity. According to Turner and Lawrence (1965, p. 157), jobs high on task identity are characterized by (1) a very clear cycle of perceived closure (that is, the job provides a distinct sense of the beginning and ending of a transformation process), (2) high visibility of the transformation to the workers, (3) high visibility of the transformation in the finished product, and (4) a transformation of considerable magnitude. Second, the job must provide the employee with the opportunity to accomplish something by using skills and abilities that he personally values. For example, an engineer feels good when he has completed the design of a new product (just as an artist feels good when he completes a painting) because he has had to use valued skills.

Jobs high on the dimension of variety would be expected to provide opportunities for workers to experience this kind of meaningfulness, since high-variety jobs typically tap a number of different skills that may be important to the employee. However, variety that does not challenge the worker would not be experienced as meaningful. Screwing many different sizes of nuts on many different colors of bolts—if this could be considered variety—would not be expected to be experienced as meaningful. In fact, Lawler and Hall (1970) present data showing that jobs can have too much variety.

Jobs may come to be experienced as meaningful to the

extent that they involve doing a whole piece of work of some significance (that is, have high task identity) and, at the same time, give employees the chance to use valued skills and abilities (that is, to be challenged). In many cases, the latter condition may be met on jobs that have high variety.

3. *The job must provide feedback about what is accomplished.* Even if the two general conditions discussed above are met, an employee cannot experience higher-order-need satisfaction when he performs effectively unless he obtains some feedback about how he is doing. Such feedback may come from doing the task itself (for example, when a telephone operator successfully completes a long distance person-to-person call), but performance feedback also may come from some other person, such as an esteemed co-worker or a supervisor. The crucial condition is that feedback must be believable to the worker, so that a realistic basis exists for the satisfaction (or frustration) of needs.

Hackman and Lawler (1971) emphasize that the major effect on employee attitudes and behavior is not from the objective state of the job characteristics discussed above but rather from how these characteristics are experienced by the employees. Regardless of the actual amount of feedback (or variety or autonomy or task identity), a worker's reactions to his job will be affected by how much of any factor he perceives that he has. Objective job characteristics are important because they do affect the perceptions and experiences of employees. But there are differences between objective job characteristics and how they are perceived by the employee; it is dangerous to assume that, since the objective characteristics of a job have been measured (or changed), the job experience of the employee has been dealt with as well.

In summary, the characteristics of jobs can establish conditions that will enhance the motivation and satisfaction of workers in certain need areas. In particular, individuals will be able to obtain meaningful personal satisfaction when they perform well on jobs that they experience as high on variety, autonomy, task identity, and feedback — the four core dimensions of job design (Hackman & Lawler, 1971).

Individual Differences in Reactions to Jobs

The discussion has emphasized that job design should have its major effect on motivation and satisfaction related to higher-order needs. This fact has some important implications for our understanding of how different individuals will react to jobs. The key to this understanding is in the strength of individuals' higher-order needs. Those people who value intrinsic outcomes such as feelings of achievement, growth, and competence should respond to jobs that are high on the four core dimensions with higher motivation and, if they perform well, with high satisfaction. However, those people who do not value these outcomes should respond to jobs that are high on the core dimensions with frustration and irritation at having too demanding a job.

The reason for this prediction is that, since job design affects mainly the attractiveness of outcomes that satisfy higher-order needs and the association of these outcomes with performance, job design will affect the motivation of only those people who are concerned with higher-order-need satisfaction. Thus, when a person who has strong higher-order needs is taken from a job that is low on the four core dimensions and placed on a job that is high on the core dimensions, his motivation and satisfaction will be different. The job that is high on the core dimensions causes him to see positive connections between good performance and outcomes he values, whereas the job that is low on the core dimensions doesn't. This factor accounts for the prediction of higher motivation on the job that is high on the core dimensions. On the other hand, when a person who doesn't have strong higher-order needs is placed on a job that is high on the core dimensions, his satisfaction and motivation shouldn't be higher than when he is placed on a job that is low on the core dimensions; both jobs should produce similar relationships between the outcomes he values and his performance. In summary, individuals with strong higher-order needs will be able to satisfy these needs when they perform effectively on jobs that are high on variety, autonomy, task identity, and feedback. Both their motivation and satisfaction should increase.

Research on the Effects of the Core Dimensions

Hackman and Lawler (1971) collected data from some 200 telephone company employees to determine why job design affects motivation. The research was designed to consider (1) the overall relationships between job characteristics and employee work attitudes and behavior and (2) whether the reaction of an employee to his work depends on the kinds of outcomes he values. Thirteen different jobs were assessed on the four core dimensions discussed above (variety, autonomy, task identity, and feedback), and the strength of the higher-order needs of employees working on these jobs was assessed. Higher-order needs were measured by asking employees how much they would like to obtain certain kinds of personal outcomes from their work (for example, feelings of personal growth, feelings of accomplishment, and so on).

The average employee in the company was found to be fairly high in self-described desire for higher-order-need satisfaction. Therefore, an overall, positive relationship between the four core job dimensions and employee work motivation, satisfaction, performance, and attendance was expected. The expectation was confirmed: in general, the "better" an employee's job (in terms of the core dimensions), the more positively he responded, both affectively and behaviorally.

Of special interest is the finding that when jobs were high on all four core dimensions, employees reported having higher intrinsic motivation to perform well. That is, the employees indicated that when they performed well on such jobs, they experienced positive, internal feelings; when they did poorly, they felt bad. Thus, it appears that jobs high on the core dimensions do establish conditions whereby some workers can obtain personally rewarding experiences by doing well on the job. Moreover, the data suggest that "doing well" is interpreted in the job context as having much more to do with work quality than with producing large quantities of work. In the study, the core dimensions did not relate either to internal pressures for high-quantity production or to the actual quantity of work produced. This is consistent with the notion that employees with strong higher-order needs feel good when they have accomplished something that they feel is meaningful; such workers would see doing high-quality work as much more of a meaningful accomplishment than simply turning out large quantities of work.

It was also interesting that the core dimensions seemed to affect most strongly the satisfaction of higher-order needs. They had no effect on factors such as social-need satisfaction and pay satisfaction. As might be expected, since higher-order-need satisfaction affects overall job satisfaction, the core dimensions were related to overall job satisfaction.

The study also tested the degree to which the strength of employees' needs affected their reactions to jobs that were high on the core dimensions. The relationship between job characteristics and the variables of attendance, motivation, and satisfaction were viewed separately for those employees whose higher-order-need strength was in the top third of the distribution of scores for all employees in the study, and for those employees whose scores were in the bottom third of the same distribution. As expected, the relationship between the core dimensions and employee attendance, motivation, and satisfaction was substantially higher for employees with strong higher-order needs than for those with weak higher-order needs.

The results of this study are helpful in understanding the effects of standardized, specialized, and simplified jobs on employee behavior, as well as the effects of job enrichment. Jobs designed according to scientific management principles tend to be low on the four core dimensions. Hence, these jobs provide no opportunity for employees to satisfy their higher-order needs, and thus employees on these jobs are not motivated to perform well by their higher-order needs. This means that if employees on these jobs are to be motivated to perform well, they must be motivated with extrinsic rewards.

Taylor and other proponents of the scientific management position realized this, and they usually installed piece-rate incentive plans when they created jobs that were low on the four core dimensions. As Chapter 6 points out, there are many limitations on the piece-rate system, one of which is that it leads to high productivity but often not to high quality. This system

can work reasonably well for those people who value money
highly. However, for people who don't value money highly but
who have strong higher-order needs, there is simply not much
motivation present to perform adequately. In fact, there may
be some motivation for them to perform poorly. As stated earlier,
assembly line workers are often able to satisfy their higher-order
needs only by developing ingenious ways to beat the system.
Apparently, beating the system in many situations is a challenging, rewarding job, whereas performing well is repetitious and
dull. Is it any wonder that employees sometimes intentionally
break down assembly lines or assemble products incorrectly?

Because jobs that are low on the four core dimensions do
not motivate or satisfy employees, they tend to produce high
turnover, high absenteeism, and low-quality work. Such jobs
are designed to fit only a portion of the work force, and those
employees who are not in that portion cause the problems that
make assembly lines less efficient. Where a well-designed incentive system is combined with jobs low on the core dimensions,
good results can be achieved if the right people are employed
(that is, people who value money and have low higher-order-
need strength). Some people like working on assembly lines and
continue to do it for years; their jobs obviously provide outcomes that are important to them. The problem is that many
people are not motivated primarily by money; they seek other
outcomes, which cannot be provided by jobs that are low on
the core dimensions.

Most job enrichment studies have involved changing jobs
that were low on the four core dimensions into jobs that are
high on the dimensions. Horizontal and vertical expansion of
jobs increases their standing on all four core dimensions. Thus,
it is not surprising that enriched jobs tend to have lower turnover and absenteeism and higher satisfaction and quality.

The Hackman and Lawler (1971) study also helps to explain the tendency for urban workers to respond less favorably
than rural workers to enriched jobs. This study found that rural
workers have stronger higher-order needs than urban workers.
Thus, it would be expected that rural workers should respond
more positively to enriched jobs, since enriched jobs provide
them with outcomes they value.

Fitting Jobs to People

The research on job design strongly suggests that if good job/people matches are to be obtained, we need to know something about both the nature of jobs and the characteristics of people. Good matching requires knowledge of both the employees' needs and the standing of the job on the core dimensions. Knowledge of employees' needs can lead to careful placement on existing jobs according to the nature of the jobs. Such a strategy could lead to improvements in the motivation, satisfaction, and tenure of employees beyond the levels that have resulted from the traditional practice of selecting and placing employees largely on the basis of skill and ability data.

But a somewhat more radical approach is often necessary. Traditionally, job design has been considered pretty much inviolate. People have been selected and perhaps crunched a bit to fit into existing jobs, but jobs have only rarely been changed to be better fits for the people who work on them. This must happen more often if jobs are to be more satisfying and motivating. A high degree of flexibility in how jobs are designed and defined must be combined with the customary emphasis on selecting and placing employees.

A strategy that emphasizes job redesign may be especially good if, as seems likely, too many jobs are low on the core dimensions. If a good job fit is to be achieved for most people, there must be a good balance between the number of jobs that are low on the core dimensions and the number of people who fit these jobs. Unfortunately, much evidence suggests that this balance does not exist; there simply are too many boring, repetitive jobs. What is more, the situation is likely to get worse as the education level and standard of living in our society continue to rise. The only practical solution is to redesign many jobs so they are higher on the core dimensions. However, unless adopted and implemented with great care, job redesign can cause organizational chaos — everyone's job might be different, and rational coordination within the organization can be severely affected. Indeed, even to begin to implement large-scale changes in job design would require much flexibility and resilience on the part of an organization.

Alderfer's (1967) data taken from one large organization show that there is a strong interaction between the way jobs are structured and the interpersonal relationships between superiors and subordinates. Although employees working on relatively complex jobs (including jobs that had been enlarged recently) were more satisfied with the opportunities they had to use their personal skills and abilities than were employees working on less complex jobs, they were substantially more dissatisfied with the respect from superiors. Alderfer suggests that one reason for the decay in superior/subordinate relationships when jobs were made more complex is that complex jobs are intrinsically more difficult to supervise and performance on such jobs is more difficult to evaluate. Unless supervisors are able to deal effectively with the emotion-laden evaluation problems (in this case, they apparently were not), the relationships between managers and subordinates would be expected to deteriorate.

A recent study (Lawler, Hackman & Kaufman, 1973) found results similar to those reported by Alderfer. A job was changed so that it was higher on two of the four core dimensions. The result was a decrease in the quality of the interpersonal relationships in the work group. Apparently, this change disrupted the traditional interpersonal relationships in the work group, and the employees had difficulty establishing new, equally satisfying relationships. The supervisors were particularly unhappy about the change. This is a crucial point, because often superiors are not in favor of job enrichment for many reasons. The most important reason is that when the supervisor's job is not enlarged, he doesn't have the autonomy, task identity, and so on in his job that he has to give his subordinates if their jobs are to be enlarged. Vertical job expansion can be especially threatening to the supervisor, since it usually means that some of his tasks are given to his subordinates. In turn, this forces the supervisor to redefine his job, puts pressure on him to manage in a different way, and may even make his position unnecessary.

Working with tight controls and low autonomy, which he does not pass on to his subordinates, the supervisor can act as an insulator between the rest of the organization and his subordinates. However, this obviously is a difficult role to play, and few managers can perform it well. Therefore, large-scale job enlargement is impossible in many organizations, unless it starts at the top. However, this approach is often resisted, since it usually results in a reduction in the number of management levels and the elimination of some managerial jobs.

Job Design and Organization Design

The way an organization is structured, the management style it uses, and the kind of products it produces set important limits on the latitude an organization has in designing its jobs. Consider, for example, an organization that is designed and operated according to classical Weberian bureaucratic principles. Burns and Stalker (1961) call such organizations mechanistic systems. They are characterized by (1) rigid breakdown into functional specialties, (2) precise definition of duties, responsibilities, and power, and (3) a well-developed command hierarchy through which information filters up and decisions and instructions flow down. In other words, mechanistic systems tend to be "tall," with power and authority centralized at the top and with clearly defined and enforced organizational rules and procedures.

The options realistically open for such organizations in designing jobs are restricted. For example, mechanistic systems could not institute vertical expansion without disrupting the rational coordination of the organization. When jobs are vertically expanded, workers are given authority and responsibility to make a maximum number of their own decisions about how they do their work, the pace they set, and (to a more limited extent) the goals they establish for their performance. In a mechanistic system, these decisions are clearly the responsibility and prerogative of management. Employees are the doers and in no sense the decision makers or the planners.

Horizontal expansion of jobs might be attempted in mechanistic organizations, since horizontal job enlargement is restricted to expanding the scope of the job (for example, by giving the employees added duties that would increase the variety in their work). But even horizontal expansion would present

some problems in a mechanistic system. Most mechanistic organizations have a high degree of functional specialization, which
would have to be broken down to expand jobs horizontally.

An alternative form of organizational design is the organic
system. Organic systems are more adaptable; communications
within the hierarchy are more in the nature of consultation than
the passing up of information and the passing down of orders
and directions. Power tends to be equalized as much as possible throughout the organization, and the chief executive of the
organization is not seen as omniscient and all-powerful. Lines
of authority are generally specified but flexible and may be
changed as organizational needs change on either a temporary
or permanent basis. Organic systems tend to be decentralized
and relatively "flat," with individuals at lower levels given the
option of managing or performing the work in ways not necessarily consistent with what is being done in other parts of the
organization. In other words, consistency is not a central value
for the organization. Organic systems tend to be amenable to
jobs that are expanded in both horizontal and vertical directions. Such organizations have the capability of designing jobs
in many ways throughout the organization without introducing organizational chaos. In addition, organic organizations are
much more able to adjust job designs to individual needs on
either a temporary or semipermanent basis than mechanistic
organizations.

Figure 7.1 presents some of the expected consequences
of congruence and incongruence between organizational design
and job design. Since the characteristics of individual employees
(especially the strength of their desires for growth-need satisfaction) are important in determining how people react to their
work, individual differences are included in the figure as well.
The figure has three aspects: (1) organizational design (organic
versus mechanistic), (2) job design (simple and routine versus
enriched), and (3) individual need strength (high growth needs
versus low growth needs).

Two cells in the figure reflect general congruences: cell 2
(mechanistic design, simple and routine jobs, and low-growth-
need employees) and cell 7 (organic design, enlarged jobs, and

Figure 7.1. Predicted Relationships Among Illustrative Types of Organizational Design, Job Design, and Employee Characteristics.

	SIMPLE, ROUTINE JOBS	ENRICHED JOBS
MECHANISTIC ORGANIZATIONAL DESIGN	**(1) High-Growth-Need Employees** — The individual feels underutilized and overcontrolled. Predict high frustration, dissatisfaction, absenteeism, and turnover. / Congruence in the classical mode. Predict effective performance, adequate levels of satisfaction, and adequate attendance levels if extrinsic reward system is effective. / **Low-Growth-Need Employees (2)**	**(3) High-Growth-Need Employees** — Predict that the individual responds well to his job but chafes at perceived over-control by the organization. / Contradictory Cues / Predict that the individual responds to cues from the organization and that he does not deal effectively with his job. / **Low-Growth-Need Employees (4)**
ORGANIC ORGANIZATIONAL DESIGN	**(5) High-Growth-Need Employees** — Predict that the individual responds to the cues in the organization and that he chafes at the restrictiveness of his job. Predict he will try to have the job changed and succeed, or resign. / Contradictory Cues / Predict that the individual responds to the cues in his job and that he performs reasonably adequately if extrinsically motivated— but that he is constantly uneasy and anxious about the perceived unpredictability of management. / **Low-Growth-Need Employees (6)**	**(7) High-Growth-Need Employees** — Congruence in the job enrichment mode. Predict very high quality performance, high satisfaction, good attendance, and low turnover. / The individual is overwhelmed by organizational and job demands. Predict withdrawal from the job or overt hostility and inadequate job performance. / **Low-Growth-Need Employees (8)**

Source: Adapted from Porter, Lawler, & Hackman, 1975.

high-growth-need employees). In both cases, generally adequate performance and satisfaction is predicted, with expectations somewhat higher for cell 7. Cells 1 and 8 are opposite of one another: in cell 1, an individual with high growth needs is faced with an entirely constraining situation regarding both his job and his organization; in cell 8, an individual with low growth needs is faced with many opportunities that he would not know how to deal with. Thus, it is predicted that individuals in cell 1 will feel underutilized, frustrated, dissatisfied, and probably will leave the organization; individuals in cell 8 will feel overwhelmed by organizational and job demands and will have great difficulties adapting to the work situation.

Cells 3 through 6 are characterized by contradictory messages: the job provides one set of cues to the worker, and the organization provides a second and contradictory set of cues. Conditions in these cells actually exist in relatively few organizations. The prediction (which is not based firmly on existing theory or data) is that, in these situations, individuals will tend to respond to and act in accordance with those cues that are congruent with their own needs. Thus, high-growth-need individuals will tend to respond to cues provided by their jobs in cell 3 and to organizational cues in cell 5; low-growth-need people will tend to respond to the organization in cell 4 and to the job in cell 6. However, in none of these cases would fully adequate performance be expected, nor would it be predicted that employees would be well satisfied with their work. In every case in cells 3 through 6, contradictory cues are present about what kinds of behavioral strategies are appropriate, and dealing with this conflict undoubtedly will tend to frustrate the achievement of good performance and the development of satisfaction.

It should be emphasized that the "types" of people, organizational designs, and job designs presented in Figure 7.1 are to some extent caricatures of the real world; pure types of any of the three categories simply do not exist. It is more useful and valid to think of the cells as end points on a continuum rather than as meaningful types in themselves.

Job designs are also limited by the kind of product an organization produces. Most products can be produced only in a limited number of ways. To conceptualize this, we can view jobs as being located along a continuum, which we will call the automation continuum. At one end of the continuum is unit production performed by individual craftsmen. At the other end is the process-, or completely automated, production facility, where the worker controls vast amounts of automated equipment. Mass production, or assembly line, jobs fall at the middle, since they are neither highly automated nor highly individualized. Unit production jobs tend to be high on the core dimensions and are quite satisfying, involving, and motivating to the worker. They provide the employee with responsibility for production of an entire product and enable him to take justifiable pride in his work. Jobs in automated plants can also be high on the core dimensions because high skill levels are required. Moreover, the workers — even at the lower skill levels — feel that they are controlling the production process. Thus, despite their basic differences, jobs at both ends of the automation continuum are high on the core dimensions.

Mass production has the worst features of both the unit-production and the automated-production processes. It tends to create jobs that are low on the four core dimensions. It has the physical working-with-the-product that is characteristic of unit production, but this work is so simplified that it provides no variety or challenge. Mass production often involves the use of complex machines but provides the worker with little or no control over the machines.

Moving jobs away from the center of the continuum toward either end should make them higher on the core dimensions. This involves a reversal of the historic movement from unit production to process production and the movement from whole jobs to specialized jobs. However, two important limiting factors in any organization's ability to move its jobs away from mass production are the type of product produced and the most economic method of production.

Figure 7.2 presents one way to visualize these factors. The figure shows where the production zones of four products fall on an automation continuum. These production zones cover all the methods on the continuum by which the product can feasibly be produced. For example, chemicals can be produced in a zone extending from mass production to process production. Airplanes can be produced on a unit basis and to some extent on a mass production basis. Typewriters have a slightly broader zone, since much of their production can be automated.

Figure 7.2. Production Zones.

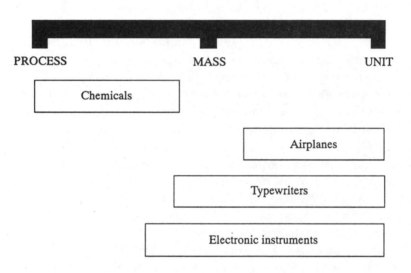

The important point is that once a zone has been developed for a product, the production method should be chosen in terms of what best fits the people who are available to do the work. In some cases, this may involve moving the job from the center of the continuum to the unit-production end. In the production of automobiles, a move toward greater automation may be needed in many cases, although unit production may be possible in other cases. The overriding objective in any change effort should always be to increase the fit between the individual's needs and the design of the job.

In summary, job design has an important effect on the satisfaction and motivation of those workers who are concerned with higher-order-need satisfaction. Because of this, it is important that organizations design jobs to fit the needs of their employees. Good job/people matches yield large dividends in both organizational effectiveness and individual need satisfaction. Finally, job design can have a strong impact on the interpersonal relationships that exist in an organization. Interpersonal relationships will be considered further in the next chapter, which focuses on the impact interpersonal relationships have on job performance and job satisfaction.

eight

Interpersonal Influences

The hierarchical nature of the complex organization produces many different types of interpersonal relationships. The most heavily researched has been the superior/subordinate relationship. Less frequently studied but also of great importance are peer-group relationships. Many other relationships have not been studied extensively (for example, line/staff relationships and customer/client relationships); for our purpose this does not present a serious problem, since the major interpersonal influences on motivation and satisfaction seem to come from the peer group and the leader. Thus, this chapter will focus first on how peer groups and leaders influence motivation and then on how they influence satisfaction.

Interpersonal Influences on Motivation

Interpersonal factors influence motivation in many complex and diverse ways. Chapter 6 discussed how rewards such as pay and promotion can influence extrinsic motivation, and Chapter 7 discussed how job design can influence intrinsic motivation. Interpersonal factors seem to influence both intrinsic and extrinsic motivation. In a sense, both Chapters 6 and 7 were concerned

with interpersonal influences on motivation. The superior plays
a crucial role in administering rewards such as pay and promotion; he usually makes the decision about who will get a pay
raise, and he is responsible for the performance evaluation on
which pay raises and promotions are based.

The superior also plays a crucial role in the area of job
design. In addition to his responsibility for organizing tasks into
jobs, his behavior after the job is designed helps to define the
employee's job. Feedback and autonomy are two of the four core
dimensions described in Chapter 7. By his behavior, the superior
influences how much of each of these dimensions is present on
the job, although his influence is limited by the actual design
of the job. He can give or withhold feedback, and he can give
or withhold autonomy. In the case of autonomy, the superior
can often turn a poor job into a motivating job by letting the
subordinates define their own approach to the work. On the other
hand, he can also turn a motivating job into a boring, repetitive job by supervising his subordinates closely and restricting
their autonomy. Because the superior can influence both the
administration of pay and promotion and the design of jobs,
he is an important factor in both intrinsic and extrinsic motivation.

The members of a work group typically play a less important role in the design of jobs and in the administration of
the organization's formal rewards and punishments than do superiors. This is not to say, however, that they play a trivial role.
Their collective behavior does influence the amount of autonomy each individual experiences on his job and the amount of
feedback he receives. The work group members can either aid
or hinder an individual's efforts to perform well, thus influencing the likelihood that the individual will receive both intrinsic
and extrinsic rewards. The work group members can also influence the administration of rewards such as promotion and
pay through their evaluation of the individual's performance.
Organizations are often hesitant to promote and reward employees who are not respected by their peers, and thus work
groups can often prevent individuals from receiving rewards.

The influence of peer groups and leaders on motivation is
not limited to their ability to influence job design and the giving

of formal extrinsic rewards and punishments. Both the leader and the peer group potentially can give extrinsic rewards other than pay and promotion. They can give praise and social acceptance, which often are valued more than pay and promotion. The research on pay incentive plans mentioned in Chapter 6 showed that interpersonal rewards given by peer-group members often are valued highly and can influence motivation. Other research to be reviewed in this chapter shows that leaders have an equal or perhaps greater ability to give extrinsic rewards than peer-group members.

In addition to their impact on job design, leaders can influence intrinsic motivation in another way. Organizational methods of decision making strongly influence the kind of intrinsic rewards that are associated with effectively carrying out the decisions. Certain leadership styles seem to result in positive rewards, such as feelings of self-esteem and competence being tied to good performance. How this occurs will be a major focus of discussion in this chapter.

Peer groups also play an important role in determining how motivated people will be to carry out decisions. Evidence shows that group decisions are different from individual decisions—both in terms of content and in terms of how people feel about them. It appears that group decision making can influence the kind of intrinsic rewards that are tied to performance. More rewards seem to be tied to good performance when decisions about performance are made on a group basis than when these decisions are made on an individual basis.

Figure 8.1 summarizes how leadership style and peer-group relationships can influence motivation by influencing both the intrinsic and the extrinsic rewards that are associated with performance. Two of the four ways that leadership and peer groups can influence motivation have already been discussed in Chapters 6 and 7; the other two ways will be emphasized in this chapter.

It is important to remember that the best leadership style is not always the one that leads to the highest motivation. A certain leadership style may lead to the highest motivation but not to the highest job performance. Performance is influenced

Figure 8.1. Interpersonal Influences on Motivation.

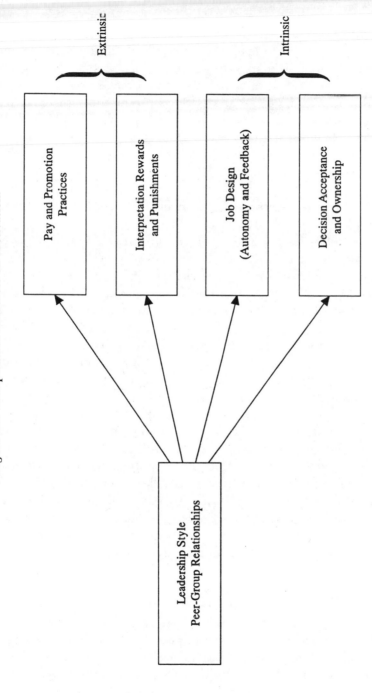

by many things other than motivation. For example, a very democratic approach to leadership might lead to low performance but high motivation in a situation in which such leadership consumes a great deal of time and leads to decisions that are not optimal in terms of factors such as production efficiency and financial investment. Sometimes, a leader who is authoritarian in his behavior can make better and faster decisions than a democratic leader; as a result, the authoritarian leader obtains better performance (Argyris, 1953).

Interpersonal Influences on Satisfaction

Because leadership style and peer-group relationships have a strong influence on the reception of both intrinsic and extrinsic rewards, they also influence satisfaction. Leadership style, in particular, has a strong influence on the kind of intrinsic rewards a person receives and thus is related to higher-order-need satisfaction, since it determines whether a subordinate will have his social needs satisfied through his relationship with his superior. Further, it can indirectly influence the kind of relationships an employee has with his peers. Leaders can behave in ways that set peers against each other or in ways that increase group cohesiveness and social-need satisfaction.

In addition to influencing the outcomes individuals actually receive, leadership style can influence their perceptions of what they should receive. For example, the supportive supervisor who gives positive feedback can increase his subordinates' view of their inputs and thereby indirectly influence the subordinates' perception of what they should receive. Because leadership style can influence both the outcomes people receive and what they feel they should receive, it can influence the satisfaction of many needs, especially social needs.

Peer-group relationships seem to have the most power to influence social-need satisfaction. The peer group is potentially the major source of friendship opportunities for an employee. The acceptance and support of peer-group members are often sufficient to satisfy an individual's social needs. Peer-group relationships can influence the individual's perceptions of what he should receive. Especially in terms of extrinsic rewards, the group can raise as well as lower a person's perception of what he should receive. For example, a supportive, accepting peer group can raise a person's perception of what he should receive in terms of a pay increase or a promotion — just as a negative, critical peer group can lower this perception.

Figure 8.2 summarizes how leadership style and peer-group relationships can influence satisfaction by influencing the kinds of rewards people receive as well as their perception of what they should receive, which in turn are shown as influencing satisfaction. The figure is based on the assumption that leadership style and peer-group relationships influence the satisfaction of certain higher- and lower-order needs and thus influence overall job satisfaction.

Leadership Style and Motivation

Now that we have considered on a general level how superiors can influence the motivation and satisfaction of their subordinates, we will look at how the specific behaviors of leaders affect subordinates. In doing this, we will focus on how leadership behavior affects $P \rightarrow O$ beliefs and the reception of rewards. However, we must consider first some of the approaches that have been used in describing leadership behavior.

Patterns of Leadership Behavior

A number of different approaches to describing and classifying leadership behavior have been developed over the 30 or more years during which leadership has been the subject of empirical investigation. Many of the early studies of leadership distinguished among authoritarian, democratic, and laissez-faire leadership styles. In their classic study of boys' clubs, Lewin, Lippitt, and White (1939) defined these leadership styles as follows: in authoritarian leadership, the leader makes all the important decisions without consulting the subordinates; in democratic leadership, the leader encourages group discussion and group decision making; in laissez-faire leadership, the leader

Figure 8.2. Interpersonal Influences on Satisfaction.

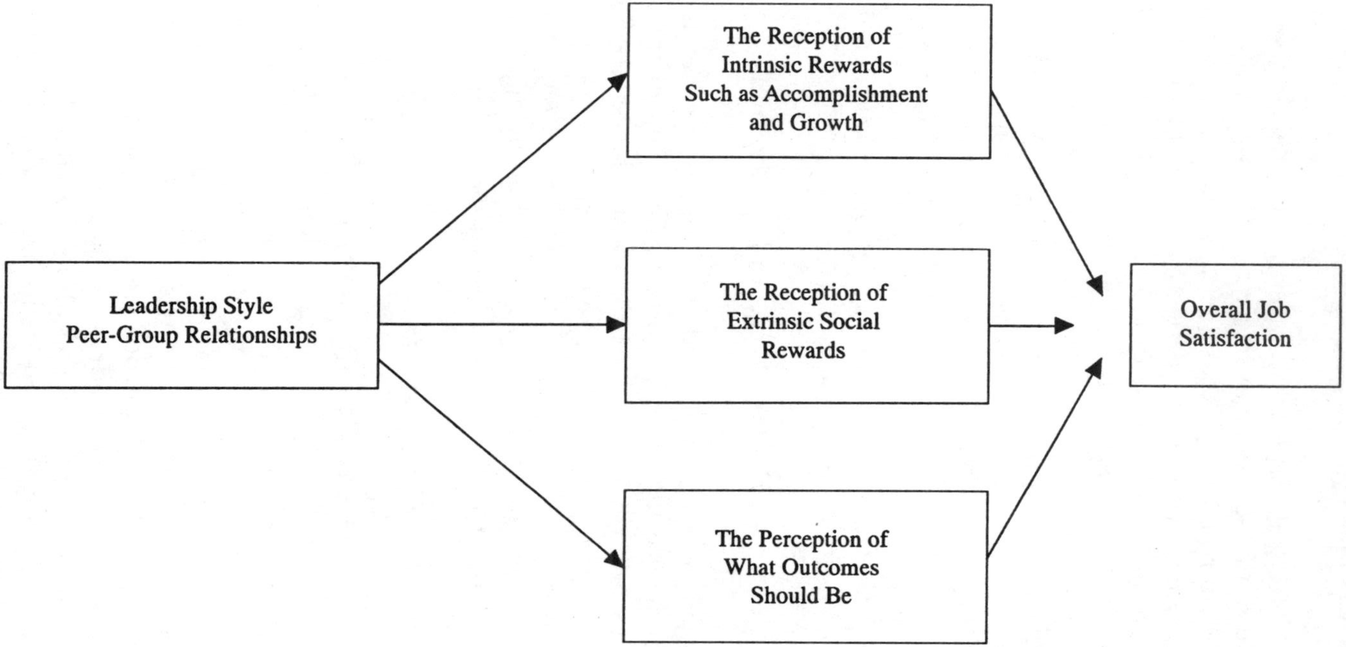

is largely passive. Since 1939, the authoritarian-democratic distinction has been used in many studies of leadership, and there is now much research that shows the effects of these styles on both motivation and satisfaction.

In the late 1940s, a group at the University of Michigan began a series of studies of leadership style that led them to distinguish between employee-centered supervisors and production-centered supervisors (Katz, Maccoby & Morse, 1950). Supervisors who emphasize the production or technical aspects of the job and who seem to consider employees primarily as people to get the work done are called production centered. Supervisors who take an interest in employees and consider them as individuals are called employee centered. A production-centered supervisor answered a question on the most important part of his job by saying, "Well, the most important part is to get the reports out. The biggest thing is to get the work out" (p. 21). A supervisor classified as employee centered said, "Well, there are two things — keeping the section running smoothly, keeping the clerks happy, keeping production up, making impartial assignments of work, making the proper decisions on some difficult cases involving some payments and maybe a premium that hadn't been paid before" (p. 21). This classification system has been used in a number of studies and has undergone some changes in recent years.

At the same time the Michigan group was conducting studies, researchers at Ohio State University began to study leadership. After an extensive analysis of the behavior of leaders, they decided that two dimensions could be used to describe much of leadership behavior. One of these they called initiation and the other consideration. According to them, a leader could be either high or low on initiation and high or low on consideration. They defined the terms as follows (Fleishman and Harris, 1962):

> *Consideration* includes behavior indicating mutual trust, respect, and a certain warmth and rapport between the supervisor and his group. This does not mean that this dimension reflects a superficial "pat-on-the-back," "first-name-calling" kind of human

relations behavior. This dimension appears to emphasize a deeper concern for group members' needs
and includes such behavior as allowing subordinates
more participation in decision making and encouraging more two-way communication.

Structure (initiation) includes behavior in which
the supervisor organizes and defines group activities and his relation to the group. Thus, he defines
the role he expects each member to assume, assigns
tasks, plans ahead, establishes ways of getting things
done, and pushes for production. This dimension
seems to emphasize overt attempts to achieve organizational goals [pp. 43–44].

In another series of leadership studies, Fiedler has been
concerned with the kind of situational factors that influence the
effectiveness of different leaders. Fiedler measures leadership
style by asking leaders to describe their least preferred co-workers
with a number of adjectives. The resulting measure is called
an LPC score. The problem with Fiedler's measure is that it
is not clear what kind of behavior characterizes low and high
LPC leaders. Because of this, some of the research is difficult
to interpret in terms of our approach to motivation. At one time,
Fiedler (1964) described low-LPC leaders as managing and controlling, and high-LPC leaders as permissive and considerate.
However, in his later works, he has dropped these distinctions.

As originally stated, the Ohio State and Michigan approaches to classifying leadership behavior had much in common. Employee centeredness was similar to consideration, and
production centeredness was similar to initiating structure; but
there was an important difference in how they were seen to be
related. Originally, the Michigan group argued that a leader
should be described as falling somewhere along a single continuum varying from production oriented to employee oriented.
Thus, if a person was high on production orientation he was
low on employee orientation, and vice versa. The Ohio State
research, on the other hand, argued for two dimensions. Thus,
a person could be high on both initiation and consideration,
low on both, or high on one and low on the other.

In a 1960 article that included the results of studying a tractor factory, Kahn altered the Michigan view in a way that made it very similar to the Ohio State approach. According to Kahn,

> In the studies on the insurance company and on the railroad, we had treated employee-centered and production-centered supervision as if they were the two opposite ends of a single continuum. We had assumed, in other words, that as a supervisor became more production oriented, he must of necessity become less employee oriented. The research data from the tractor company suggested instead that the quality of being employee centered should be regarded as theoretically independent dimensions of supervision. Thus, we may, for convenience, think of a four-celled table, with each cell representing a kind of supervision that combines differently the attributes of employee orientation and production orientation [p. 282].

Thus, at the present time, the results of both the Ohio State and Michigan studies agree that the critical behaviors a leader demonstrates can be described in terms of two dimensions. This is a significant conclusion, given the great amount of research that was done at Ohio State and Michigan. More recently, Blake and Mouton (1964) made these same dimensions the basis for their approach to organization development. This raises the important question of how these dimensions relate to the other major approach to classifying leadership behavior—the distinction between authoritarian and democratic leadership.

Research typically has been focused on either the initiation and consideration dimensions or the authoritarian-democratic distinction. Few studies have tried to relate these approaches, although they do seem to be related. The definition of consideration contains some of the elements of democratic participation. For example, high consideration is defined as including good two-way communication and mutual trust. Thus, it would seem that the democratic leader would be high on consideration, and he would be high on initiation if he were task oriented. In Figure 8.3, the high-consideration/high-initiation cell is labeled democratic or participative. The low-consideration/high-initiation cell is labeled authoritarian because of the strong emphasis in authoritarian management on getting things done without including or worrying about people. The low-consideration/low-initiation cell is labeled laissez-faire for obvious reasons, and the high-consideration/low-initiation cell is labeled human relations because of the dominant emphasis on keeping people happy.

Figure 8.3. Classification of Leadership Styles.

INITIATION

		High	*Low*
CONSIDERATION	*High*	Democratic or Participative	Human Relations
	Low	Authoritarian	Laissez-Faire

A number of other approaches to classifying leadership behavior have been suggested. However, those presented in Figure 8.3 have been used in most of the research studies on leadership; thus, the following discussion will focus on their relationship to motivation.

Initiation, Consideration, and Motivation

Many writers have asserted that considerate, employee-oriented supervisors tend to obtain better productivity from their subordinates. For example, Likert (1959) states that the supervisor who obtains the highest productivity is "supportive, friendly, and helpful rather than hostile" and endeavors to treat people in a "sensitive, considerate way." There is some evidence of a positive relationship between productivity and supervisor consideration; however, the evidence fails to offer consistent support for this point of view. Based on our motivation model, we can find little reason to expect that consideration, alone, should affect motivation. Just being nice to people does not change their $P \rightarrow O$ beliefs about working hard and performing effectively. However, in combination with other behaviors, consideration may have this effect. Before discussing this issue, let us consider some of the studies of the relationship between consideration and productivity.

The original study by the Michigan group (Katz et al., 1950) found a strong relationship between consideration and productivity. The highly productive supervisors were typically characterized as employee centered because they concentrated on the human-relations aspects of their jobs, and they described people management as the most important part of their jobs. A second study by the Michigan group essentially replicated these results (Katz, Maccoby, Gurin & Floor, 1951). Again, the men in high-productivity work groups described their supervisors as not being punitive and as taking a personal interest in them, helping them by training them for higher-level jobs.

Some of the Ohio State studies also found a strong relationship between consideration and productivity (Korman, 1966a). Other studies have shown that initiation is strongly related to effectiveness. However, many studies have found either no relationship between consideration and productivity or a negative relationship, and the relationship between initiation and productivity has also varied from one study to another. Korman (1966a) concludes his literature review of initiation and consideration by pointing out that neither style seems to be consistently related to productivity. He further states that we need to know more about the conditions under which these relationships exist or do not exist. Vroom (1964) states that "measures of the amount of consideration shown by a supervisor for his subordinates are frequently positively related to the effectiveness of the work unit" (p. 214), but he, too, notes that the results are inconsistent and that different situations probably require different leadership styles.

A minimum level of initiation seems necessary for any kind of extrinsic motivation to be high. To tie rewards to performance, someone must define what kind of behavior is expected and measure the behavior. This is usually the superior's task, and the more he does this (that is, the more initiation he practices), the more possibility there is that extrinsic motivation will be high. By itself, however, initiation behavior should not be expected to increase motivation; motivation should be increased only if the initiation behavior results in extrinsic rewards being tied to good performance. Thus, it is not surprising that initiation of structure and performance are related under some conditions and unrelated under others.

As has been noted, there is no reason to expect that consideration should always lead to higher motivation and higher productivity. By itself, consideration does not affect the relationship between either intrinsic or extrinsic rewards and effective performance. Thus, it is not surprising that studies have failed to find a consistent relationship between motivation and consideration. However, under certain conditions, the amount of consideration shown by a leader might be expected to relate to motivation. Considerate behavior is a potential reward and might serve as a motivator if its reception were made contingent on effective performance. The person who expects to be praised and supported, regardless of his performance, will be no more motivated than the person who will not be praised or supported, regardless of his behavior. On the other hand, the person who wants to receive praise and support and receives them only when he performs well will have different $P \rightarrow O$ beliefs, and should be more motivated than the person who always or never receives praise and support.

Instead of studying how and when consideration is given, researchers have simply looked at how much consideration is given, which could be one reason for the inconsistent findings. Based on our motivation model, we would predict a positive relationship between consideration and productivity when consideration depends on performance, and a zero relationship when it doesn't. Supervisors who combine high initiation with high consideration would seem to come closer to practicing conditional consideration than other leaders. These supervisors concentrate on defining their relationships with subordinates, in addition to getting the work done. Thus, to a large extent, their approval and acceptance might depend on the subordinates' performance. This leads to the prediction that the most effective leader should be the one who combines initiation and consideration in a way that influences his subordinates' $P \rightarrow O$ beliefs.

Unfortunately, little evidence exists to validate the last prediction. Few studies have looked at the joint influence of consideration and initiation on productivity. One applicable study is that of Kahn (1958). According to him, data from many of the Michigan studies suggest that productivity differences are related to the degree to which supervisors convince their subordinates that effective performance leads to supervisory approval.

> Supervisors who have actually achieved high levels of productivity have done so in part by making such behavior on the part of the employee a path to supervisory approval and a condition for the exertion of supervisory influence. For example, among employees in a tractor factory, those in the high-producing groups were more likely to say that their foreman considered high productivity one of the most important things on the job. Employees in low-producing groups more often said that other things were equally or more important to their foreman. The implication of such a finding is that the high-producing supervisor not only wants to attain high productivity but has successfully communicated to his employees that at least one of the paths to supervisory approval is to produce at a high rate [p. 69].

In another relevant study, Evans (1970) found a relationship between both initiation and consideration and employees' $P \rightarrow O$ beliefs. (However, these relationships were found in only one of two samples, and his data do not explain this.) Thus, some evidence does show that, in combination, high consideration and high initiation can increase motivation by tying supervisory approval to effective performance. High consideration and high initiation seem to be effective because they create strong extrinsic motivation based on social needs; thus, our motivation model would predict that they should influence the motivation of only those people who want social rewards from their superior.

There are still unanswered questions about the conditions under which initiation and consideration lead to higher motivation. The conclusion that motivation is higher (for people who value social approval) when consideration is made conditional is only a partial answer. It says nothing about how initiation and consideration relate to intrinsic motivation. Some possible answers are provided by the following discussion of research on power equalization.

Power Equalization and Motivation

Democratic management and participative management are approaches to leadership that lead to a reduction in the power differential between superiors and subordinates. Many writers argue that engaging in power equalization results in increased employee motivation. In fact, many studies show that power equalization can and often does result in higher productivity. The classic study by Lewin et al. (1939) showed that, in terms of overall productivity, democratic leadership was superior to laissez-faire leadership and almost equal to authoritarian leadership. However, the democratically led children continued to work when the leader left the room, whereas the autocratically led children did not. This suggests that the autocratically led children were motivated extrinsically but the democratically led children were motivated intrinsically.

Later studies of the effectiveness of democratic leadership have shown it to be superior to other styles. Coch and French (1948) found that participation led to a more productive work group. Those employees who participated in the design of a technological change learned their new jobs more quickly, produced more, and showed less resistance to the change. Strauss (in Whyte, 1955) did a fascinating study of a work group that painted toys in a factory. Originally, the work pace was controlled by a belt that ran at a constant speed. The situation was changed so the employees could decide to set the belt at a speed that would result in increased productivity; they did, and production went up dramatically. However, this had several negative effects. The extra production in the paint room created a pile-up in front and a vacuum behind, and both results were unwelcome to the adjoining departments. The company's wage structure was shaken because the workers in this group were on a piece-rate plan, and their wages were suddenly high in comparison with other workers' wages. The company took back the right to control productivity; as a result, most of the workers in this group quit.

Many studies have shown that under some conditions power equalization does not lead to higher motivation and productivity. French, Israel, and As (1960) tried to replicate the Coch and French study in a Norwegian plant and obtained insignificant results. In a large-scale field experiment, Morse and Reimer (1956) studied the relative effectiveness of authoritarian and democratic leadership styles in a clerical setting. Two groups of workers were placed under a democratic style of leadership, and two were placed under an authoritarian style. All groups improved their productivity. Likert (1961) has argued that the democratic approach would have proved superior if the experiment has continued.

> The results . . . give every reason to believe that had the clerical experiment been continued for another year or two, productivity and quality of work would have continued to increase in the participative program, while, in the hierarchically controlled program, productivity and quality of work would have declined as a result of the hostility, resentment, and turnover evoked by the program [p. 69].

However, over the period during which the study took place, the democratic approach was not superior. Furthermore, this is not an isolated study; other studies have found the authoritarian style to be as good as or better than the democratic style (for example, see Vroom, 1964; Argyris, 1953). It is hardly surprising that in many cases autocratic leadership is in fact superior to democratic leadership. The authoritarian leader is often in a better position than the democratic leader to influence extrinsic motivation. Because he is free to give and withhold extrinsic rewards, such as pay and promotion, he can tie many of these rewards to performance. This will create a strong motivation to produce, if the workers value the extrinsic rewards and see their connection to good performance. The authoritarian leader also has a time advantage because participation uses up a considerable amount of time that could be used in directly productive activities.

In many ways, it is surprising that democratic leadership does sometimes lead to higher productivity. If people were motivated only by extrinsic rewards, skillful authoritarian leadership might be always superior to democratic leadership. The fact that it isn't always superior highlights the importance of intrinsic motivation and decision quality in influencing performance. Both of these factors must be high if performance is to be high, and authoritarian leadership doesn't always lead to either the highest intrinsic motivation or the highest-quality decisions with respect to level of productivity and methods of production. Vroom (1964) states that power equalization "can increase the quality of decisions made, the strength of group norms regarding execution of the decisions, and the worker's 'ego involvement' in the decisions. Each of these three effects seems to be a frequent — but probably not a necessary — consequence of increased influence in decision making by subordinates" (p. 229).

In Strauss' study (in Whyte, 1955), participation led to the employees setting higher work standards, which shows that participation can increase decision quality. What determines whether participation will lead to improved decision quality? Two important factors appear to be crucial. The first is the amount and kind of information that the subordinates have;

often, subordinates simply don't have the information they need in order to make high-quality decisions. The second is the kind of decision involved. Where the goals of the work group conflict with those of the organization, the workers cannot be counted on to make what the organization would consider a high-quality decision. A good example is provided by the Morse and Reimer (1956) study described earlier. In this clerical situation, it was found that the best way to increase efficiency was to cut the staff by 25 percent. The autocratic leader had no trouble making this decision, but the participative groups were very reluctant to come to this decision. They finally decided to reduce the staff by not replacing workers who left and by looking for transfer opportunities. In short, it is not safe to assume that higher-quality decisions and higher productivity are a necessary consequence of democratic leadership.

The study of Lewin et al. (1939) showed that participation can influence intrinsic motivation. The democratically led children seemed to be so involved and committed to their work that they continued to produce even when the extrinsic evaluator (their supervisor) wasn't present. Vroom (1964) has offered an interesting explanation of why participation affects motivation.

> People become ego involved in decisions in which they have had influence. If they have helped to make a decision, it is their decision, and the success or failure of the decision is their success or failure. Intuitively, it would appear that the amount of personal involvement of people in decisions is dependent on the amount of influence they have had in the decision and on the extent to which they pride themselves on their ability to make that kind of decision. If, for example, a person who conceives himself to be a brilliant scientist shares in the making of a decision that he believes requires scientific judgment, the outcome of that decision is a test of the adequacy of his self-conception. A successful decision confirms his self-concept; an unsuccessful decision threatens it [p. 228].

Vroom's statement is similar to the discussion in Chapter 5 of the effects of participation in performance appraisal. In terms of our motivation model, our explanation of why participation affects motivation would be that participation changes the $P \rightarrow O$ beliefs of subordinates.

There is also evidence that the influence of power equalization may be partially accounted for by its effect on group norms. Apparently, when leadership is participative, norms favorable to high productivity are more likely to develop. Coch and French (1948) stressed the importance of group norms in their study of the successful use of participation. Lewin (1947) stressed that group discussion and decision making are usually superior to lectures in changing behavior because they affect group norms. Apparently, when participation takes place, norms develop that lead the group members to reward behavior that is supportive of the group decision and punish behavior that isn't. This, of course, has a direct effect on the extrinsic motivation of the employees to carry out the decision.

Evidence shows that participation does not always lead to increased motivation. In a classic study, Vroom (1960) showed that the effects of participation are moderated by a worker's need for independence. Vroom found that workers with little need for independence were not motivated by participation. The failure of the French et al. (1960) study to replicate the earlier Coch and French (1948) study illustrates that participation is ineffective when the work group is not in favor of it. Because the group didn't favor participation, the use of it failed to affect the group norms.

Because the effect of power equalization on motivation is largely a function of its impact on intrinsic motivation, it will influence only certain people. People who do not value the intrinsic rewards affected by power equalization will not be influenced by it. Similarly, its influence on group norms does not assure that it can influence everyone's motivation. It can influence only those people who value the extrinsic rewards that groups can give.

In summary, power equalization has the potential to increase the motivation of employees who (1) have strong needs for independence, competence, and self-esteem, (2) are members of a work group that favors participation, and (3) value the social rewards that groups can offer. Power equalization has the potential to lead to higher-quality decisions when (1) employees have relevant information, (2) time is available for adequate discussion, and (3) the self-interest of employees does not conflict directly with the interests of the organization. Finally, power equalization will lead to higher productivity when it results in both improved decision making and higher motivation.

Leadership Style and Satisfaction

The research on motivation shows that the superior represents an important source of rewards. If rewards have the kind of impact on satisfaction that was specified in Chapter 4, satisfaction should be related to leadership style. In fact, as we shall see in the following discussion, leadership style and satisfaction have been found to be related.

Consideration and Satisfaction

Many studies have been concerned with the relationship between satisfaction and the amount of consideration shown by a leader. Not surprisingly, there is evidence that consideration is positively related to satisfaction. Considerate supervisors behave in ways that will lead their subordinates to receive more rewards, especially in the interpersonal area. According to Fleishman and Harris (1962), considerate behavior includes "mutual trust, respect, and a certain warmth and rapport between the supervisor and his group" (p. 43). In short, the considerate supervisor is concerned with his subordinates' needs. Thus, he would be expected to have satisfied subordinates who, because of the effects of satisfaction, would be expected to have low absenteeism and turnover rates.

Many of the early Ohio State studies reported a significant relationship between amount of consideration and satisfaction (for example, see Fleishman, Harris, & Burtt, 1955; Halpin & Winer, 1957). Likert (1961) studied relationships between many behaviors and employee satisfaction in a public-utility company (see Table 8.1) and found considerate behavior to be associated with high satisfaction. In other, more recent studies, similar consideration/satisfaction relationships were found (Wager, 1965; House, Filley, & Kerr, 1971).

**Table 8.1. Relationship Between
Supervisor's Behavior and Subordinates' Attitudes.**

Supervisory behavior	*Percentage of employees in work groups with favorable atttiudes who report that their supervisors engage in the stated activity*	*Percentage of employees in work groups with unfavorable attitudes who report that their supervisors engage in the stated activity*
Recommends promotion, transfers, pay increases	61	22
Informs men on what is happening in the company	47	11
Keeps men posted on how well they are doing	47	12
Hears complaints and grievances	65	32
Thinks of employees as human beings rather than as persons to get the work done	97	33
Will go to bat or stand up for me	87	30
Usually pulls for the men or for both the men and the company, rather than for himself or for the company only	86	29
Takes an interest in me and understands my problems	81	29
Is really part of the group; interests are the same as those of the people in the group	66	16
Likes to get our ideas and tries to do something about them	62	17

Source: Adapted from *New Patterns of Management* by R. Likert. Copyright © 1961 by McGraw-Hill Book Company. Used by permission of the publisher.

If amount of supervisor consideration is related to employee satisfaction, there should be a relationship between consideration and factors such as grievances, turnover, and absenteeism, which also are related to satisfaction. Figure 8.4 shows the relationship found by Fleishman and Harris (1962) between turnover and employee consideration. Figure 8.5 shows the joint effects of consideration and initiation (structure) on grievance rates as found by these researchers. High consideration is associated with low grievance rates and high initiation is associated with high grievance rates. However, when consideration is high, high initiation does not lead necessarily to high grievance rates; only when consideration is low does high initiation lead to high grievance rates. Apparently, large amounts of consideration can nullify the negative effects of high initiation.

Under certain conditions, no positive relationship may exist between satisfaction and consideration. Pelz (1951) states that when leaders are low on upward influence (power), considerate behavior on the part of the leader may not cause greater employee satisfaction. Pelz concluded that

> if an influential supervisor attempts to help employees achieve their goals, his efforts will tend to succeed. Concrete results will be achieved, and therefore employee satisfaction will rise. But — according to the data — if a noninfluential supervisor tries to get the same result, his efforts may often fail. Employees' expectations will be frustrated, and consequently their satisfaction will not rise and may even fall [p. 216].

Similar findings were reported by Wager (1965). He studied lower-level white-collar workers and found that high-upward-influence leaders were more effective in using a considerate leadership style than low-influence leaders were. In both the Pelz and Wager studies, the leaders were operating in a hierarchical organization where their ability to satisfy their subordinates' needs depended on their ability to influence the rest of the organization.

Figure 8.4. Relation Between Consideration and Turnover Rates.

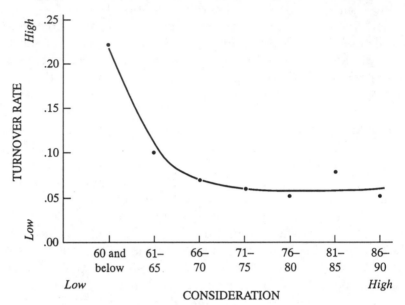

Source: From Fleishman, E. A., & Harris, E. F. Patterns of leadership behavior related to employee grievances and turnover. *Personnel Psychology,* 1962, *15,* 43–56. Copyright © 1962 by Personnel Psychology, Inc. Reprinted by permission.

The impact of consideration on employee satisfaction is also affected by how much employees value the kind of rewards the supervisor can control. Even the supervisor with high upward influence is limited in the kind of rewards he can influence. He can affect many interpersonal and other extrinsic rewards but he has less influence over the reception of some important, intrinsic rewards. Thus, if an employee is motivated largely by intrinsic rewards, the amount of consideration his supervisor shows may not have a significant effect on his feelings of overall job satisfaction.

In general, more considerate supervisors tend to have more satisfied subordinates. However, there are exceptions; the relationship depends on the supervisor's power in the organization and the kind of rewards that are important to the subordinates.

Figure 8.5. Combinations of Consideration
and Structure Related to Grievances.

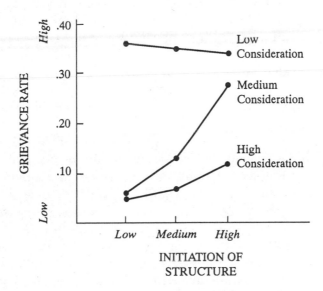

Source: From Fleishman, E. A., & Harris, E. F. Patterns of leadership behavior related to employee grievances and turnover. *Personnel Psychology,* 1962, *15,* 43–56. Copyright © 1962 by Personnel Psychology, Inc. Reprinted by permission.

Power Equalization and Satisfaction

Why should participation and democratic leadership be associated with high job satisfaction? First, some people have strong needs for independence, and participation in decision making can help satisfy these needs. In addition, when people participate, they have a chance to influence decisions so that the decisions provide them with the outcomes they desire. In an early study, Jacobson (1951) found that workers were more satisfied with those foremen and shop stewards who allowed them to participate in decision making. Morse and Reimer (1956) compared satisfaction scores for authoritarian and democratic groups and found that the democratic groups had higher satisfaction scores even though they were not more productive.

In an interesting study, Marrow, Bowers, and Seashore (1967) reported the efforts of a company to change the leadership style of managers in a newly acquired division. A more participative leadership style was put into effect, which seemed to increase the satisfaction and effectiveness of the employees. A follow-up several years later revealed that the leadership change persisted and the employees still showed high levels of satisfaction.

Several studies have shown that when participation and democratic management are practiced, absenteeism and turnover rates are lower. A relationship between participation and absenteeism and turnover would be expected because of the strong relationship between satisfaction and absenteeism and turnover. Wickert (1951) compared attitudes of telephone operators and service representatives who quit with those who stayed. Those who remained were significantly more likely to report that they had chances to make decisions on their jobs and that they were making an important contribution to the company's success. Other studies (for example, Ross & Zander, 1957) comparing employees who quit with those who stayed found that those who stayed felt that they had more autonomy and that they were kept better informed about what went on in the organization.

The finding that participation strongly affects autonomy satisfaction leads to the prediction that only people who have strong needs for autonomy will respond with increased satisfaction to a power-equalization leadership style. Several studies support this view. In an indirect test, Trow (1957) found that subjects with a strong need for independence expressed lower satisfaction than other subjects with roles in which they were made highly dependent on others. In Tannenbaum and Allport's (1956) study, employees were placed under authoritarian leaders while others were placed under democratic leaders. The employees' personalities were assessed, and the employees were classified on the degree to which they were likely to respond to authoritarian and democratic leadership. The employees receiving the leadership style to which they were suited by their personalities were more satisfied than those receiving the style to which they were not suited. In addition, those who were more satisfied wanted to continue under the leadership style they received during the study.

Vroom (1959, 1960) has provided the most complete test of the view that the effect of leadership style on satisfaction depends on the personalities of the subordinates. In a large package-delivery firm, Vroom measured the strength of the subordinates' needs for independence and their degree of authoritarianism. According to other research findings, high-authoritarian people prefer strong, directive leadership and carefully controlled, unambiguous situations (Adorno et al., 1950). Vroom's data showed that when low-authoritarian subordinates who had a high need for independence were led in a participative way, they were more satisfied. However, the same was not true for high-authoritarian people who had a low need for independence.

The research evidence on leadership clearly makes the point that some people want to be told what to do and not asked what should be done. When they are asked, they become uncomfortable and flee from the responsibility involved. Every manager who has tried participation has found that some of his subordinates don't want it. However, the number of employees who don't want to participate may be decreasing. Several studies have shown that the level of authoritarianism is decreasing in the American society (for example, see Hall, 1971; Ondrack, 1971).

In summary, power equalization does lead to higher employee satisfaction. It is associated most strongly with higher satisfaction of autonomy needs, and it leads to lower absenteeism and turnover. However, these positive effects occur only when the people involved have strong needs for independence and are low on authoritarianism.

Group Influences on Motivation

The Western Electric studies first called attention to the strong impact that groups and group norms can have on productivity and motivation (Roethlisberger & Dickson, 1939). In the relay-assembly test room, a group was observed to develop norms that were supportive of high productivity and that were basically pro-management. In this group, productive behavior was rewarded by the group. The actual productivity and motivation of the group was high and continued to increase during the course of the study. In the bank-wiring observation room, the researchers found a different set of conditions. As in the relay-assembly test room, strong norms existed about production; however, these norms were anti-management and anti-production. As one worker explained,

> There's another thing; you know, the fellows give the fast workers the raspberry all the time. Work hard, try to do your best, and they don't appreciate it at all. They don't seem to figure that they are gaining any by it. It's not only the wiremen, the soldermen don't like it either. . . . The fellows who loaf along are liked better than anybody else. Some of them take pride in turning out as little work as they can and making the boss think they're turning out a whole lot. They think it's smart [p. 418].*

Production in this room was restricted by the employees and stayed at a constant, low level during the course of the study. When an employee broke the norms of the group and engaged in productivity that was considered too high, he was usually severely reprimanded and subjected to considerable abuse. For example, the following incident was observed by the researchers.

> W_8: (To W_6) Why don't you quit work? Let's see, this is your fifth row today. What are you going to do with them all?

Management and the Worker by Fritz Roethlisberger and William Dickson. Copyright © 1939 and 1967 by the President and Fellows of Harvard College. This and all other quotes from the same source are reprinted by permission of Harvard University Press.

W$_6$: What do you care? It's to your advantage if
I work, isn't it?

W$_8$: Yeah, but the way you're working you'll get
stuck with them.

W$_6$: Don't worry about that. I'll take care of it.
You're getting paid the sets I turn out. That's
all you should worry about.

W$_8$: If you don't quit work I'll bing you. (W$_8$ struck
W$_6$ and chased him around the room.)

Observer: (A few minutes later) What's the matter,
W$_6$, won't he let you work?

W$_6$: No. I'm all through though. I've got enough
done [pp. 422–423].

This example illustrates how groups influence motivation through their ability to control the giving and receiving of social outcomes. According to our motivation model, this means that those people who do not value the kind of social outcomes groups have to give will not be influenced by the group. Whyte (1955) presents supporting evidence for this point in his description of the rate-buster. Despite the fact that these employees were pressured by the group to restrict their productivity, they were highly productive. Why? According to Whyte, they simply didn't care about the rewards and punishments the group members had to give; thus, the group was powerless to influence them.

It has been suggested that highly cohesive work groups will be more productive than less cohesive ones. As we have seen, this is not necessarily true. However, cohesive groups should have more ability to influence motivation and productivity. Because of the high level of mutual friendship and respect in cohesive groups, the outcomes that the group controls are valued by the members of the group; as a result, the group can have a strong influence on motivation. This influence will not necessarily be positive. Since some cohesive groups influence their members to be anti-management and anti-production, cohesive groups cannot be expected to always be more productive than noncohesive groups.

Because cohesive groups have more ability to influence motivation, we would expect them to perform differently than noncohesive groups. Seashore (1954) found that, although cohesive groups were not significantly more productive, they did differ from low-cohesive groups in some important ways. Due to the effects of group norms on productivity, most individuals in cohesive groups produced at the same level, and cohesive groups showed more variance in group production rates. When all the members of a cohesive group produced at a high level, the production of the group was high; when they produced at a low level, the production of the group was low. On the other hand, because members of low-cohesive groups were producing at different levels, none of the low-cohesive groups was ever very high or very low on productivity. In low-cohesive groups, low producers offset high producers, and the productivity of the group tended to be in the middle. Seashore tried to determine what distinguished the high-producing, cohesive groups from the low-producing, cohesive groups. He found a difference in group norms; the high-producing groups were more supportive of high productivity. Unfortunately, he was unable to specify why the different norms developed.

A laboratory study by Schachter, Ellertson, McBride, and Gregory (1951) shows how cohesiveness affects the amount of influence a group has on the productivity of its members. This study also illustrates how group norms influence productivity. High- and low-cohesive groups were created, with each group consisting of three people. Group members were told that their job was to produce cardboard checkerboards. The job consisted of three tasks, and each member would work on one task in a separate room. The members could communicate only by notes. The experimenter intercepted the notes and substituted prewritten notes that were delivered at specified times. Some of the notes were designed to encourage the workers to increase production; other notes encouraged decreased production. Examples of the former are "Can you hurry things up a bit?" and "Time is running out, let's really make a spurt." Examples of the latter are "Let's try to set a record—the slowest subjects they ever had" and "We've done a lot of these things, let's take it easy now."

Table 8.2 shows the results of the study. A positive number indicates that production increased as a result of the notes, and a negative number indicates that production decreased. The notes affected production as expected, having the largest effect in the cohesive group. In a follow-up study, Berkowitz (1954) tried to determine if the effect of the notes would continue after they were no longer being sent. He replicated the results of the original study and found that the effect did persist. Since the subjects had no reason to believe that other members of the group had changed their minds, they still expected that acceptance and approval from the group depended on their being either a high or low performer, and they performed accordingly. It would have been interesting to see whether, by switching the messages, productivity would have been increased in the negative group and decreased in the positive group. Based on our motivation model, we would predict these reactions.

Table 8.2. Mean Change in Production Level Following Induction.

Experimental conditions	Mean change
High cohesiveness, positive induction	+5.92
Low cohesiveness, positive induction	+5.09
High cohesiveness, negative induction	−2.16
Low cohesiveness, negative induction	− .42

Source: After Schachter, Ellertson, McBride, & Gregory, 1951, p. 234.

In summary, groups have the power to influence employee motivation and productivity because they control outcomes that are valued by most people. For example, group members can reward certain behaviors by expressing verbal approval, and punish others by rejecting people who demonstrate them. Cohesive groups have more influence on motivation and productivity than noncohesive groups, because cohesive groups are more effective at giving and withholding rewards for two major reasons. First, cohesive groups can act with more unanimity (rejection by one means rejection by all); second, they influence the reception of highly valued outcomes (acceptance or rejection by a cohesive group is an important outcome to most people).

However, groups cannot influence the performance of people who do not value the outcomes controlled by the groups.

To know how groups will influence motivation, we must know the kind of norms that exist in the group. We must know what kinds of behavior will be rewarded and what kinds of behavior will be punished. What determines the kind of reward practices and norms that will develop in groups has not been extensively researched. One study (Lawler & Cammann, 1972) suggests that how much employees trust the organization has an important influence on group norms. Data from this study show that democratically led groups are more likely than autocratically led groups to believe and trust management and to develop norms and practices that favor production.

Group Influences on Satisfaction

Because groups control attractive outcomes, they can influence satisfaction as well as motivation. How they will influence satisfaction is predicted by the satisfaction model presented in Chapter 4, which points out that the more positive social outcomes a person receives, the more satisfied he should be, particularly in the area of social need. In their classic study of the automobile assembly line, Walker and Guest (1952) found that satisfaction was related to the kinds of opportunities for social interaction provided by the job. Fewer interaction possibilities meant lower satisfaction. Hackman and Lawler (1971) found that workers on jobs with few opportunities for social interaction reported less social-need satisfaction than workers on jobs with extensive opportunities. They also found that opportunity for social interaction did not affect satisfaction in other need areas. Other studies have shown that jobs providing greater opportunities for social interaction tend to have lower turnover and absenteeism rates than jobs providing few opportunities (Vroom, 1964). This finding is consistent with the research showing that satisfaction influences absenteeism and turnover.

By itself, interaction does not necessarily lead to increased satisfaction. Interaction can be either pleasant or unpleasant. To lead to satisfaction, it must be pleasant. We would expect that those workers who are accepted by the group and who, as a result, receive positive responses should be more satisfied than those who aren't accepted. This relationship should be especially strong in cohesive groups. One study found that only 43 percent of the "isolates" (nonaccepted members) in a work group were highly satisfied with their jobs, whereas 75 percent of the accepted members of the work group were highly satisfied (Zaleznik, Christensen, & Roethlisberger, 1958). Other studies have reported similar findings as well as the finding that turnover is directly related to group acceptance.

Many studies have shown that group size is strongly related to satisfaction, absenteeism, and turnover (Porter & Lawler, 1965). Large groups are characterized by high turnover, high absenteeism, and low satisfaction, although they are not necessarily characterized by low performance. One hypothesis of why large groups should have lower rates of satisfaction is that social interactions are spread over more people in large groups. Thus, although the individual members of large groups experience the same amount of interaction, they experience less intense, less accepting, and less meaningful interaction. Larger groups tend to be lower on cohesiveness, which also suggests that less meaningful social interaction takes place in large groups. In some ways, small groups may coerce people to develop deeper, more meaningful relationships; because membership is smaller, people have more time to talk to each other on a one-to-one basis.

How much is total satisfaction influenced by the kinds of rewards a group can offer? Many authors argue that social rewards are of crucial importance. For example, Mayo (1945) states that "man's desire to be continuously associated in work with his fellows is a strong, if not the strongest, human characteristic" (p. 111). Likert (1961) comments that "to have a friendly, supportive relationship day in and day out with one's colleagues is more important to most people than relatively minor financial rewards" (p. 15). Because of individual differences in how important social needs are, work-group relationships probably have considerable effect on overall satisfaction for some people and little effect for others.

In summary, groups do seem to influence job satisfaction

because they satisfy people's social needs. Frequency of social interaction is related to satisfaction, but not all interaction is satisfactory. Interaction in small groups and interaction that constitutes social acceptance of a person are most likely to be experienced as satisfactory.

Leadership Style and Organizational Effectiveness

Leadership style has an important influence on organizational effectiveness because it influences both intrinsic and extrinsic motivation, as well as satisfaction, absenteeism, and turnover. It also plays a crucial role in determining the kind of norms groups will develop toward productivity. Evidence suggests that motivation and satisfaction are highest when democratic leadership is practiced. Why, then, don't all leaders use a power-equalization leadership style? The many reasons are worth enumerating because they raise some important points about the determinants of leadership style, the effectiveness of different styles, and the determinants of organizational effectiveness.

Even though it usually produces the highest satisfaction and motivation, democratic leadership is not always the most effective. It is time-consuming, and time is not always available. Further, subordinates don't always have the information they need to make good decisions, and they cannot always be counted on to make decisions that put the interests of the organization above their own interests. Finally, some individuals simply are uncomfortable with power equalization and don't respond to it. Thus, a democratic leadership is not always the best one. Admittedly, except when people with low needs for independence are being dealt with, power equalization usually does produce the highest motivation and satisfaction. But motivation and satisfaction are not enough; high-quality decisions are needed. Thus, from the point of view of organizational effectiveness, democratic leadership is not always appropriate or desirable.

Is democratic leadership practiced often enough? Many writers (for example, Miles, 1965; Haire, Ghiselli & Porter, 1966) agree that democratic management is not always appropriate but go on to argue convincingly that it is used less often than it should be. The reason it is used less often than it should be is suggested by our motivation model. Like most behavior in organizations, leadership behavior is motivated behavior, and the too-small amount of democratic leadership observed in organizations can be explained in motivational terms. At one time, a person's leadership style was considered a relatively fixed facet of his personality. As it became clear that people did change their leadership styles, leadership training became popular, and it was thought that leaders would practice more democratic management if they were trained to do so. Many studies now show that training may not change a person's leadership style once he is back on the job. Although training is often necessary if a person is to become a democratic leader, it is not sufficient. Leadership behavior is controlled by the rewards and punishments that exist in the work setting. Unless democratic leadership behavior is rewarded in the work setting, leaders will not be motivated to behave in a democratic manner.

Some consistency is imposed on most leaders' behavior because they are capable of behaving in only a limited number of ways, but the same leader will and often does behave differently when faced with different work situations. What determines how he will behave? Primarily, the rewards given by his superiors and subordinates determine his behavior. Subordinates try to influence their superiors to behave in more considerate and more democratic ways. For example, Moore and Smith (1952) found that subordinates—in this case, members of the Air Force—judged officers as good leaders if they were high on consideration. Thus, subordinates represent a force in the work environment that supports and rewards democratic management. However, they are usually the second most influential force in the work environment. The leader's superior controls many rewards that the group doesn't. For example, he may influence promotion and pay increases. What kind of behavior do superiors typically value? Superiors feel their subordinates are doing a good job of leading their subordinates when they supervise closely and keep tight control. Thus, "the leader is subject to conflicting demands from above and below" (Berelson

& Steiner, 1964, p. 372). Because the leader's superior controls
more rewards than his subordinates, the superior is in a position to motivate the leader; thus, a suboptimal amount of democratic leadership is practiced. To increase the amount of democratic leadership, organizations must do three things. First,
in their selection process, they must screen out people who are
not capable of behaving in a democratic manner. Second, they
need training courses designed to teach leaders how to function
in a democratic manner. Finally, they must create an organization climate that is supportive of democratic leadership. This
is difficult and often can be done only by a large-scale change
in the way the organization is run.

    In summary, no leadership style is correct for all situa-
tions or all individuals. As we will see in Chapter 9, this has
some important implications for how organizations should think
about motivation. Less democratic management is practiced in
organizations than is warranted because higher-level managers
do not feel that their subordinates who are managers should practice democratic management. Thus, the motivation to practice
democratic management is not present. Finally, the behavior
of leaders appears to be determined by training, by relatively
permanent personality and ability factors, and by the rewards
available in the situation.

nine

Overview:
Motivation in Organizations

Inherent in all approaches to the management of organizations are assumptions concerning the motivation of employees; different prescriptive approaches can be distinguished on the basis of these assumptions. The essence of management is influencing behavior, which is a function of ability and motivation. Thus, being able to influence the motivation of employees is crucial in the effective management of organizations. Not surprisingly, this ability is given considerable attention in most discussions concerned with how organizations should be managed. Vroom and Deci (1970) identify three "managerial or organizational strategies for stimulating motivation" (p. 11). By reviewing and assessing these three approaches in terms of our discussion so far, we will have a good overview of the thoughts of most writers who have been concerned with how motivation in organizations should be managed. The discussion of these approaches will lead to a new approach, which is more congruent with the research reviewed in this book.

Organizational Approaches to Motivation

The first approach that Vroom and Deci identify is the paternalistic approach. This approach

. . . assumes that people will be motivated to perform their jobs effectively to the extent to which they are satisfied with these jobs. The more one rewards workers, the harder they will work. The greater the extent to which an employee's needs are satisfied in his job, the greater the extent to which he will respond, presumably with gratitude or loyalty, by producing effectively on that job.

The essence of this approach is to make the organization a source of important rewards — rewards for which the only qualification is membership in the organization. In other words, the rewards which are utilized in this approach might be termed unconditional rewards in the sense that the amount of rewards that any individual receives is not dependent in any clear-cut way on how he behaves within the organization, but rather on the fact that he is a member of that organization [p. 11].*

Instead of paternalistic, this approach might be called the gratuity approach to management. Its key assumption is that satisfaction leads to performance. Although this approach has never been dominant, it has enjoyed periods of great popular acceptance, especially following the Western Electric studies. Many people interpreted these studies as supporting the view that satisfaction leads to performance, which encouraged some people to argue for a gratuity approach to motivation. The popularity of this approach decreased after the Brayfield and Crockett (1955) literature review, which showed little relationship between satisfaction and performance. Thus, this view had its greatest popularity from approximately 1939 to 1955.

One appealing facet of the paternalistic approach is that it makes clear-cut statements about what organizations should do to motivate workers. Furthermore, the recommended actions

*Vroom, V., and Deci, E. *Management and Motivation.* Copyright © 1970 by Penguin Books, Inc. This and all other quotes from the same source are reprinted by permission.

are usually feasible. Motivating employees is simply a matter of giving them — regardless of their performance — good working conditions, fair wages, and a secure job. It is also important to treat employees with respect and to be concerned about their problems. Most companies adopting this approach provide extensive fringe-benefit packages, considerate supervision, across-the-board wage increases, and promotions based largely on seniority.

The second approach outlined by Vroom and Deci is the scientific-management approach to motivation, which

> . . . is based on the assumption that a person will be motivated to work if rewards and penalties are tied directly to his performance; thus, the rewards are conditional rather than unconditional. In short, they are attached to and made contingent upon effective performance [p. 13].

This approach suggests some practical actions that organizations should take to motivate people. The clearest application of this approach is in the area of pay administration, where it conflicts with the paternalistic approach. It argues strongly for wage-incentive plans that tie pay to performance. The archetypes of this approach are the piece-rate incentive systems that are used on lower-level jobs. This approach also argues for promoting on the basis of merit and for using extrinsic rewards, such as approval of supervisors and stock-option plans, to recognize and reward people for good performance. An emphasis on status symbols (for example, large offices and impressive titles) and special awards (for example, Salesman-of-the-Year) is also consistent with this approach.

> The methodology of this approach constitutes an external-control system. It is necessary to define the standards to be used in the allocation of the rewards and penalties in as objective or measurable a fashion as possible. These standards may be formulated in terms of the methods used by the individual when

carrying out his job or in the results which he
achieves. It is also necessary to monitor the behavior
of the individual to observe the extent to which these
standards are attained or adhered to. The final in-
gredient of the system is the consistent allocation
of the rewards and penalties based on the observa-
tions of performance [p. 13].

The scientific management approach gained a great deal
of popularity during the early part of this century. Over 70 percent of the firms in the United States had piece-rate pay-incentive
plans during the 1930s. In the last 20 years, acceptance of this
approach has decreased, as reflected in the decreasing popularity of pay-incentive systems. Now, less than 40 percent of the
firms in the United States have piece-rate pay-incentive systems.

The third approach has appeared in the last 20 years. It
is well described by McGregor (1960), Likert (1961), and Argyris (1957).

> . . . it has frequently been termed participative
> management. Whereas paternalistic management
> assumed that man can be induced to work out of a
> feeling of gratitude to the system, and the external-
> control system associated with scientific manage-
> ment assumed that man can be induced to work
> by the expectation of gain for doing or the expec-
> tation of loss for not doing, participative manage-
> ment assumes that individuals can derive satisfac-
> tion from doing an effective job per se. They can
> become ego-involved with their jobs, emotionally
> committed to doing them well, and take pride from
> evidence that they are effective in furthering the ob-
> jectives of the company [Vroom & Deci, 1970, p. 15].

It is more difficult to specify what managers must do to practice participative management than to practice paternalistic or
scientific management. However, the participative approach
does have implications for how jobs should be designed and how

leaders should behave. It argues for the use of power-equalization strategies, democratic management, and vertically expanded jobs.

On matters that affect a work group, the supervisor does not make decisions autocratically and issue orders to subordinates; he meets with subordinates as a group and shares the problems with them. He encourages them to participate with him in finding solutions to these problems. This opportunity to participate in the decision-making process is assumed to create involvement or commitment to the decision on the part of subordinates and enhance identification with corporate goals and objectives.

The participative approach argues for designing jobs that are high on the four core dimensions. The assumption is that when people determine how to do their own jobs, they will be motivated to perform well because they will be challenged by their jobs. Few of the discussions on participative management deal with how extrinsic rewards such as pay and promotion should be handled. The motivation for effective performance is expected to come from the task or from the interpersonal processes that take place and not from how the organization mediates rewards. In short, the emphasis is on creating conditions under which effective performance can be a goal rather than a means to the attainment of some other goal, and the philosophy is one of self-control or self-regulation rather than organizational control.

Now that we have reviewed the paternalistic, scientific, and participative management approaches, the remaining question is: How valid are they? The answer can be obtained by looking at the major research findings presented in this book. These findings are summarized in the following section and then compared to the three management approaches in the next section.

Motivation: An Overview and Summary

Evidence presented in Chapters 5, 6, 7, and 8 showed that motivation is influenced by $E \rightarrow P$ and $P \rightarrow O$ beliefs and by outcome valence. Since motivation was shown to change when these three factors change, it seems safe to conclude that motivation is influenced by these three factors.

Our analysis of the research findings has shown that motivation is influenced by the nature of the individual and by the policies and practices of the organization. Lewin (1935) emphasized that behavior is a function of the characteristics of both the person and the environment. His approach to describing the determinants of behavior is still accurate and useful. The research on motivation in organizations shows that motivated behavior is influenced by the characteristics of both the environment and the person. All the components of our motivation model ($E{\rightarrow}P$, $P{\rightarrow}O$, and V) have been shown to be influenced by organizational practices, as well as by the nature of the person.

Employees' $P{\rightarrow}O$ beliefs concerning money are strongly influenced by organizational pay practices. People who work in organizations in which pay is based on performance have different $P{\rightarrow}O$ beliefs than people who work in organizations in which pay is not performance based. The research also shows that $P{\rightarrow}O$ beliefs of people within the same organization vary. Because of individual differences in needs, personality, and so on, different people perceive the same situation differently. In Chapter 7, attractiveness of outcomes such as achievement was shown to be partially a function of the environment and partially a function of the person. Certain tasks can arouse achievement motivation in people only if they have the capacity for this motivation. $E{\rightarrow}P$ beliefs were also shown to be influenced by environmental factors, such as task design, and by individual characteristics, such as self-esteem.

Although none of the three factors in our motivation model may be said to be more important than the others, two of the three — $P{\rightarrow}O$ beliefs and valences — may deserve the most attention from organizations. People are constantly forming and acting on $P{\rightarrow}O$ beliefs, which seem to play the key role in determining which behavior people will try in order to achieve their goals. The attractiveness of outcomes plays the crucial role in influencing which type of outcomes people seek. Interestingly, people's $P{\rightarrow}O$ beliefs are influenced mostly by their environment, whereas people's outcome valences are more a function of their personal background and need state. Thus, organizations can influence people's $P \rightarrow O$ beliefs more easily than their outcome valences.

In some cases, $P \rightarrow O$ beliefs do diverge from reality; because of this, organizations can never completely control the kinds of $P \rightarrow O$ beliefs their members have. However, organizations can establish clearly visible reward systems that will be seen in similar ways by most people. Evidence shows that organizations can strongly influence people's $P \rightarrow O$ beliefs, causing an increase in motivation. One practical implication of this is that organizations should consider the impact of new policies and practices on people's $P \rightarrow O$ beliefs before instituting them. Each new action potentially can influence $P \rightarrow O$ beliefs and, as a result, can increase or decrease motivation. Organizations that hope to have highly motivated employees should not take actions that will reduce the degree to which positive outcomes are seen to result from good performance.

Organizational influence on outcome valence is more limited but still possible. Giving employees a large quantity of certain rewards can change their need states and thereby influence the attractiveness they attach to certain outcomes. Organizations can design the work environment in ways that will arouse certain needs. Still, the influence of these approaches is limited because the strength of people's needs is relatively fixed and is affected by many things beyond the control of the organization. Perhaps the best way organizations can influence valence is through the selection process. The potential exists for hiring people on the basis of their needs and thus controlling the kinds of outcomes valued by employees. It is difficult to do this successfully, however, because there is a paucity of ways in which need strength can be successfully measured at the time of selection.

Because the major components in the motivation model are determined by many factors, large individual differences are to be expected in how people respond to organizational situations. Much of this can be attributed to large and relatively stable differences in how people value outcomes. For example, jobs high on the four core dimensions are reacted to favorably by people with strong higher-order needs and unfavorably by people who do not have strong higher-order needs. The research on pay shows that not everyone responds to pay-incentive plans by being more productive; only those people who value money highly seem to react this way. If we are able to understand motivation in organizations, we must realize the important role of individual differences. Individual differences exist, and because of them most organizational policies and practices will meet with more than one reaction from employees.

Finally, the research supports the model of satisfaction presented in Chapter 4. Satisfaction seems to be a function of the rewards a person receives. It does not appear to be a direct cause of performance. However, motivation can be influenced indirectly if satisfaction comes about as a result of good performance; in such cases, satisfaction influences employees' $P \rightarrow O$ beliefs, which in turn influence motivation. Satisfaction does seem to be related to turnover and absenteeism. Satisfied employees see more rewards associated with their jobs; thus, satisfaction is associated with the motivation to come to work because it influences people's beliefs about the rewards associated with coming to work. The motivation to come to work is influenced in turn by people's beliefs about the consequences of coming to work.

A Critical Evaluation of the Approaches

Testing the three motivation approaches against the research shows that all contain an element of truth. However, they all fail to provide a satisfactory basis on which to develop an adequate general approach to motivation. Each approach is incomplete and partially incorrect. They all focus on one strategy for motivating people, thereby ignoring the fact that no one system will fit everyone. What is more, none of the approaches considers the negative side effects it produces.

The paternalistic approach has the least support in scientific literature. Its basic assumption has not been supported by research. It assumes that satisfaction can cause good performance because satisfied employees will be more motivated. Research indicates no reason to believe that increased satisfaction, alone, will lead to increases in either motivation or performance. The paternalistic approach fails to deal with individual differences in motivation and to explain why factors such as pay-incentive systems and enriched jobs can motivate people. One aspect of the paternalistic model is supported by research; high satisfaction does seem to reduce turnover and absenteeism. Even here, however, there is a problem with this approach. It argues for keeping everyone happy and for rewarding people the same. The evidence indicates that this may be impossible. Better performers feel that they deserve more rewards than poorer performers. If they are rewarded the same as poorer performers, they are dissatisfied and may quit. Thus, the paternalistic approach can create conditions in which turnover and dissatisfaction are centered among the best performers. In short, the paternalistic model not only contains a crucial erroneous assumption but is incomplete. The organization that adopts this approach may end up with a satisfied work force characterized by low turnover among the poor performers, low absenteeism, and little motivation to perform.

The scientific management approach to motivation is supported by much of the theory and research presented in this book. Establishing a clearly visible relationship between valued extrinsic rewards and good performance does increase motivation and performance. In Chapter 3, our motivation model proposed that $P \rightarrow O$ beliefs are important determinants of performance. In Chapter 6, pay-incentive systems were shown to increase both motivation and performance. It was also stressed that other extrinsic rewards can and do influence motivation if they are important and if they are tied to performance.

The weakness of the scientific management approach lies in what it fails to say. It fails to explain how jobs can intrinsically motivate people or why participative management increases motivation under certain conditions. It also fails to point out that incentive systems can have many side effects and thus may not lead to the predicted increases in production. This approach ignores the fact that extrinsic rewards are not highly important to everyone, and thus not everyone will be motivated by extrinsic-reward systems. The scientific management approach makes erroneous statements about both job design and leadership. It says that pay-incentive systems in combination with specialized, standardized, and simplified jobs will produce the greatest performance — a statement that was discredited in Chapter 7. It also says that authoritarian leadership produces the best results, which is not always the case, as shown in Chapter 8.

Overall, the scientific management approach has proven to be inadequate because it ignores important individual and situational differences. It relies only on extrinsic rewards, even though extrinsic rewards are effective motivators only for those people who value them and only in certain situations. The use of extrinsic rewards requires that good performance measures be available and that organizations have control over the rewards. In many situations, adequate performance measures do not exist and cannot be obtained. For example, in organizations offering a service, in higher-level jobs, and in jobs that involve the cooperative effort of several people, the results of work are difficult to quantify and measure.

Like the scientific management approach, the participative approach can be criticized most severely on the basis of what it fails to account for. It correctly points out that certain approaches to job design can increase motivation and that, in some cases, participative decision making can increase motivation and satisfaction. However, this approach fails to give extrinsic rewards a significant role in motivating people. It also fails to point out that not everyone responds positively to an enlarged job or to the opportunity to participate in decision making. Thus, the participative approach has nothing to say about how to motivate people who do not desire interesting work and involvement in decision making.

The participative approach is keyed to motivating those people who are interested in satisfying their higher-order needs at work, whereas the scientific management approach is keyed to motivating those people who are interested in satisfying their lower-order needs at work. Unfortunately for both the participative and scientific management approaches, most organizations are composed of some higher-order-need people and some lower-order-need people. Further, most people who work in organizations probably are interested in satisfying both kinds of needs. As Schein (1965) has pointed out, it is time we stopped thinking in terms of social man and self-actualizing man and started thinking in terms of "complex man." Complex man has many needs; to motivate him, an approach must recognize the diversity of these needs. Unfortunately, the paternalistic, scientific management, and participative approaches are not designed to do this.

Are the Approaches Incompatible?

These approaches to motivation have been discussed as though they are incompatible and an organization must choose among them. To some extent, they are incompatible. The paternalistic approach, in particular, is incompatible with the others. The paternalistic approach emphasizes uniformity of rewards, whereas the scientific management approach argues for basing rewards on performance. Obviously, it is impossible to base rewards on performance while giving across-the-board rewards. The scientific management approach and the participative approach seem to have the most validity, and they are not completely incompatible. Both approaches are based on the principle that motivation will be high when valued rewards are tied clearly to performance. They differ in the kind of rewards with which they are concerned—extrinsic or intrinsic. The emphasis of the scientific management approach on external control, simplified jobs, and autocratic supervision does conflict with the participative approach. Carried to its extreme, the scientific management approach calls for careful specification of how tasks are to be done and for the development of nonchallenging jobs, which is inconsistent with the development of intrinsic motivations.

However, rewards can be allocated on the basis of performance even though jobs are not simplified and even though employees are given a chance to participate in decision making. In short, to base rewards on performance, work need not be designed in such a way that planning and control is separated from the doing. People can be rewarded on the basis of their productivity in enriched jobs as well as in simplified jobs. The difference is that, in enriched jobs, the results of the work — rather than the process by which it is done — must be focused on, since specifying and rewarding the work process is inconsistent with participative management. Rewarding on the basis of performance is not inconsistent because rewards can be distributed in a participative manner. In fact, participation can increase the validity of the appraisal process. Thus, the participative and scientific management approaches are not completely incompatible.

The Combination Approach

If an organization combined the participative and scientific management approaches, its employees would be both challenged by their jobs and rewarded on the basis of their performance. They would be involved in both the design of their jobs and the decision of what objective measures should be used to evaluate their job performance. Further, they would be active participants in the process of evaluating their own performance. Thus, the organization that combined these two approaches would be characterized by enriched jobs, participative decision making about reward allocation, and rewards based on performance.

However, such a combination approach would still suffer from one weak point: it simply is not applicable to all people or all situations. Some jobs cannot be enlarged; further, performance on some jobs is impossible to measure, and some people don't want to participate in decision making. Other people don't value extrinsic rewards. The combination approach is perfect for the person who is comfortable with participation and who has strong higher- and lower-order needs. The approach fits Schein's (1965) complex man very well. Unfortunately, not everyone fits the complex man model.

One solution is to select only those people who fit the "right" motivational pattern. However, there are several problems in doing this. First, it is often difficult to identify at the time of selection those people who are right for this approach.

The selection instruments currently available are not that good. Second, selecting the right people demands that the organization have a large number of applicants relative to the number of positions it has to fill. In many cases, organizations do not have the luxury of choosing among many applicants. Finally, this strategy demands that it be legally acceptable for organizations to reject people on the basis of their motivational patterns. Many recent laws and court decisions have restricted organizations' rights to use psychological tests for selection purposes. Particularly questioned has been the use of personality and interest tests, which would have to be used if the organization were to select on the basis of motivational patterns. In summary, better selection would seem to represent at best only a partial solution to the problems presented by individual differences in motivational patterns.

The Individualized Organization

What, then, is the best approach to motivating employees? The paternalistic approach, the scientific management approach, the participative approach, and the combination approach fail to take individual differences sufficiently into account. The only generally valid motivation strategy would appear to be one that fits the motivation system to the individual. Operationally, such a system means that some individuals would work on enriched jobs, and others would work on jobs designed according to the principles of scientific management. Some employees would work under pay-incentive systems, and others would not. Thus, rather than trying to motivate everyone in the organization with the same approach, the organization would recognize the importance of individual differences and try to individualize management to fit the nature of its work force; each employee would be motivated by the approach or combination of approaches that best fits his needs.

What must organizations do to adopt an individualized approach? First, they must do a good job of assessing their employees, and they must carefully analyze each employee's job. To do this effectively, they must gather valid data on the nature of employees' needs and create more comprehensive descriptions of their jobs. Describing the physical aspects of a job is not enough; the psychological aspects must be described, too. The kinds of needs jobs affect, the kinds of rewards they offer, and the management climate surrounding them must be described. It is difficult for organizations unilaterally to make valid decisions about where a person will fit, even if good person and job descriptions are developed. For effective placement, organizations must establish a counseling relationship with employees in which employees have a chance to influence the type of job they are given. This approach is desirable for two reasons: (1) unless they are given this opportunity, employees are not likely to give valid data about themselves, and such data are crucial to the placement process; (2) employees can and will make valid decisions about which jobs will fit them if they have realistic descriptions of the nature of the jobs. As shown in Chapter 5, when employees have the chance, they will pick jobs that provide them with the opportunity to obtain the outcomes they value; this is desirable, since it means that they will pick jobs that are potentially motivating and satisfying for them.

Next, organizations must create different kinds of work situations, all of which meet one crucial condition: the reception of some outcome or outcomes valued by a group of employees is contingent on good performance. Within one organization, some jobs should be enriched, and others should not. Pay-incentive plans should be in effect in some places, but not in others. In some situations, democratic leadership should be practiced; in other situations, authoritarian leadership should be practiced. Although many organizations have this variety, they don't attempt to place employees in suitable jobs, and they often don't have enough of some kinds of situations. As stated in Chapter 7, organizations often don't have enough enriched jobs relative to the number of people who would respond to enriched jobs. At the managerial level, they often don't have enough jobs in which pay is based on performance relative to the number of managers who would respond to a pay-incentive system. Democratic management is seldom practiced to the extent it should be.

Individualization demands that a variety of work situations be created, but the variety need not be infinite and unmanageable. No situation should be created that doesn't relate important rewards to performance. This is a crucial limiting condition because only if this condition exists can high satisfaction and high motivation be achieved. It rules out many situations. For example, a situation in which extrinsic rewards are not related to performance and the job is repetitive should not be created because motivation will not be high. The necessary degree of variety of situations can be somewhat reduced by screening potential employees during the initial selection process. For example, the organization could not hire certain kinds of people because their needs are not compatible with the kind of job situations the organization is willing to create. This could be accomplished to some extent by self-selection if employees were told what the job situation is like.

Obviously, it is difficult for any organization to know just how many of each kind of job situation it will need, since selection will never be perfect and people change. Thus, organizations must encourage employees to design their own work situations within the limits specified above. This kind of personalization process goes on anyway, but what is suggested here is that it be encouraged and supported by the organization. As some of the research reviewed in this book has shown, employees can design their own pay system, and they can help design their own jobs. One very effective way to arrive at a good individual/organization fit is to have the individual design the role he has in the organization.

It will not be easy for organizations to individualize their motivation systems. The system has to be somewhat complicated because people are complicated. Because people differ in many ways and each person is unique, complete individualization would demand that a unique job situation be created for every person. What is more, since people are continually changing and developing, true individualization would require that the job situation of each person be constantly changing. For these and other reasons, complete individualization of jobs will probably always remain a goal to be strived for rather than an accomplished reality, but it is a goal that is very much worth striving for. It holds the promise of greater individual need satisfaction and greater organizational effectiveness — two objectives worth achieving. In a time when society is becoming more and more dominated by large, complex organizations, it is very important to recognize the uniqueness and worth of each human being. The individualized approach does recognize this and provides a refreshing contrast to the unidimensional assumptions of the other approaches about the nature of man.

References

Adams, J. S. Toward an understanding of inequity. *Journal of Abnormal Psychology*, 1963, *67*, 422–436.

Adams, J. S. Injustice in social exchange. In L. Berkowitz (Ed.), *Advances in experimental social psychology*. Vol. 2. New York: Academic Press, 1965.

Adorno, T. W., Frenkel-Brunswik, E., Levinson, D. A., & Sanford, R. N. *The authoritarian personality*. New York: Harper & Row, 1950.

Alderfer, C. P. An organizational syndrome. *Administrative Science Quarterly*, 1967, *12*, 440–460.

Alderfer, C. P. An empirical test of a new theory of human needs. *Organizational Behavior and Human Performance*, 1969, *4*, 142–175.

Alderfer, C. P. *Existence, relatedness, and growth: Human needs in organizational settings*. New York: The Free Press, 1972.

Alderfer, C., & McCord, C. Personal and situational factors in the recruitment interview. *Journal of Applied Psychology*, 1970, *54*(4), 377–385.

Allport, G. W. *Becoming: Basic considerations for a psychology of personality*. New Haven: Yale University Press, 1955.

Alper, T. G. Task-orientation vs. ego-orientation in learning and retention. *American Journal of Psychology,* 1946, *38,* 224–238.

Argyris, C. *The impact of budgets on people.* New York: Controllership Foundation, 1951.

Argyris, C. *Executive leadership.* New York: Harper & Row, 1953.

Argyris, C. *Personality and organization.* New York: Harper & Row, 1957.

Argyris, C. *Integrating the individual and the organization.* New York: John Wiley, 1964.

Atkinson, J. W. Towards experimental analysis of human motivation in terms of motives, expectancies, and incentives. In J. W. Atkinson (Ed.), *Motives in fantasy, action, and society.* Princeton, N.J.: Van Nostrand Reinhold, 1958.

Atkinson, J. W. *An introduction to motivation.* Princeton, N.J.: Van Nostrand Reinhold, 1964.

Atkinson, J. W., & Reitman, W. R. Performance as a function of motive strength and expectance of goal attainment. *Journal of Abnormal and Social Psychology,* 1956, *53,* 361–366.

Ayllon, T., & Azrin, N. H. The measurement and reinforcement of behavior of psychotics. *Journal of Experimental Analysis of Behavior,* 1965, *8,* 357–383.

Babchuk, N., & Goode, W. J. Work incentives in a self-determined group. *American Social Review,* 1951, *16,* 679–687.

Beer, M., & Gery, G. J. *Pay systems preferences and their correlates.* Paper presented at the American Psychological Association Convention, San Francisco, August 1968.

Berelson, B., & Steiner, G. A. *Human behavior: An inventory of scientific findings.* New York: Harcourt Brace Jovanovich, 1964.

Berkowitz, L. Group standards, cohesiveness, and productivity. *Human Relations,* 1954, *7,* 509–519.

Berliner, J. S. The situation of plant managers. In A. Inkeles & K. Geiger (Eds.), *Soviet Society: A book of readings.* Boston: Houghton Mifflin, 1961.

Berlyne, D. E. Arousal and reinforcement. In D. Levine (Ed.), *Nebraska symposium on motivation.* Lincoln: University of Nebraska Press, 1967.

Bexton, W. H., Heron, W., & Scott, T. H. Effects of decreased variation in the sensory environment. *Canadian Journal of Psychology,* 1954, *8,* 70–76.

Bindra, D. *Motivation: A systematic reinterpretation.* New York: Ronald Press, 1959.

Blake, R. R., & Mouton, J. S. *The managerial grid.* Houston: Gulf Publishing Co., 1964.

Blood, M. R., & Hulin, C. L. Alienation, environmental characteristics, and worker responses. *Journal of Applied Psychology,* 1967, *51,* 284–290.

Brayfield, A. H., & Crockett, W. H. Employee attitudes and employee performance. *Psychological Bulletin,* 1955, *52,* 396–424.

Breer, P. E., & Locke, E. A. *Task experience as a source of attitudes.* Homewood, Ill.: Dorsey Press, 1965.

Brenner, M. H., & Lockwood, H. C. Salary as a predictor of salary: A 20-year study. *Journal of Applied Psychology,* 1965, *49,* 295–298.

Burnett, F. An experimental investigation into repetitive work. *Industrial Fatigue Research Board Report No. 30.* London: H. M. Stationery Office, 1925.

Burns, T., & Stalker, G. M. *The management of innovation.* London: Tavistock Publications, 1961.

Butler, R. A. Discrimination learning by rhesus monkeys to visual-exploration motivation. *Journal of Comparative and Physiological Psychology,* 1953, *46,* 95–98.

Campbell, H. Group incentives. *Occupational Psychology,* 1952, *26,* 15–21.

Campbell, J. P., Dunnette, M. D., Lawler, E. E., and Weick, K. E. *Managerial behavior, performance, and effectiveness.* New York: McGraw-Hill, 1970.

Carter, M. *Into work.* Baltimore: Penguin, 1966.

Coch, L., & French, J.R.P. Overcoming resistance to change. *Human Relations,* 1948, *1,* 512–532.

Cofer, C. N., & Appley, M. H. *Motivation: Theory and research.* New York: John Wiley & Sons, 1964.

Cohen, A. K. *Deviance and control.* Englewood Cliffs, N.J.: Prentice-Hall, 1966.

Collins, O., Dalton, M., & Roy, D. Restriction of output and social cleavage in industry. *Applied Anthropology,* 1946, *5* (3), 1–14.

Cowles, J. T. Food tokens as incentives for learning by chimpanzees. *Comparative Psychology Monograph,* 1937, *14* (No. 71).

Cravens, R. W., & Renner, K. E. Conditioned appetitive drive states: Empirical evidence and theoretical status. *Psychological Bulletin,* 1970, *73,* 212–220.

Crespi, L. P. Quantitative variation of incentive and performance in the white rat. *American Journal of Psychology,* 1942, *55,* 467–517.

Crespi, L. P. Amount of reinforcement and level of performance. *Psychological Review,* 1944, *51,* 341–357.

Dalton, M. The industrial "rate-buster": A characterization. *Applied Anthropology,* 1948, *7,* 5–18.

Despain, D. Let workers write the pay checks. *Nations Business,* 1945, *33* (July), 23.

Drucker, P. F. *The practice of management.* New York: Harper & Row, 1954.

Dubin, R. Industrial workers' worlds: A study of the "central life interests" of industrial workers. *Social Problems,* 1956, *3,* 131–142.

Dubin, R. *The world of work.* Englewood Cliffs, N.J.: Prentice-Hall, 1958.

Dunnette, M. D., Campbell, J. P., & Hakel, M. D. Factors contributing to job satisfaction and job dissatisfaction in six occupational groups. *Organizational Behavior and Human Performance,* 1967, *2,* 143–174.

Dyson, B. H. Whether direct individual incentive systems based on time-study, however accurately computed, tend over a period to limitation of output. Paper read at the spring conference, British Institute of Management, London, 1956.

Englander, M. E. A psychological analysis of vocational choice: Teaching. *Journal of Counseling Psychology,* 1960, *7,* 257–264.

Evans, M. G. The effects of supervisory behavior on the path-goal relationship. *Organizational Behavior and Human Performance,* 1970, *5,* 277–298.

Fiedler, E. E. A contingency model of leadership effectiveness. In L. Berkowitz (Ed.), *Advances in experimental social psychology,* Vol. 1. New York: Academic Press, 1964.

Fleishman, E. A., & Harris, E. F. Patterns of leadership behavior related to employee grievances and turnover. *Personnel Psychology,* 1962, *15,* 43–56.

Fleishman, E. A., Harris, E. F., & Burtt, H. E. *Leadership and supervision in industry.* Columbus: Ohio State University, Bureau of Educational Research, 1955.

Ford, R. N. *Motivation through the work itself.* New York: American Management Association, 1969.

French, E. G. Some characteristics of achievement motivation. *Journal of Experimental Psychology,* 1955, *50,* 232–236.

French, J.R.P., Israel, J., & As, D. An experiment on participation in a Norwegian factory. *Human Relations,* 1960, *13,* 3–19.

Fromm, E. *Escape from freedom.* New York: Holt, Rinehart & Winston, 1941.

Gardner, B. B. *Human relations in industry.* Homewood, Ill.: Richard D. Irwin, 1945.

Gardner, J. W. *No easy victories.* New York: Harper & Row, 1968.

Glickman, A. S., Hahn, C. P., Fleishman, E. A., & Baxter, B. *Top management development and succession.* New York: Macmillan, 1968.

Goldstein, K. *The organism.* New York: American Book, 1939.

Goldthorpe, J. H., Lockwood, D., Bechhofer, F., & Platt, J. *The affluent worker: Industrial attitudes and behaviour.* Cambridge University Press, 1968.

Grove, E. A., & Kerr, W. A. Specific evidence on origin of halo effect in measurement of employee morale. *Journal of Social Psychology,* 1951, *34,* 165–170.

Haber, R. N. Discrepancy from adaptation level as a source of affect. *Journal of Experimental Psychology,* 1958, *56,* 370–375.

Hackman, J. R., & Lawler, E. E. Employee reactions to job characteristics. *Journal of Applied Psychology,* 1971, *55,* 259–286.

Haire, M. *Psychology in management.* New York: McGraw-Hill, 1956.

Haire, M., Ghiselli, E. E., & Gordon, M. E. A psychological study of pay. *Journal of Applied Psychology Monograph,* 1967, *51* (4, Whole No. 636).

Haire, M., Ghiselli, E. E., & Porter, L. W. *Managerial thinking: An international study.* New York: John Wiley & Sons, 1966.

Hall, C. S., & Lindzey, G. *Theories of personality.* New York: John Wiley & Sons, 1957.

Hall, D. T. Potential for career growth. *Personnel Administration.* May–June, 1971, *34,* 18–30.

Hall, D. T., & Lawler, E. E. Unused potential in research and development organizations. *Research management,* 1969, *12,* 339–354.

Halpin, A. W., & Winer, B. J. A factorial study of the leader behavior descriptions. In R. M. Stogdill and A. E. Coons (Eds.), *Leader behavior: Its description and measurement.* Columbus: Ohio State University, Bureau of Business Research, Research Monograph, 1957, No. 88, 39–51.

Harlow, H. F. Mice, monkeys, men, and motives. *Psychological Review,* 1953, *60,* 23–32.

Harlow, H. F. The nature of love. *American Psychologist,* 1958, *13,* 673–685.

Herzberg, F., Mausner, B., Peterson, R. O., & Capwell, D. F. *Job attitudes: Review of research and opinion.* Pittsburgh: Psychological Service of Pittsburgh, 1957.

Herzberg, F., Mausner, B., & Snyderman, B. *The motivation to work.* (2nd ed.) New York: John Wiley & Sons, 1959.

Hickson, D. J. Motives of work people who restrict their output. *Occupational Psychology,* 1961, *35,* 110–121.

Hofstede, G. H. *The game of budget control.* Assen, Netherlands: Royal Van Gorcum, 1967.

Hoppock, R. *Job satisfaction.* New York: Harper & Row, 1935.

Horney, K. *Neurosis and human growth.* New York: W. W. Norton, 1950.

House, R. J., Filley, A. C., & Kerr, S. Relation of leader consideration and initiating structure to *R* and *D* subordinates' satisfaction. *Administrative Science Quarterly,* 1971, *16,* 19–30.

Hulin, C. L., & Blood, M. R. Job enlargement, individual differences, and worker responses. *Psychological Bulletin,* 1968, *69,* 41–55.

Hull, C. L. *Principles of behavior.* New York: Appleton-Century-Crofts, 1943.

Hull, C. L. *A behavior system.* New Haven: Yale University Press, 1952.

Jacobson, E. *Foreman-steward participation practices and worker attitudes in a unionized factory.* Unpublished doctoral dissertation, University of Michigan, 1951.

Jones, M. R. (Ed.) *Nebraska symposium on motivation.* Lincoln: University of Nebraska Press, 1955.

Kahn, R. L. Human relations on the shop floor. In E. M. Hugh-Jones (Ed.), *Human relations and modern management.* Amsterdam: North-Holland, 1958.

Kahn, R. L. Productivity and job satisfaction. *Personnel Psychology,* 1960, *13,* 275–286.

Katz, D., Maccoby, N., Gurin, G., & Floor, L. G. *Productivity, supervision, and morale among railroad workers.* Ann Arbor: University of Michigan, Institute for Social Research, 1951.

Katz, D., Maccoby, N., & Morse, N. *Productivity, supervision, and morale in an office situation.* Ann Arbor: University of Michigan, Institute for Social Research, 1950.

Katzell, R. A. Personal values, job satisfaction, and job behavior. In H. Borow (Ed.), *Man in a world of work.* Boston: Houghton Mifflin, 1964.

Keys, A., Brozek, J., Henschel, A., Mickelsen, O., & Taylor, H. *The biology of human starvation.* Minneapolis: University of Minnesota Press, 1950. 2 vols.

Klein, S. M., & Maher, J. R. Education level and satisfaction with pay. *Personnel Psychology,* 1966, *19,* 195–208.

Korman, A. K. "Consideration," "initiating structure," and organizational criteria—A review. *Personnel Psychology,* 1966, *19,* 349–362. (a)

Korman, A. K. Self-esteem variable in vocational choice. *Journal of Applied Psychology,* 1966, *50,* 479–486. (b)

Kornhauser, A. *Mental health of the industrial worker: A Detroit study.* New York: John Wiley & Sons, 1965.

Kuriloff, A. H. *Reality in management.* New York: McGraw-Hill, 1966.

Langer, W. C. *Psychology and human living.* New York: Appleton-Century-Crofts, 1937.

Lawler, E. E. Managers' attitudes toward how their pay is and should be determined. *Journal of Applied Psychology,* 1966, *50,* 273–279.

Lawler, E. E. The multitrait-multirater approach to measuring managerial job performance. *Journal of Applied Psychology,* 1967, *51,* 369-381.

Lawler, E. E. Job design and employee motivation. *Personnel Psychology,* 1969, *22,* 426-435.

Lawler, E. E. *Pay and organizational effectiveness: A psychological view.* New York: McGraw-Hill, 1971.

Lawler, E. E., & Cammann, C. What makes a work group successful? In A. Morrow (Ed.), *The failure of success.* New York: Amacom, 1972.

Lawler, E. E., & Hackman, J. R. The impact of employee participation in the development of pay incentive plans: A field experiment. *Journal of Applied Psychology,* 1969, *53,* 467-471.

Lawler, E. E., Hackman, J. R., & Kaufman, S. Effects of job redesign: A field experiment. *Journal of Experimental Social Psychology,* 1973, *3,* 49-62.

Lawler, E. E., & Hall, D. T. Relationship of job characteristics to job involvement, satisfaction, and intrinsic motivation. *Journal of Applied Psychology,* 1970, *54,* 305-312.

Lawler, E. E., & Porter, L. W. Perceptions regarding management compensation. *Industrial Relations,* 1963, *3,* 41-49.

Lawler, E. E., & Porter, L. W. Predicting managers' pay and their satisfaction with their pay. *Personnel Psychology,* 1966, *19,* 363-373.

Lawler, E. E., & Porter, L. W. The effect of performance on job satisfaction. *Industrial Relations,* 1967, *7,* 20-28.

Lawler, E. E., & Suttle, J. L. A causal correlational test of the need hierarchy concept. *Organizational Behavior and Human Performance,* 1972, *7,* 265-287.

Lecky, P. *Self-consistency: A theory of personality.* New York: Island Press, 1945.

Lewin, K. *A dynamic theory of personality.* New York: McGraw-Hill, 1935.

Lewin, K. Group decision and social change. In T. M. Newcomb & E. L. Hartley (Eds.), *Readings in social psychology.* New York: Holt, Rinehart & Winston, 1947.

Lewin, K., Dembo, T., Festinger, L., & Sears, P. Level of aspiration. In J. McV. Hunt (Ed.), *Personality and the behavior disorders.* New York: Ronald Press, 1944.

Lewin, K., Lippitt, R., & White, R. K. Patterns of aggressive behavior in experimentally created social climates. *Journal of Social Psychology,* 1939, *10,* 271–299.

Likert, R. A motivational approach to a modified theory of organization and management. In M. Haire (ed.), *Modern organization theory: A symposium of the foundation for research on human behavior.* New York: John Wiley & Sons, 1959.

Likert, R. *New patterns of management.* New York: McGraw-Hill, 1961.

Lincoln, J. F. *Incentive management.* Cleveland: Lincoln Electric Company, 1951.

Locke, E. A. What is job satisfaction? Paper presented at the American Psychological Association Convention, San Francisco, September 1968.

Locke, E. A. What is job satisfaction? *Organizational Behavior and Human Performance,* 1969, *4,* 309–336.

Lyden, F. J., & Miller, E. G. (Eds.) *Planning, programming, and budgeting: A systems approach to management.* Chicago: Markham, 1968.

McClelland, D. C. Measuring motivation in phantasy: The achievement motive. In H. Guetzkow (Ed.), *Groups, leadership, and men.* Pittsburgh: Carnegie Press, 1951.

McClelland, D. C. *The achieving society.* Princeton: Van Nostrand Reinhold, 1961.

McDougall, W. *An introduction to social psychology.* London: Methuen & Co., 1908.

McGregor, D. An uneasy look at performance appraisal. *Harvard Business Review,* 1957, *35* (3), 89–94.

McGregor, D. *The human side of enterprise.* New York: McGraw-Hill, 1960.

March, J. G., & Simon, H. A. *Organizations.* New York: John Wiley & Sons, 1958.

Marks, A.R.N. An investigation of modifications of job design on an industrial situation and their effects on some measures of economic productivity. Unpublished doctoral dissertation, University of California, Berkeley, 1954.

Marriott, R. Size of working group and output. *Occupational Psychology,* 1949, *23,* 47–57.

Marrow, A. J., Bowers, D. G., and Seashore, S. E. *Management by participation.* New York: Harper & Row, 1967.

Martin, N. H., & Strauss, A. L. Patterns of mobility within industrial organizations. *Journal of Business,* 1956, *29,* 101–110.

Maslow, A. H. A theory of human motivation. *Psychological Review,* 1943, *50,* 370–396.

Maslow, A. H. *Motivation and personality.* New York: Harper & Row, 1954.

Maslow, A. H. *Toward a psychology of being.* (2nd ed.) Princeton: Van Nostrand Reinhold, 1968.

Maslow, A. H. *Motivation and personality.* (2nd ed.) New York: Harper & Row, 1970.

May, R. *Man's search for himself.* New York: W. W. Norton, 1953.

Mayo, E. *The social problems of an industrial civilization.* Cambridge, Mass.: Harvard University, Graduate School of Business Administration, 1945.

Metzner, H., & Mann, F. Employee attitudes and absences. *Personnel Psychology,* 1953, *6,* 467–485.

Meyer, H. H., Kay, E., & French, J.R.P. Split roles in performance appraisal. *Harvard Business Review,* 1965, *43* (1), 123–129.

Miles, R. C. Learning in kittens with manipulatory, exploratory, and food incentives. *Journal of Comparative and Physiological Psychology,* 1958, *51,* 39–42.

Miles, R. E. Human relations or human resources? *Harvard Business Review,* 1965, *43* (4), 148–163.

Mobley, W. H., & Locke, E. A. The relationship of value importance to satisfaction. *Organizational Behavior and Human Performance,* 1970, *5,* 463–483.

Moore, J. V., & Smith, R. G. Aspects of non-commissioned officer leadership. Working paper, U.S. Air Force Human Resources Research Center, Technical Report No. 52–53, 1952.

Morse, N. C. *Satisfactions in the white-collar job.* Ann Arbor: University of Michigan, Institute for Social Research, Survey Research Center, 1953.

Morse, N. C., & Reimer, E. The experimental change of a major organizational variable. *Journal of Abnormal Social Psychology,* 1956, *52,* 120–129.

Morse, N. C., & Weiss, R. The function and meaning of work and the job. *American Sociological Review,* 1955, *20,* 191–198.

Murray, E. J. *Motivation and emotion.* Englewood Cliffs, N.J.: Prentice-Hall, 1964.

Murray, H. A. The effect of fear upon estimates of the maliciousness of other personalities. *Journal of Social Psychology,* 1933, *4,* 310–329.

Murray, H. A. *Explorations in personality.* New York: Oxford University Press, 1938.

Odiorne, G. S. *Management decisions by objectives.* Englewood Cliffs, N.J.: Prentice-Hall, 1965.

Office of Strategic Services Assessment Staff. *Assessment of men.* New York: Holt, Rinehart & Winston, 1948.

Ondrack, Daniel A. Examination of the generation gap: Attitudes toward authority. *Personnel Administration,* May-June, 1971, *34,* 8–17.

Opinion Research Corporation. *"Productivity" from the worker's standpoint.* Princeton: Opinion Research Corporation, 1949.

Organization for Economic Cooperation and Development. *Wages and labor mobility.* Paris: Author, 1965.

Pelz, D. C. Leadership within a hierarchical organization. *Journal of Social Issues,* 1951, *7* (3), 49–55.

Porter, L. W. A study of perceived need satisfactions in bottom and middle management jobs. *Journal of Applied Psychology,* 1961, *45,* 1–10.

Porter, L. W. Job attitudes in management: I. Perceived deficiencies in need fulfillment as a function of job level. *Journal of Applied Psychology,* 1962, *46,* 375–384.

Porter, L. W. Job attitudes in management: II. Perceived importance of needs as a function of job level. *Journal of Applied Psychology,* 1963, *47,* 141–148.

Porter, L. W. *Organizational patterns of managerial job attitudes.* New York: American Foundation for Management Research, 1964.

Porter, L. W., & Lawler, E. E. Properties of organization structure in relation to job attitudes and job behavior. *Psychological Bulletin,* 1965, *64,* 23–51.

Porter, L. W., & Lawler, E. E. *Managerial attitudes and performance.* Homewood, Ill.: Irwin-Dorsey Press, 1968.

Porter, L. W., Lawler, E. E., & Hackman, J. R. *Behavior in organizations.* New York: McGraw-Hill, 1975.

Puckett, E. S. Productivity achievements—A measure of success. In F. G. Lesieur (Ed.), *The Scanlon Plan.* Cambridge, Mass.: MIT Press, 1958.

Quinn, R. P., Staines, G., & McCullough, M. Job satisfaction in the 1970's: Recent history and a look to the future. *Manpower Monograph,* 1973.

Raiffa, Howard. *Decision analysis: Introductory lectures on choices under uncertainty.* Reading, Mass.: Addison-Wesley, 1968.

Reich, C. *The greening of America.* New York: Random House, 1970.

Rhode, J. G., Sorensen, J. E., & Lawler, E. E. *A study of professional staff turnover in public accounting firms.* 1975.

Riesman, D. *The lonely crowd.* New Haven: Yale University Press, 1950.

Roethlisberger, F. J., & Dickson, W. J. *Management and the worker.* Cambridge, Mass.: Harvard University Press, 1939.

Rogers, C. R. *Client-centered therapy: Its current practice, implications and theory.* Boston: Houghton Mifflin, 1951.

Rogers, C. R. *On becoming a person.* Boston: Houghton Mifflin, 1961.

Rosenberg, M. *Occupations and values.* Glencoe, Ill.: Free Press, 1957.

Ross, I. E., & Zander, A. F. Need satisfaction and employee turnover. *Personnel Psychology,* 1957, *10,* 327–338.

Roszak, Theodore. *The making of a counter culture.* Garden City, N.Y.: Doubleday, 1969.

Rotter, J. B. Generalized expectancies for internal versus external control of reinforcement. *Psychological Monographs,* 1966, *80* (1), 1–28.

Roy, D. Quota restriction and gold bricking in a machine shop. *American Journal of Sociology,* 1952, *57,* 427–442.

Schachter, S. *The psychology of affiliation.* Stanford, Calif.: Stanford University Press, 1959.

Schachter, S., Ellertson, N., McBride, D., & Gregory, D. An experimental study of cohesiveness and productivity. *Human Relations,* 1951, *4,* 229–238.

Schaffer, R. H. Job satisfaction as related to need satisfaction in work. *Psychological Monographs,* 1953, *67* (14, Whole No. 364).

Scheflen, K. D., Lawler, E. E., & Hackman, J. R. Long-term impact of employee participation in the development of pay incentive plans: A field experiment revisited. *Journal of Applied Psychology*, 1971, *55*, 182–186.

Schein, E. H. *Organizational psychology*. Englewood Cliffs, N.J.: Prentice-Hall, 1965.

Schultz, G. P. Variations in environment and the Scanlon plan. In F. G. Lesieur (Ed.), *The Scanlon Plan*. Cambridge, Mass.: MIT Press, 1958.

Scott, W. E. The behavioral consequences of repetitive task design: Research and theory. In L. L. Cummings & W. E. Scott (Eds.), *Readings in organizational behavior and human performance*. Homewood, Ill.: Richard D. Irwin, 1969.

Seashore, S. *Group cohesiveness in the industrial work group*. Ann Arbor: University of Michigan, Institute for Social Research, Survey Research Center, 1954.

Simon, H. A. *Administrative behavior*. (2nd ed.) New York: Macmillan, 1957.

Smith, P., Kendall, L., & Hulin, C. *The measurement of satisfaction in work and retirement*. Chicago: Rand McNally & Company, 1969.

Smock, C. D., & Holt, B. G. Children's reactions to novelty: An experimental study of "curiosity motivation." *Child Development*, 1962, *33*, 631–642.

Snygg, D., & Combs, A. W. *Individual behavior*. New York: Harper & Row, 1949.

Sofer, C. *Men in mid-career: A study of British managers and technical specialists*. Cambridge: Cambridge University Press, 1970.

Stone, C. H. The personality factor in vocational guidance. *Journal of Abnormal and Social Psychology*, 1933, *28*, 274–275.

Svetlik, B., Prien, E., & Barrett, G. Relationships between job difficulty, employee's attitude toward his job, and supervisory ratings of the employee's effectiveness. *Journal of Applied Psychology*, 1964, *48*, 320–324.

Tannenbaum, A. S., & Allport, F. H. Personality structure and group structure: An interpretive study of their relationship through an event-structure hypothesis. *Journal of Abnormal Social Psychology*, 1956, *53*, 272–280.

Tausky, C., and Dubin, R. Career anchorage: Managerial mobility motivations. *American Sociological Review*, 1965, *30*, 725–735.

Taylor, F. W. *The principles of scientific management*. New York: Harper & Row, 1911.

Thorndike, E. L. *Animal intelligence: Experimental studies*. New York: Macmillan, 1911.

Titmus, R. M. *The gift relationship*. New York: Pantheon Books, 1971.

Tolman, E. C. *Purposive behavior in animals and men*. New York: Century Co., 1932.

Trow, D. B. Autonomy and job satisfaction in task-oriented groups. *Journal of Abnormal Social Psychology*, 1957, *54*, 204–209.

Turner, A. N., & Lawrence, P. R. *Industrial jobs and the worker*. Boston: Harvard University School of Business Administration, 1965.

Viteles, M. S. *Motivation and morale in industry*. New York: W. W. Norton, 1953.

Vroom, V. H. Some personality determinants of the effects of participation. *Journal of Abnormal Social Psychology*, 1959, *59*, 322–327.

Vroom, V. H. *Some personality determinants of the effects of participation*. Englewood Cliffs, N.J.: Prentice-Hall, 1960.

Vroom, V. H. *Work and motivation*. New York: John Wiley & Sons, 1964.

Vroom, V. H. Organizational choice: A study of pre- and post-decision processes. *Organizational Behavior and Human Performance*, 1966, *1*, 212–225.

Vroom, V. H., & Deci, E. L. *Management and motivation*. Baltimore: Penguin Books, 1970.

Wager, L. W. Leadership style, influence, and supervisory role obligations. *Administrative Science Quarterly*, 1965, *9*, 391–420.

Walker, C. R., & Guest, R. H. *The man on the assembly line*. Cambridge, Mass.: Harvard University Press, 1952.

Wanous, J. P. *An experimental test of job attraction theory in an organizational setting*. Unpublished doctoral dissertation, Yale University, 1972. (a)

Wanous, J. P. Occupational preferences: Perceptions of valence and instrumentality and objective data. *Journal of Applied Psychology*, 1972, *56*, 152–155. (b)

Wanous, J. P., & Lawler, E. E. Measurement and meaning of job satisfaction. *Journal of Applied Psychology*, 1972, *56*, 95–105.

Weitz, J. Job expectancy and survival. *Journal of Applied Psychology*, 1956, *40*, 245–247.

Weitz, J., & Nuckols, R. C. The validity of direct and indirect questions in measuring job satisfaction. *Personnel Psychology*, 1953, *6*, 487–494.

White, B. F., & Barnes, L. B. Power networks in the appraisal process. *Harvard Business Review*, 1971, *49* (3), 101–109.

White, R. W. Motivation reconsidered: The concept of competence. *Psychological Review*, 1959, *66*, 297–333.

Whyte, W. F. *Human relations in the restaurant industry.* New York: McGraw-Hill, 1948.

Whyte, W. F. *Money and motivation.* New York: Harper & Row, 1955.

Wickert, F. R. Turnover and employees' feelings of ego-involvement in the day-to-day operations of a company. *Personnel Psychology*, 1951, *4*, 185–197.

Williamson, E. G. *How to counsel students.* New York: McGraw-Hill, 1939.

Wolfe, J. B. Effectiveness of token-rewards for chimpanzees. *Comparative Psychology Monograph*, 1936, *12*, 15.

Woodworth, R. S. *Dynamic psychology.* New York: Columbia University Press, 1918.

Wyatt, S. *Incentives in repetitive work: A practical experiment in a factory.* (Industrial Health Research Report No. 69) London: H. M. Stationery Office, 1934.

Yoder, D. *Personnel management and industrial relations.* Englewood Cliffs, N.J.: Prentice-Hall, 1956.

Zaleznik, A., Christensen, C. R., & Roethlisberger, F. J. *The motivation, productivity, and satisfaction of workers: A prediction study.* Boston: Harvard University, Graduate School of Business Administration, 1958.

Zeaman, D. Response latency as a function of the amount of reinforcement. *Journal of Experimental Psychology*, 1949, *39*, 466–483.

Index